ALSO BY ADA LOUISE HUXTABLE

Classical New York

Pier Luigi Nervi

The preparation of this book was assisted by a
grant from the Graham Foundation for
Advanced Studies in the Fine Arts, Chicago.

Will They Ever Finish Bruckner Boulevard?

Ada Louise Huxtable

WILL THEY EVER FINISH BRUCKNER BOULEVARD?

Preface by Daniel P. Moynihan

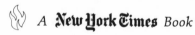 *A* **New York Times** *Book*

THE MACMILLAN COMPANY, NEW YORK, NEW YORK

COLLIER-MACMILLAN LTD., LONDON

All of the material in this book first appeared in The New York Times. *Dates of the original publications are given in the back of the book.*

To my husband

CONTENTS

Contents

PART II / ARCHITECTURE

Contents

LIST OF ILLUSTRATIONS

List of Illustrations

PREFACE

"Lechery, lechery!" *quoth Thersites, "still wars and lechery! Nothing else holds fashion."* In general, a good rule. True, surely, of Elizabeth's London: Shakespeare may be relied on in such matters. Doubtless also true of Helen's Troy. Of Ada Louise Huxtable's New York, however, a third theme of preoccupation must be recorded: that of the city itself.

This is something new. And increasingly, of course, it may be said to be true not only of the Great Metropolis, but of the culture itself. Out of a past of seeming invincible indifference to any qualities, good or bad, of the urban environment, Americans of a sudden find themselves fascinated, horrified, seized with the subject.

In Ada Louise Huxtable's words, "People have been looking at the environment, as environment, for only a very short time. It has always been there, but it has finally been recognized as something that is terribly responsive to acts of will and judgment that have an endless impact on the state of humanity." It would be easy to underestimate the dimensions of this change, ascribing it, for example, to the noisome but transitional state of a certain number of cities in the aftermath of the automobile, or to the difficulties that have accompanied certain internal migrations, or even to the restrained but intense and stimulating fury of the writings of Huxtable herself and the very few but very important writers like her who have followed in Lewis Mumford's tradition of a sustained, unsparing, hands-on critique of the mess we have made of things. But something more is involved, something that gives to this collection of essays a setting and significance of large and special consequence. Kenneth E. Boulding has described it in terms of an emergent style of social self-awareness:

> This movement of the social system into self-consciousness is perhaps one of the most significant phenomena of our time, and it represents a very fundamental break with the past, as did the development of personal self-consciousness many millennia earlier.

Huxtable is writing about—helping to shape—what is in effect a new sensibility, one which in its ultimate meanings assumes the form also of a new morality.

At the core of Huxtable's thinking is the struggle of good and evil, but a confused and inconclusive struggle waged on a darkling plain of issues only dimly perceived and rarely understood. Ambiguity is all; and something very like original sin sets limits to what actually will happen that are insanely short of what man can and does conceive. Her book indeed is almost a primer on the process. At the outset we are told that the environment may be recognized "as something that is terribly responsive to acts of will and judgment." Whereupon follow essay upon essay in which the failure of will and the failure of judgment are recorded. One is reminded of the opening sentence of Samuel Beckett's *Murphy*, in which the ancient theme of Ecclesiastes is evoked with the peculiar spiritual despondency of the twentieth century: "The sun shone, having no alternative, on the nothing new."

What in particular is nothing new is the fact of decline and fall in human affairs. The ability to locate an event on the curve of rising and declining fortunes is almost the first requirement of architectural journalism, and it is here that Huxtable has no equal. A powerful, pervasive sense of history informs her judgments throughout. Buildings are seen to exist in space, but also in time, and the more powerful perspective will typically be found along the latter dimension, certainly so in these essays. Hence the essays that follow combine almost lyric reports of things that are new and agreeable, even on occasion grand, reports of rising cities and theories and reputations, with somber accounts of deterioration and destruction. In no one thing is this process more conspicuous than in the deterioration of public architecture over the past half century, and on no single point is Huxtable more poignant—or implacable. The standard liberal mind has been curiously indifferent or oblivious to this process. This is doubtless in part due to the fact that, as she comments, the institutions that teach the American elites to *think* about the modern world are altogether unconcerned with teaching them to *look* at it. One also has the impression that a certain type of Victorian Gothic and later Beaux Arts architecture came to be associated with political conservatism on the one hand and, given a curious liberal asceticism in these matters, to represent a weakness for display, even an indifference to human needs, on the other hand. Great buildings and public spaces were not seen as a human need, and are not. In any event, twentieth-century America has seen a steady, persistent decline in the visual and emotional power of its public buildings, and this has been accompanied by a not less persistent decline in the authority of the public order. This many of us know, but only Huxtable could capture the process in the precise moment of transmutation. Where? When? In Jersey City. At the moment the judges left the marble colonnaded chambers of the turn-of-the-century Hudson County Courthouse for new, functional efficient modern quarters next door. Right-thinking Americans will have seen this as a long overdue disengagement with a corrupt and archaic past for a hopeful and enlightened future. Not Huxtable: she alone reports how much has been lost and what little has been gained. Decline and fall and failure are the repeated fact and constant theme of this book.

Not less central is the recurrent theme of paralysis. Will they ever finish Bruckner Boulevard, that indeterminate artery that always seems to be on the way or in the way if you're traveling north from Manhattan? Every city must have one such: a public project that somehow can't be focused, can't be finished. A "they" out there somewhere who can't be reached or won't be bothered. At some point in the course of the twentieth century our capacity to make effective urban decisions began to vitiate. Largely in the name of greater responsiveness, government became fundamentally less responsible. An ominous quiet has now settled on cities everywhere, *as nothing happens*. Nothing—or almost nothing—in those very places where only yesterday *everything* happened.

I write on a Sunday afternoon in Washington. Earlier in the day, thinking of this book and this theme, I drove to 7th and T Streets, N.W., one of the areas badly burned out in the "civil disturbance" that followed the assassination of Dr. King in April, 1968. On taking office the following January, President Nixon found in his capital city that *not a single building destroyed in the riots had been rebuilt*. Every resource of modern government had been made available for the reconstruction effort. A Reconstruction Development Corporation was established, foundation funds raised, a staff recruited. The planning agency, the land agency, the urban renewal agency, joined in. The burned-out corridors were precisely, lovingly mapped. Damage was assessed. Plans were drawn. Meetings held. Speeches. More meetings. More speeches.

But *nothing happened*. Somehow the city could not even organize itself to clear away the ruined buildings.

As a gesture, on his eleventh day in office the President went out to 7th and T Streets and proposed that one building lot immediately adjoining a school yard be cleared and converted, for the time being at least, into a simple playground. It was proposed that the site be named for a black school principal who had just been murdered in another school nearby.

It was only a gesture, but meant to have meaning. Meant to state in some palpable way that something *had* to happen. That the city could not simply leave the ruined buildings to rot and fester through another year.

And so this morning I went out to 7th and T Streets to see what had happened, and found what I knew would be the case. Nothing had happened. In fairness, work had begun. The site was cleared, a number of concrete footings were in place, two steel trusses had been raised. But in no sense was there a playground. There will be. Someday. But already the point is lost: the point that if enough people care, a playground can be put together in a fortnight.

This will be our ruin if we do not attend to it. If there is any primary reason American cities are in such trouble at this moment it is because we doubled our population in the past fifty years. It took three centuries for the first hundred million; half a century for the hundred million after that; it will take a third of a century for the next hundred million. Locating this next hundred million people will be almost the primary national work of the rest of the century. A sense of the magnitude of the effort may be had if we consider that to locate them in "new towns" would require the construction of a city the size of Tulsa every thirty days for thirty years. We have not the political energy or inventiveness to do a tenth of that. And yet the new population will come. To create a rewarding urban environment for a nation of three hundred million people is the precise task ahead. The book that follows suggests how little prepared we are for such a task.

But we are not without resources. Indeed, the task seems so great not least because of the standards the Ada Louise Huxtables of this nation set for it. You must love a country very much to be as little satisfied with it as she. You must wish very great things for a nation to be so insistent in pointing out how little prepared it is to *do* great things. So be it. The probability, of course, is that the future will be much like the past. But for all the misery we must then prepare for, we do so in the expectation that there will be a measure of splendor as well. This is about how we have been managing things. As Huxtable writes of the Secaucus Meadows into which the classical figures and shards of Pennsylvania Station were unceremoniously deposited "in a setting of macabre surrealist *vérité*," it did, after all, turn the Jersey wasteland "into a pretty classy dump."

Washington, D.C.   DANIEL P. MOYNIHAN

Introduction

A CRITIC writing for the daily press does not deal in immortality. In the classic putdown of his trade, today's words are for wrapping tomorrow's fish. If he works in the fields of architecture and urbanism, what he deals in is immediacy—the day-to-day pressures and proposals and decisions that can make or maim a city. He fights city hall, vested private interest and popular apathy with an urgency that can easily lose its meaning a few years later when his particular crises have been consigned to oblivion. His words, being newsprint, have yellowed and crumbled. The only thing more ephemeral than newsprint is the shape and condition of the world that is his concern, and which he sees as the environment.

People have been looking at the environment, as environment, for only a very short time. It has always been there; but it has finally been recognized as something that is terribly responsive to acts of will and judgment that have an endless impact on the state of humanity. The way we live, or exist, is the generator of many of the problems called the urban crisis. How we live, or exist, is what urban design and planning are all about. Esthetics is not some kind of optional extra or paste-on for pretty facades; it is the satisfaction of the needs of the body, the spirit and the senses through the way an environment looks and functions—two inseparable factors. Every

1

social plan has a form, good or bad. The art of design is an unavoidable part of every urban decision. Until this is understood as the planning process, and design is accepted as an inescapable determinant of the result, we will simply produce more environmental failures. And the urban critic will have failed as well.

The critic's role in architecture and urbanism is quite different than in any other field. For one thing, this is a relatively new field in the popular press and a growing one. The function of this broad kind of architectural criticism is educational; it must in many ways fill the gap that our schools have left so conspicuously vacant—the yawning chasm between the "educated" man's perception and understanding of the man-made world around him. Without this, no campaign for better ways of building can succeed. George Kennan, in his *Memoirs*, analyzing the areas of thought and experience opened to him by a Princeton education, noted that the one serious omission was visual instruction of any kind. "No one, to the day of my graduation," he wrote, "ever taught me to look understandingly at a painting, or a tree, or the facade of a building."

The critic in this field, where everything is transient and temporal, hopes that something may testify to his efforts. He hopes that he may have taught someone to see. He would like to feel that there is just a chance that he may have changed some degree of practice, helped effect some shift in philosophical base, revised the climate of thought and feeling to some small extent or influenced public awareness to the point where the world those few years later may be a bit more in the image of the kind of life and environment (again, they cannot be separated) for which he has fought his battles. He expects no miracles but he is an optimist with some fairly tough beliefs. In architecture and urbanism those beliefs must be based on history, art and humanism. They must have strong ties to modern sociology and technology. And they must be grounded in a knowledge of the past for the shifting present and the uncertain future.

This book is a selection from the work of the six or seven years that I have been producing analysis and evaluation for *The New York Times*. What I really want to say in assembling these pieces is that, like Kilroy, Huxtable was here. They are a record of a continuing professional passion, of an occasional mitigating triumph in a job of unending frustration, a testament to involvement and, it is hoped, evidence of a vision. Critics are not by nature existentialists;

if they accepted things as they are, they would be in some other business. But only mock philosophers pretend to provide answers for the questions they raise; the purpose is to provoke thought and the possibility of solutions.

Criticism of this sort has an unavoidable messianic sound. Instead of dealing in the pleasant esoterica of esthetics, one finds oneself at querulous and sometimes tiresome odds with ignorance, bureaucracy, cupidity and political and personal opportunism. One becomes a scold, and that can be deadly. Without redeeming wit, this kind of criticism can also be a bore. With shifting climates and conditions, it can soon seem jejune.

But if the obsessions of the journalistic critic are quickly obsolete, what does not become obsolete are his standards—those philosophical and esthetic yardsticks by which he measures his subject and his world as acts of art or blasphemy. The architecture critic cannot be enamored of fashionable polemics. It may be tempting to make a small, rarefied splash in the upper intellectual stratosphere but it will not matter. In the long run, what he has to say must matter or he might as well not say it. His reality is compounded of politics, economics and human fallibility. He is essentially a pragmatist, but one with professional principles that become over-familiar to the constant reader, who is hit repeatedly on the head with them.

If his standards are to be relevant, however, they must not be absolute. If they were inflexible or unchanging in these revolutionary times, they would produce judgments of instant obsolescence and supreme fallaciousness. It is no measure of a critic's worth whether or not he has changed his mind. If he has not to some degree, it is more a measure of his lack of growth in a field of stunning transmutation. But I find that I do not feel that I wish or need to take back a word that I have written here; the only revisions have been some updating of tenses and figures, the occasional vanity of a smoother or emphasizing phrase, and an expansion of the Pop Architecture theme into a more recently developed concern for whatever functional lessons about twentieth-century life an otherwise appalling Pop environment can teach us.

"The only way the critic can improve his capacity for making the right kind of choices is by continued exertions," Edouard F. Seckler, the art historian, has said. "He must match his sensuous and mental equipment time and again against new phenomena in a spirit of openness and with a willingness to bring his full being to bear in each case. He may have to revise his criteria in the light of a new creation, for the architect may have established something which is not amenable to treatment in a critic's established terms and the critic forever has to fit into a new context. He remains a concerned observer in search of possibilities for a positive interpretation of the present."

I have written as a concerned observer in search of possibilities for a positive interpretation of the present. I believe in the present, partly because, like Mount Everest, it is here and partly because, as a historian, I see it, in spite of the cataclysmic problems that have resulted from a series of concurrent human and scientific revolutions, as one of the greatest and most challenging periods in history. It is the age in which man has reached first the clouds and then the moon. It is the age of the skyscraper, when new technologies have finally made it possible for him to build as high as he has dreamed of doing since the beginning of time—but it is also the age that has turned the dream of a better world into a fouled environment. When, in the past, we of the critical press have pointed out the price of wasting our natural and technological resources and sabotaging our skills, we have been dismissed as idealists. We are the realists now.

Part I / The Urban Scene

The World of the Absurd

CITY life and city problems have come to Antarctica. In some kind of record for nest-fouling, urban sprawl has turned McMurdo Station into an urban horror in a brief ten years. This may be a standing backjump record for ruining the environment.

"A smoking garbage dump and junkyard litter the shore of a once picturesque inlet, power lines from the nuclear plant deface the stark, wind-swept and lifeless hills that so awed and impressed explorers 50 years ago," a reporter noted. The answer? A McMurdo redevelopment program, naturally.

Every year sees megalopolis, the urban smear that is staining the entire American northeast and blurring city boundaries everywhere, relentlessly on its way to ecumenopolis, or a totally urbanized world, according to planner Constantinos Doxiadis. (The Greeks had a word for it and still do. Any trend or truism dressed up in classical etymology becomes a charismatic concept for the intellectually susceptible. It has the authority of a sermon from the Acropolis.)

Ecumenopolis may take a little while, but we'll get there. We are getting to the moon first, of course, although only one thing is sure about that and none of the scientific prognostications mention it. When we get there, we'll make a mess of it.*

* Man the explorer made it to the moon on July 20, 1969, and became man the litterer as he jettisoned electronic equipment, waste and wrappings.

7

Today's city, where mistakes are made on an Olympian scale
(THE NEW YORK TIMES BY SAM FALK)

Meanwhile, back at the foundations and universities, studies of the city proliferate and more are promised. In a brilliant review of "Taming Megalopolis," planner and architect Clive Entwistle envisions "continuing and increasing and ever more expensive 'research' projects to the horizons of urban space and post-graduate time."

The pinned butterfly of urban phenomena, the dissected and annotated crisis, substitute handily for solutions. Few studies have the jolting pertinence of a Moynihan analysis of the Negro family in American society. Most are pretentious and fatiguingly detailed enshrinements of the obvious or ordinary, properly impressive to those who are awed by Greek-root words. "Before the buzz of refined scholarship," Entwistle concludes, "the decision makers, engineers and politicians stand abashed and emasculated."

"Trend is not destiny," Lewis Mumford has warned in one of his periodic blasts on the urban scene from his sanctuary in the non-urban hills, quoting Albert Mayer's book *The Urgent Future.* "Progress," said *The New York Times* editorially, is an idea that needs to be "challenged."

All this makes it quite clear where we are. We are obviously in the world of the absurd. The black urban comedy continues to be played out in the research institutes and the black urban tragedy goes on in the ghettos while Rome, and Detroit and Newark, burn.

Disaster is charted as destiny and objective, scholarly truth. Progress consists of making the same mistakes, but on an Olympian scale. Research builds abstract monuments to itself. Funds are made available for "prototype studies" while untouched problems take their toll of the human heart and the urban world. In government agencies, policy set at the top is reversed by bureaucracy at the bottom.

We pollute the country with the refuse of the affluent society. In Washington, D.C. it has been found that there is more gold per ton of fly ash in the refuse dumps than in commercial mines. At McMurdo we have the apotheosis of absurdity; we have destroyed the environment while studying it. The reality of the world of the absurd can't be touched by anything in the imagination of man.

There is hope, of course. We can press that precious garbage into construction blocks and build with them, according to promising new processes, rather than face slow strangulation from the detritus of prosperity. Eventually we may be able to move to a $4 billion experimental city being studied by ten industries and three Federal agencies in Minnesota. We can enter the research cloisters in handsome parts of the countryside where megalopolis waits to spring.

But for now we substitute the high-level make-work of scholars for responsibility and action. It is a face-saving, if not city-saving, evasion. For value judgments we embrace more esoteric studies of the natural chaos of "the scene." The administrator, politician or planner who holds convictions enough to battle for solutions—and solutions are always partial, imperfect, debatable and without guarantees—must be an extraordinary combination of gutter tough and intellectual visionary. He does it, surprisingly, in an age of cynicism, because he cares.

What he deals in is the environment, an "in" word in the crisis of cities that is a poorly understood concept at best. As a word, it is meaningless. Its comprehension is a visual, emotional, sensuous, physical and visceral process; it is the direct, three-dimensional, individual and collective experience of one's surroundings; the sum total of external conditions and influences affecting life for better or worse.

In a city the environment is made by man. "Made by Man" should be stamped across the blank towers and arid open spaces that are the equally barren contribution of both public and luxury housing at the two extremes of the scale. (One has art, the other has vandalism in the lobby.) "Made by Man" should be branded on rotting piers and scabrous waterfront. It should be emblazoned on city-maiming expressways and the shadowed slums beneath them. It all comes off the drawing board at the start, whatever subsequent overlays of social disaster may add rich varieties of human blight.

The urban world is a conscious act; it is the work of some hand and eye and mind, no matter how mindless it may appear. The original blight was the designer's, the builder's, the developer's, the engineer's or the architect's, whatever economic, political or legislative pressures or incentives may have set the standards or the style.

What is being designed privately and publicly with alarming consistency is instant blight. We are building blight for the next hundred years. The environment is being sealed systematically into sterility and its social problems are being compounded and immortalized by substandard design. The failure of the environment is our theme.

11

New York, The Death-Wish City

Death by Development

THEY are terse headline notices—"Three Town Houses Bought by High-Rise Builder," "Midtown Expansion Forcing Music Street to Sing Swan Song," "Real Estate Deal in Village." On the surface, a factual, newsprint chronicle of urban change; underneath, the death of a city by "development."

There was a time when, Candide-like, New Yorkers bought the arguments of progress that this was all for the best in the best of all possible worlds. As their favorite neighborhoods were pulled out from under their feet to be replaced by the profitable sterility of the standard real estate model, wisdom came, slowly and painfully. It was the grass-roots, or rather cement-roots, wisdom of bitter experience, but it paralleled the more cerebral lessons being taught in planning schools and environmental studies and redundant urban symposia: without variety of function and humanity of scale, the city becomes monstrous and insupportable.

Take "Three Town Houses Bought by High-Rise Builder." The three houses were in the center of the 79th to 80th Street block on Fifth Avenue, flanked by apartment buildings at either corner. The

79th Street tower is a brand-new skyscraper that makes a pathetic gesture toward the elegance of its older neighbors with somber brick and elementary stone trim. The three town houses were of richly detailed masonry in variations of turn-of-the-century French taste—Gothic, classical and Beaux Arts. The story will end, perfectly predictably, when another new apartment house replaces them.*

The story started when the 79th Street skyscraper displaced a landmark building, the Brokaw mansion. The little Gothic town house that stood for a while next to it like some piece of bungled surgery had been built to match the mansion. The Brokaw house went down over the howls of preservationists who were unable to find a way to make that magnificent white elephant useful in today's cut-rate, computer society after the institutional owners had exchanged it for a pocketful of cash. The new apartment house quickly became known as New York's most expensive cooperative. Next to the Gilded Age mansions, it represents a kind of architectural poverty for the affluent.

In addition, it represents irreversible environmental damage. A brutal breaking of the streetscape, both historically and esthetically, is the developer's most notable achievement. That block was part of one of the city's finest, continuous landmark group of mansions, an irreplaceable row that stretched from the Duke House at 78th Street to the Stuyvesant House at 79th Street, crossing to the Brokaw house and ending at the 80th Street corner. Until the 79th Street tower was built, this magnificent urban complex was tied together by a unified street line and the facing park and an incredible period richness of material and detail. These low buildings against a large sky, tinted gold and lavender at dusk or bathed in an extra measure of sun and light, had a civilized beauty. That beauty has been violated. Nor is there any guarantee that some of the succulent real estate of the remaining 78th Street block is not vulnerable, in spite of current institutional uses.

A second environmental tragedy illustrated here is the destructive force of the new zoning when it is applied literally and without adjustment to specific urban conditions. A feature of the 79th Street apartment house is a wraparound corner plaza. Open plazas oppo-

---

* The apartment house went up in the spring of 1969.

site the open space of Central Park are an absurdity. But this awk-ward, meaningless windswept setback from the street gives the builder a bonus of extra rentable floors in a taller tower. Builders, notoriously, are not urbanists. This trend can destroy the little that New York has of genuine urban elegance or greatness, its few handsome avenues and sophisticated plazas.

In New York, neighborhoods fall like dominoes. Everyone knows about the small electrical supply stores uprooted by the World Trade Center; the thrift and antique shops chased by the apartment builders from Third Avenue; the small businesses, bars and coffee dealers displaced from the lower Manhattan waterfront by office construction; the artists' lofts eliminated in the Village for more luxury apartments.

What follows demolition is preordained by the divine right of development. There will be the same new buildings out of the same old mold, sleekly commercial or shoddily residential; and in the ground floor store space of all, as if by some holy decree, there will be banks.

Even an expanding Rockefeller Center has repudiated the su-perior planning principles of organized massing and multi-level cir-culation that added a superb urban heart to midtown. Its subsequent preoccupation has just been to make the facades blend. Somehow, it fell over Sixth Avenue on the way to 48th Street.* New York, anyone? Come and get it before it is too late. This seems like a death-wish city.

Sometimes We Do It Right

When it is good, New York is very, very good. Which is why New Yorkers put up with so much that is bad.

When it is good, this is a city of fantastic strength, sophistica-tion and beauty. It is like no other city in time or place. Visitors and even natives rarely use the words "urban character" or "en-

---

*Publicity plus persuasion by the city, using zoning bonuses as incentive, resulted in the addition of a mid-block passage behind these new Sixth Avenue buildings to accommodate shops, restaurants and pedestrian uses.

vironmental style," but that is what they are reacting to with awe in the presence of massed, concentrated steel, stone, power and life. It is a quality of urban greatness that may not solve racial or social tension or the human or economic crises to which a city is prone, but it survives them.

In this sense, one small piece of downtown Manhattan is very, very good. For a demonstration of New York at its physical best, go to Broadway between Cedar and Liberty streets and face east. You will be standing in front of the new building at 140 Broadway, one of the handsomest in the city, and you will not be able to miss the twenty-eight-foot high vermilion steel cube by Isamu Noguchi that balances on one point in front of it, at the north end of a travertine plaza.

Look to your left (Liberty Street) and you will see the small turn-of-the-century French pastry in creamy, classically detailed stone that houses the neighboring Chamber of Commerce. To your right (Cedar Street) is a stone-faced building of the first great sky-scraper period (pre-World War I through the 1930's).

Move on toward the East River, following the travertine plaza that flows elegantly on either side of the slender new shaft, noting how well the block size of the marble under foot scales the space. Surprisingly, the site and the fifty-two-story tower are trapezoidal in shape.

At Broad Street, the 140 Broadway plaza stops and Chase Manhattan Plaza begins. There is an unfortunate wall between them, due to abrupt changes in ground level and the fact that the architects of both buildings, Skidmore, Owings and Merrill, had no idea when they did Chase in the early 1960's that they would be doing the adjoining building less than a decade later.

But the open space continues, even with this barrier. Closing it and facing Chase's gleaming sixty-story tower across Liberty Street is the stony vastness of the 1924 Federal Reserve Building by York and Sawyer, its superscaled, cut limestone, Strozzi-type Florentine facade making a powerful play against Chase's bright aluminum and glass. A more conventional masonry-faced structure walls the plaza to the south.

There will be still more open space west of 140 Broadway, following the same axis. Just opposite the new building is the U.S. Steel site, where the Singer Building stood. That landmark loss to

The urban drama at its best (EZRA STOLLER)

New York's skyline will be replaced by a skyscraper by the same architects who have done Chase Manhattan and 140 Broadway, Skidmore, Owings and Merrill.

The architects and owners have received approval from the City Planning Commission to adjust the zoning of the two-block site to extend the present pedestrian channel farther toward the Hudson River. The Liberty-Cedar block west of Broadway will be another open plaza, paralleling the existing one. The new skyscraper will be constructed on the block to the north.

Still farther west, slightly off this axis, will be the giant World Trade Center twin towers and plaza. For much of this, underground connections are being planned.

The result, a striking slice through one of the densest, most dramatic cityscapes in the world, is a stunning success in terms of urban design. For once, the losses, such as the Singer Building, are at least being balanced by rational gains. For once, there has been intelligent, sensitive capitalization on one of this century's most fantastic urban phenomena. Instead of thoughtless destruction through new construction, there is a calculated relationship between past and present and between buildings and spaces.

This small segment of New York compares in effect and elegance with any celebrated Renaissance plaza or Baroque vista. The scale of the buildings, the use of open space, the views revealed or suggested, the contrasts of architectural style and material, of sculptured stone against satin-smooth metal and glass, the visible change and continuity of New York's remarkable skyscraper history, the brilliant accent of the poised Noguchi cube—color, size, style, mass, space, light, dark, solids, voids, highs and lows—all are just right. These few blocks provide (why equivocate?) one of the most magnificent examples of twentieth-century urbanism anywhere in the world.

Not the least contribution is the new building, for which Gordon Bunshaft was partner-in-charge at S.O.M. One forty Broadway is a "skin" building—the kind of flat, sheer, curtain wall that it has become chic to reject. Younger architects, off on a wild, Arthurian search for the *nouveau* picturesque, and an uninformed public that never understood or accepted what was happening have turned their backs on one of the miracles of modern building: the skyscraper wall reduced to gossamer minimums of shining, thin material hung on a frame of extraordinary strength through superb contemporary technology.

The significance and beauty of this achievement are not dimmed by the instances of its commercial prostitution as the unjustly denigrated "glass box." It is still one of the great developments and most remarkable expressions in all of architectural history from Stonehenge to the present. It has produced some masterpieces and made a lot of commercial building palatable. One forty Broadway is a commercial building, not a monument. Here the skin is handled with suave expertise.

It is New York's ultimate skin building. The wall is held unrelentingly flat; there are no tricks with projecting or extended mullions; thin and flush, they are used only to divide the window glass. The metal spandrel facing, in one smooth piece, echoes the placing of structural steel and seeks no "artful" plasticity. The taut, shiny-dark sleekness of matte black aluminum and gleaming bronze glass is an architectural statement of positive excellence as well as a foil for the ornate masonry around it. The quiet assurance of this building makes even Chase look a little gaudy.

What next? Probably destruction. One ill-conceived neighboring plaza will kill this carefully calculated channel of related space and buildings. Seagram was semi-sabotaged by the recent construction on its south; it can happen here. It only takes one opening in the wrong place, one "bonus" space placed according to current zoning (read "business") practice, to ruin it all.

Space is meaningless without scale, containment, boundaries and direction. The fabled massing of the Wall Street skyscrapers has been given masterful urban definition by the architects' ordering of these few blocks of new construction. It has been done by concerned, coordinated effort. This is planning, whether it is merely fortuitous or foresighted. It is the opposite of non-planning, or the normal pattern of New York development. See and savor it now, before it is carelessly disposed of.

Lower Manhattan Expressway: Where It Goes, Nobody Knows

The word on the Lower Manhattan expressway is that it is going to be poisonous.* Well, that is no surprise to a lot of us who have considered the whole idea of a Lower Manhattan expressway poisonous for some time. The warning is that its covered stretches— which represent the result of a long and bitter battle to depress the road rather than rend Manhattan asunder with an elevated Chinese wall—will produce air polluting fumes of more than acceptable noxiousness. One could probably do a dandy dissertation on levels of acceptable noxiousness in overpolluted New York.

The battle of the Lower Manhattan expressway, which has raged for twenty-eight years, was "settled" by the incoming Lindsay

* The Lower Manhattan expressway project was killed by Mayor Lindsay in July, 1969.

administration's "acceptance" of the road on the condition that it be built as a depressed highway, recasting it in the role of urban benefactor instead of urban assassin. (The cases of inner-city destruction by expressway are too numerous and well known to recount. Almost every one is a demonstrated environmental catastrophe.)

The in-and-out, over-and-under proposal that has come out of this attempt to defang the monster makes no one very happy. Ducking subways, utilities and the water table, it struggles above and below ground in a series of curious compromises of tortuous complexity, complete with enough entrances, exits and connections to turn Lower Manhattan into a concrete no man's land. Displaced people will now number in the low thousands rather than the high thousands. It is a question of degree: do you kill a city or maim it?

At present, the mess—and all except die-hard road lovers admit it is one—is undergoing a year's special planning study. The administration has given the problem to a highly creative architect, Shadrach Woods, hoping that the application of genius may turn up a miracle of some sort. Anyone who thinks New Yorkers lack faith has no idea of how many miracles are prayed for every day.

Meanwhile the traffic studies pile high. One thing is quite clear with or without them: you can go uptown and downtown some of the time, with luck, but you can rarely go across town. That is a truth of New York life, but it is particularly true of Lower Manhattan. Cars and trucks pour off the bridges and struggle gelatinously to the tunnels and vice versa.

The traffic studies prove that most of Lower Manhattan crosstown traffic is "interstate," which means that 90 per cent Federal funds are available for the expressway's construction. Then they prove that most of the traffic is local after all and that the expressway is needed primarily just to get to the other side. They prove that traffic will be routed around rather than through Manhattan as a result of building the expressway, and they also prove that traffic will go directly to Manhattan destinations because of it. Slice it any way you want.

Only one thing is really proved—that there is a monumental and complex traffic problem for which Nostradamus might reliably predict a future pattern. And one thing is not proved at all—that the expressway, at the expense of city-maiming, is going to solve it.

There is a Parkinson-type law that once you provide a super-route you do not just speed the already stuck cars on their way; you acquire a lot of new traffic. How much more non-Manhattan traffic will be attracted that would, or should, use Lower Manhattan as an interstate shortcut is a question that just won't go away. Or why that traffic should be dumped in Brooklyn. What will happen to the capacity of the Lincoln and Holland tunnels is another. How much more traffic can be shunted to still other congested Manhattan streets is one more.

A Port Authority statement made in favor of construction of the expressway some years ago claimed that the tunnels could, at that time, handle all traffic "which *must* travel between New Jersey and Manhattan." (Port Authority italics. Motorist vows on the necessity of their trips would ostensibly be handled by Port Authority toll collectors.) It was explained that nothing would be helped by enlarging the tunnels "and so dumping more traffic on the already overburdened streets of Manhattan."

The Port Authority's reasoning is incontrovertible. It applies equally well to the Lower Manhattan expressway.

What concerns us most of all is something that has been least discussed: the irreversible damage to the fabric of the city along the expressway route. There is a prevalent thought that depressing the road eliminates blight. This is not so, or only relatively so, to the degree that getting rid of a city-dividing superstructure is an improvement. But the social and physical fabric of the city along the proposed route has been deteriorating for the past twenty-eight years. This is the blight that comes from being fingered for an expressway route, with the uncertain future of the area its only certainty.

Properties are not kept up; improvements are not made. Residential and business tenants share the insecurity that sends everything downhill. Twenty-eight years of this can do a lot of damage. Along the Lower Manhattan expressway route there once was a healthy community and its remains are still there—blighted by the expressway before it ever got built.

The route is fixed where it will do the most possible historical and architectural damage. A line on a map does not begin to indicate the amount of destruction that will take place. To get the cars on and off that "line," supporting and servicing construction must extend far beyond it. Not only will the entire north side of Broome

Street go for the expressway's cross-island path but so will sections of many streets beyond.

The area is known to historians as the Cast-Iron District, a mid-to-late-nineteenth-century structural and architectural development of particular importance to American building. Part will be destroyed and the rest irreparably mutilated. The Haughwout Store on the northeast corner of Broome Street and Broadway, noted in many histories of architecture, is doomed. Greene Street, a uniquely intact enclave of iron architecture, will be hopelessly dismembered. One of the most respected critics and historians, Nikolaus Pevsner, informed a group of Americans visiting England that "there is a veritable museum of cast iron architecture in downtown New York, a greater concentration than anywhere else in the world."

"Are you aware of this?" he asked. "Do you recognize its unique quality? Are you letting the public know about it?"

The answers to Dr. Pevsner's questions, except for the efforts of a few persistent members of the architectural press, are no, no and no. The Landmarks Commission has designated the Haughwout Store and held other hearings. The highway people did go so far, a few years ago, as to commission a survey of the buildings. The city knows that some of them contain flammable materials of industries of less than good housekeeping habits, which has led to some particularly tragic fires. Hell's Hundred Acres is the catchy popular name given to the district as a result, ignoring its history, culture and some important economics.

For still another city survey came up with the information that this near miraculous nineteenth-century survival forms a valuable economic neighborhood. Small businesses of above-average stability occupy irreplaceable low-rent loft space behind those handsome, rhythmic, cast-iron colonnades of shabby Victorian elegance. These necessary businesses, of the kind that the city has been losing, also give essential, hard-to-find employment to marginally skilled minority workers.

So—stack up economics, environment, sociology, art, history and people against that line across the map. If there is no guarantee, there must at least be a reasonable certainty that some problems

---

(OVERLEAF) A route that will do the most possible
historical and architectural damage
(SY FRIEDMAN, ZODIAC PHOTOGRAPHERS)

are really going to be solved by the huge expenditure of funds and urban assets. We wouldn't bet our money on it, and what is being gambled with is the city itself.

Lincoln Center: Adding Up the Score

Although architecture and design must be broken in, like new shoes, until they have settled normally into the city's pattern of use, some assessments of Lincoln Center can be made. It is time to ask the $165.4 million question: what hath money, hopes, dreams and talent wrought? It may seem churlish to ask at all, in view of the fact that on any busy evening Lincoln Center is an agreeable place, full of light and movement and the tangible promise of varied entertainments.

What we have, architecturally, are four buildings designed to accommodate opera, drama, dance, musical theater, concerts and film festivals—no small cultural package. Three played it safe: Philharmonic Hall, the State Theater and the Metropolitan Opera are lushly decorated, conservative structures that the public finds pleasing and most professionals consider a failure of nerve, imagination and talent.

With a totally new esthetic and technology, the twentieth century is making dramatic contributions to the history of the art of building. But not here. The only buildings where one senses the possibilities are the Juilliard School and the Vivian Beaumont Theater. Standing in front of the theater, with its strong, structural good looks and the fronting pool and Henry Moore sculpture, the visitor sees one of the few honestly contemporary vistas in the place.* This is the sole moment that lifts the spirit of those to whom the twentieth century is a very exciting time to be alive and for whom the fleeting sensuosity of lighting effects and matching travertine is not enough. Even the Beaumont Theater formula was done better by Mies at Barcelona in 1929.

By contrast, however, the *retardataire* fussiness and esthetic indecision of the rest become painfully clear: a gift wrap job of

* The completion of the Juilliard School in 1969 strengthened this aspect and added Lincoln Center's best building.

What hath money, hopes, dreams and talent wrought?
(THE NEW YORK TIMES BY MEYER LIEBOWITZ)

travertine trim and *passe partout* colonnades applied to basic boxes in a spatial composition new with the Renaissance and reworked six decades ago by the Beaux Arts. In the most depressing sense, the Lincoln Center complex has defaulted as contemporary architecture and design.

Fortunately, the scale and relationship of the plazas is good, and they can be enjoyed as pedestrian open spaces, a value that may well increase with use and age. This and the massive amounts of entertainment that will be provided are its major successes.

There are other successful features. In real estate terms, it's a smash. Values of Lincoln Center and adjoining land have risen dramatically, and will continue to increase. According to certain renewal standards that have wide currency in metropolitan circles,

25

a lot of nice, shiny new buildings are replacing a lot of shabby, substandard old buildings, and that, in simplistic terms, looks good.

But there is serious question as to whether this is successful urban renewal. A bulldozer operation cleared the way for the cultural center and the new private office buildings, motels and luxury apartments that it has sparked. The most serious accusation leveled at Federally aided renewal, that it has failed to replace the stock of low and middle income housing that it destroys, holds true here.

Some renewal specialists and planners offer the alternative of scattered cultural facilities combined with new housing and urban services for the necessary social and physical rehabilitation of neighborhoods rather than the creation of cultural complexes. The idea that the cultural facility is a tool, rather than an end in itself, deserves thoughtful attention, even if it offers less immediate monumental gratification of the current cultural megalomania gripping most communities.

In further terms of urban planning, Lincoln Center has been created on a traffic island of converging avenues that is pure circulatory horror and the situation worsens constantly as new buildings open. The underground parking that repeats the tangle above ground is neither the corrective nor the supporting circulation design that should have been part of the original scheme. Murmurings by the city of remedial traffic measures have thus far failed to make any substantial improvement.

There is, finally, the question of culture, around which the whole complex revolves. If we define culture as average to expertly executed established and familiar fare, available to many people in maximum comfort, Lincoln Center is providing an impressive amount of it.

But there is no culture without creativity, and there is no meaningful culture of any period without that vital spark of fresh ideas and new forms that, fanned into brilliance by the greater epochs, becomes the enduring expression of an age. This is art, and culture, whether it appears in a cellar, a slum, or the back room of a bar. It has not appeared in Lincoln Center.

It is, after all, by the standards of art that all art must be judged. As entertainment, Lincoln Center promises to be an operational success.* By creative measurement, much of its product and most of

* Three years later (in 1969), Lincoln Center was in serious economic trouble.

26

its plant are an artistic failure. And that is why its expensively suave, extravagantly commonplace presence is making a great many people in the fine and performing arts profoundly uneasy.

World Trade Center: Who's Afraid of the Big, Bad Buildings?

On balance, the World Trade Center may not be the city destroyer that it has been popularly represented to be; its pluses could outweigh its minuses in the complex evaluation that must be made of it. The issues are far from black and white. The proper basic question may well be whether any agency should have the right to indulge in city-building on this scale and with this freedom without obligations to the city and beyond city review.* Since the Port of New York Authority has that legal right, the pertinent issues are those of the plan. Certainly its impact is so great that it is a matter of legitimate public concern.

The project that has generated so much controversy is a $525 million, sixteen-acre complex bounded on the north and south by Vesey and Liberty streets and on the east and west by Church and West streets. It will be the largest commercial superblock in Manhattan, closing all internal streets of fifteen small blocks, with a perimeter coverage on each side equal to the distance between Fifth and Park avenues. The twin 110-story towers, each 200 feet square or about the size of a city blockfront, are flanked by four seven-story structures around a five-acre plaza. The architects are Minoru Yamasaki and Associates and Emery Roth and Sons.

The greatest storm has centered on the size of the towers, which, as everyone knows by now, will break the skyline and be the tallest buildings in the world. The argument goes that the flat-topped behemoths will destroy the beauty of the romantically spired Lower Manhattan skyline. The hue and cry equals that raised at the time those spires were built. They were attacked then as barbaric, oversized wreckers of scale and sunlight, and with the build-

---

* The question can also be asked, as public transportation worsens in New York, why the Port Authority, as a public agency, fails to do anything about it, and whether it should be in the real estate business at all.

A new skyscraper age or the biggest tombstone in the world?
(BALTHAZAR KORAB FOR NEW YORK PORT AUTHORITY)

28

ing of the (now modest) twin towers of the Equitable Building in 1914 the outcry became so great that the city's first restrictive zoning law was passed. Wall Street was a symbol of architectural transgression. The responsible intellectual community refused to forgive the design sins of those early skyscraper builders with their decorative curtain-wall classicism, fancy-dress Gothic, "senseless" spires and Halicarnassus water towers for another forty years. This is the skyline that the same intellectual community now wants to protect.

With today's engineering advances, it was only a matter of time when the skyline would be broken again. The inevitable may or may not be desirable, but it must be dealt with as a fact of life. Barring war or depression, the impact will be ameliorated by buildings of intermediate scale as history, technology, megalomania, the skyscraper and the skyline pursue their natural course.

We do not believe in embalming or Williamsburging the New York skyline. This valid and dramatic testament of the city's brutally competitive grandeur and vitality has produced an incomparable twentieth-century esthetic. What we do believe in is the absolute necessity of relating these corporate and speculative status symbols to the needs, functions and uses of the city at ground level. The rationale of planning goes far deeper than a picture of the skyline, which is not static, and which changes its composition and alignment from every viewpoint.

The World Trade Center is no Pan Am Building, muscling into an overcrowded neighborhood of maximum big-building concentration. It is closer to Rockefeller Center as a city-shaping group of structures (also rejected by the architectural community and now hailed as urban design). The area is of minimum interest to preservationists. Separate studies by the Regional Plan Association, the City Planning Commission and the consultants preparing the new Lower Manhattan plan, Whittlesey and Conklin, Wallace-McHarg Associates and Alan M. Voorhees and Associates, Inc., confirm the planning logic of the location.

Rapid transit (three subway lines and Path) and street capacity are judged to be adequate for the 50,000 employees and 100,000 visitors expected daily. The Regional Plan Association, which is conscientiously concerned with long-range planning goals and particularly with better public transportation, feels that the downtown location encourages more transit than car use and that it has the right kind and number of jobs in the right places.

The city's consultants for the Lower Manhattan plan are not exactly bankers' boys in their view of what is best for downtown New York, which includes people-oriented waterfront reclamation, parks and pedestrian streets. They nevertheless have concluded that the economic realities of Lower Manhattan are a critical issue, and that without the revitalizing emphasis of the Chase Manhattan Building, the World Trade Center and some coherent solution of the muddled Civic Center plan the continued vitality of the area is in doubt.

Regional Plan and Planning Commission studies indicate that the eight million square feet of rentable space in the Trade Center will be properly absorbed. It will be spread over six years of staged construction in a city that builds an average of five million square feet of new office space annually.

The serious issue that remains, then, is the disruption of the local business community. One of the worst unsolved problems in the renewal of cities is the loss of those healthy small enterprises of a kind and character that large-scale projects increasingly and trag- ically destroy. The situation is particularly bad in New York, and the Port Authority has done even worse with it than the average municipality. Untouched by local laws, endowed with the right of eminent domain and a sovereign state position from which it nego- tiates at an absurdly one-sided advantage with the city, the Port Authority offers only a bonus as inducement to the tenant to move, which is less liberal than the liquidation or small business displace- ment grants under Title I urban renewal.

If skill, imagination and even enlightened philanthropy were required to keep this business community as an economically and humanly viable part of downtown, they should all have been em- ployed. At this point, the default is clear and inexcusable. The public finds it less easy to excuse and the mammoth project less easy to accept because the Port Authority has not, in the opinion of many, used the power and prosperity gained from the ceding of municipal rights for the greatest municipal good. It has acted more as a private investor than as a public agency.

The Regional Plan Association points out that foreign trade is projected as a growth industry in New York and that the scale of the Center is consistent with its prospects. However, it is more

likely that the World Trade Center will function to a large extent
as an arm of the financial community, which requires more and
more automated services and quarters for them. Its use for government offices outside of Customs (1,900,000 square feet of the
10,165,000 total have been taken by New York State) is questionable
in the extreme. It could be one more blow to the reeling Civic Center.

If we come to esthetics last, there is good reason for putting
this at the bottom of the list. Buildings that have this substantial
an effect on the life patterns of the city are a great deal more than
art objects. Unless they represent design irresponsibility, which
means raising the cheap and ordinary solutions of the speculative
builder to monument status, their relationship to those life patterns
must be the primary consideration.

No one would suggest, however, that esthetics are not important in big buildings. Nor is Detroit architect Minoru Yamasaki's
work to everyone's esthetic taste. He has developed a curiously unsettling style, which involves decorative traceries of exotic extraction
applied over structure or worked into it. His choice of delicate detail on massive construction as a means of reconciling modern structural scale to the human scale of the viewer is often more disturbing
than reassuring. It makes many competent architects go to pieces.
Here we have the world's daintiest architecture for the world's biggest buildings. But no review board could refuse to pass his buildings, even if it pined for a Corbusian or Miesian masterwork.

The design has been revised significantly since it was announced.
The towers' aluminum facing on incredible three-foot four-inch
modules will still shimmer at a distance like windowless metal grilles.
The four low buildings, originally to be finished in the same aluminum, are now in a brownish concrete, tied to the towers by the
use of aluminum spandrels. At model scale, the relationship is un-
defined and disquieting.

These buildings, which were joined to provide an enclosing
arcade for the plaza, have been separated to give access to views
of the river and to the waterfront in future development when the
West Side highway will hopefully be depressed. They give the appearance of having been merely broken apart slightly. As a result,
the immense formal plaza now has subsidiary open spaces. It is
to be hoped that they will enrich rather than disrupt this awesome
area. The danger is that they could leak limp and uncoordinated
out of the five-acre vastness, as in the smaller Holford plan for the

rebuilt St. Paul's precinct in London, rather than give the intimate relief intended.

The plaza has now been reduced to an ornamental role, or a kind of huge, paved promenade for fine weather, with most circulatory and access functions relegated to the concourse level below ground. This lifelessness is frightening. All elevators start on the lower level, which also connects to rapid transit. There is a serious need now to improve pedestrian use and circulation at street level. With Church Street doubled in width, the Center becomes traffic-isolated. A tunnel to be built deep under the street will lead again to the underground concourse. A bridge over the street would bring pedestrians more easily to the plaza and make it a more physical, functioning part of the neighborhood.

The final, inescapable fact remains that architecture is now breaking scale, and style, everywhere. (There is hardly an architect who in his secret heart doesn't want to be the one to do it.) The objective historian realizes that the twentieth century is in transition to a remarkable new technology and a formidable new environment before we have learned how to handle the old ones. Who's afraid of the big, bad buildings? Everyone, because there are so many things about gigantism that we just don't know. The gamble of triumph or tragedy at this scale—and ultimately it is a gamble—demands an extraordinary payoff. The Trade Center towers could be the start of a new skyscraper age or the biggest tombstones in the world.

Columbia Gym: How Not to Build a Symbol*

Architecture creates symbols; that is one of its functions. One of its most curious symbols has been the Columbia University gymnasium. But this is not the kind of symbol anyone wanted. It stands for one of the more disturbing problems of our troubled times—

* This article was a critique and analysis of the Columbia University gymnasium, which became one of the focal issues of the spring, 1968, disturbances at the university. It was written before the student strike. Construction of the gymnasium was put off and then canceled in early 1969.

32

the deep and bitter split and many-layered misunderstanding between a privileged urban university and an underprivileged community—a division that the Ford Foundation has given Columbia $10 million to heal.

No one is neutral about the building. The university sees it as an exemplary, badly misunderstood town-gown gesture. Its opponents see it as a too concrete instance of the university's rigid physical and emotional isolationism, even when making a gesture toward the community.

It is actually a definitive demonstration of an institutional failure to comprehend and react to the human and urban attitudes and feelings that surround it. These are partly university-engendered and partly symptomatic of the times, but they have very real and inescapable meaning for the university's future planning and its tenuous community and city relationships. The story of the gym is one answer to what has gone wrong on the Heights. It is both symbol and object lesson.

The controversy revolves around two basic factors: whether or not the gym belongs in the park, and the nature of its dual school-community uses. In the heat of the fight hardly anyone looked at the building itself. It is a blockbuster. It will cover two acres of Morningside Park, reaching, with its entrances and terraces, virtually from top to bottom. (Its defenders say it will make more "usable" land, help make the park safe and form a bridge between the university and the neighborhood. Its critics call it an invasion and violation of public parkland.)

There will be three upper levels reached from Morningside Drive, above, consisting of standard academic athletic facilities for Columbia. One lower level, entered from the bottom, will contain sports facilities for community use. Entrances are separate. There is no connection between the two at any point. (Two separate buildings in one, the university explains, with Columbia paying for both and giving one back to the city for public use. Separate and unequal, say its foes: Gym Crow.)

And so it goes. The university is accused of getting bargain parkland and cutting its costs with a nominal $3,000-a-year lease. The administration answers that it is actually taking on a $3-million-plus responsibility to build and give away the community gym and provide the community athletic program at a cost of $75,000 annually. The building is estimated at $12 million, of which $1.6 million will go for the community facilities. Columbia's complaint is that nobody mentions its full financial contribution.

Nor does anyone mention, administration spokesmen point out, the immensely successful, university-sponsored program that has been going on in the park for neighborhood children for the last twelve years that the community gym will extend to a year-round, full-time activity.

The university's facilities will be too small and outmoded as soon as they are finished, claim its foes. The administration's reply is that the building is not meant to serve all 18,000 students. It is for 3,800 undergraduates. When the new gym is completed, says Jackson Smith, a compact Olympic swimmer who also happens to be the designing architect for the firm of Eggers and Higgins, "it will be the best in the country."

The administration claims that it is backed by the community "except for a few troublemakers who are not in Harlem; they are on the Heights." It is certain that the community wants the gym. "It is our number one building project," says Columbia, officially. "It will prove itself in use."

It does not take much investigation, however, to find that both community groups and university faculty are sharply divided. A kind of *noblesse oblige* keeps some high-placed dissenting faculty members from speaking up in what would be a virtual vote of no confidence in the administration. Research undertaken as one of the first Ford grant activities found that most Harlemites have never even heard of the project.

Altogether, it is an undertaking not notable for sensitivity. It is certainly not going to be a particularly sensitive building. Although the front elevation on Morningside Drive has been reduced to twenty-seven feet to make it less obtrusive than in earlier schemes, the huge masonry bulk will never blend with its rustic setting. It is in conflict just by being there.

Attempts have been made to minimize mass by studying divisions in the virtually windowless walls and by breaking up the brutal, 126-foot-high rear facade in the park with three materials— a base of park-type stone, a center section of buff brick and a top of concrete aggregate. But you can't disguise an elephant or a building in a park. While thought and care have gone into the architectural treatment, the result cannot be characterized as either inspired or sympathetic to its site.

Insensitivity has been the crux of the matter from the start. It has been "too late" for this project for at least eight years. The die was really cast with the first questionable decisions.

Faced with predictable violent opposition to relocation that would have come with normal site selection, the unpopulated park looked like an irresistible alternative. There was a "good purpose" to justify its use. Park erosion, of course, is always carried out for a good purpose. The history of the despoliation of parks and the loss of precious urban open land can be charted by good purposes. Add the problem of crime, and good purpose becomes sanctified procedure.

Fired by good intentions, the university ignored clear warnings. Opposition came immediately from civic groups on the grounds of park encroachment. Encouraged by then Parks Commissioner Robert Moses, who was always known as a doer rather than a community sympathizer, the project was pushed ahead.

In 1960–61 it was pressed through a series of actions necessary to legalize its transgressions, including public hearings, that amounted virtually to a joint railroading by city and university. Authorization for this kind of use of parkland, which is held in trust by the state for the city, must be given by the State Legislature. It cannot be obtained without a home rule message from City Council and Mayor, and then there must be a two-thirds vote of each house of the State Legislature and approval by the Governor.

These are necessary community safeguards, and they were all systematically abrogated for the university in spite of rising community opposition. After this appalling enabling legislation was obtained, a lease was signed between Columbia and the Parks Department, represented by Commissioner Moses's successor, Newbold Morris, and approved unanimously by the Board of Estimate.

To Columbia, these steps are proof of the scrupulous correctness of its proceedings. To a large public that has helped throw the parks policies of the Moses era out of the window, the procedure is proof of the outrageousness of what has had to be protested and abolished.

At the time of the lease, the building plans were included in

35

the agreement. Visibly disturbed today by the accusation of "segregated" school and community facilities, Columbia says that it was "locked into" the present plan by the 1961 lease.

The real tragedy of the whole Columbia gym affair is that this dubious and even harmful project has been carried out in good faith. It is not the product of a monstrous and evil deviousness ascribed to the university by its enemies. The institutional mentality is not diabolical. It is simply grossly imperceptive. It has meant well and behaved with consummate wrongheadedness.

Certainly the problems are not simple. The urban university is doomed to steer between the Scylla and Charybdis of community and vested interest. Whatever it decides, it is damned if it does and damned if it doesn't. And there will always be town-gown conflict, intensified by the urban crisis.

But Columbia still seems to want it both ways. It feels justified in using public parkland for a building that is perhaps one-sixth for public purposes, and in its heart it still thinks of itself as a privileged private club generously conferring certain optional, peripheral philanthropies. Today's university can never play that part again. It cannot avoid an involved and responsible role in its troubled neighborhoods. Unless there is a significant change in the basic understanding of this inescapable and critical community relationship the Ford grant program is doomed to failure.

Hard Questions for Harlem: The State Office Building Dilemma

The case of the State Office Building, known in Harlem as the SOB, has turned into Governor Rockefeller's Vietnam. It is mired in the question of community participation, or the complex matter of who speaks for the real needs and wishes of the Harlem community, or even if anyone can. And it focuses on the basic problem of physical planning: how it can meet needs and desires on the local level if it is to have any degree of environmental success.

The great disaster of "planning," for black and white communities alike, is that in the past it has almost wholly failed to do this. Meant to create a bright new world for everyone, it became, through no consciously evil act but simply by following a kind of conventional real estate wisdom, a discriminatory operation. Called renewal or redevelopment, it has been an economic rather than a social tool, aimed at a set of limited economic objectives that have been essentially destructive of anything that does not fit into a pre-conceived pattern of certain types of acceptable financial benefits, largely to business and the tax structure.

What was destroyed in the process, in too many cases, were neighborhoods, such as Boston's West End, a now-classic urban renewal catastrophe, housing that the poor could afford, which was never replaced, and the variety, humanity and stability of older sections of any city that had worked out their own modest destiny. It bulldozed the shaky structure of the "underclass," and added fuel to minority fires.

That is why the case of the State Office Building has a particular importance. It goes to the root of planning practice.

The project was headed for trouble from the time Governor Rockefeller announced it in 1966, because he was operating under an old and already dangerously outdated set of rules. The assumption then was that all major revitalizing investments were going into other parts of Manhattan, with attention turned particularly to the huge expenditures of the World Trade Center, and that Harlem should get "a piece of the action." And so the Governor announced a State plan for the 125th to 126th Street block between Lenox and Seventh Avenues, with half of the site to be a State Office Building and half a cultural center.

At the time it seemed a courageous act for the State to go in where real estate men feared to tread. And the idea of economic and social integration still had considerable general currency; it was just the Governor's bad luck and timing that black self-determination was on the rise. It was further bad luck and timing that a group of Albany legislators promptly cut the cultural center out of the plan.

Opposition started immediately and grew in 1968. In the summer of 1969 a group of activists, the Community Coalition, occupied the site to prevent construction. The State's Urban Development Corporation then offered to finance the half-block of cultural or other neighborhood facilities that had been dropped, contingent on finding "a representative community advisory committee to work with." In September the police removed the squatters and the Governor announced that he was going ahead with the office building.

In October, three proposals for housing, a school, and a variety of social and commercial services for the entire block were unveiled by ARCH, the Architects' Renewal Committee in Harlem, a group of young black advocacy planners. Advocacy planners are a new breed of professionals that works within a community to express, and advocate, its wishes, often in opposition to government or official plans. ARCH has announced itself as unalterably against a State Office Building in any form, which it considers "in clear contempt of the needs and desires of the Harlem community."

A group of Harlem businessmen proposed a development corporation. CORE offered a compromise: state offices in a tower above a substantial community center that could be "built as far as the heavens," says Roy Innis, "barring negotiations with God." Negotiations with God would appear to be easier than negotiations on the ground. It is apparently as hard to get all the factions together in Harlem as it is in Paris, and peace seems equally far away.

A few facts about the controversy won't hurt. First, the State Office Building and cultural center project as originally conceived and released by the Governor's office had about all the sparkling warmth and potential community vitality of a typical old-style urban renewal proposal. Color it black or white, that kind of block is devitalizing cities everywhere.

Second, there is that most interesting and sensational of charges hurled by the black activists—that the State Office Building presages a white takeover of Harlem. Actually, that's not nearly as far out as it sounds, if you remove the grotesque implications of white establishment conspiracy.

What it really means, is that the routine redevelopment of parts of Harlem, as such development has occurred in other marginal neighborhoods, "upgrades" land potential in a way that it makes it profitable for real estate speculators to follow. What happens then is, in a sense, "takeover"; the residents are bulldozed out for an entirely different kind of institutional, commercial and residential community. Again, color it black or white; that is precisely what has happened in some of the city's other marginal neighborhoods.

To understand that this is not pure paranoid fantasy, one must think of those parts of Harlem close to universities or hospitals, or

prime transportation centers such as 125th Street. The Harlem pro-
testors are sophisticated enough to know that the prospect of the
State Office Building was already attracting other potential outside
investors. And when they question this kind of "revitalization" by
asking "For whom?"—it is the same question being asked by social
planners who have watched the process of dispossessing neighborhoods before.

Fact number three: the state has radically revised its position
as to what can and should be put on the 125th Street block, even to
the extent of considering the interiors of the State Office Building
almost as a blank check for community-oriented services. Moreover,
the state, in the form of the Urban Development Corporation, is now
in virtually complete agreement with most of those who are claiming
to speak for Harlem in the only area of general consensus—definition
of what the community needs. That is housing and community and
commercial facilities. Both sides suffer from a current malady:
intransigence. Apparently the Governor has to have a State Office
Building, no matter what the four walls contain, in part because he
has already spent so much money on it. For the community it has
become an odious symbol that must go.

Which leaves the Governor with his Vietnam. If he withdraws,
and plans the development of the block without the State Office
Building, he loses. Or does he? If the building is accepted by Harlem
but used as a chance to drive a bargain for what it wants, the
community loses. Or does it? Can there be an honorable, negotiated
peace? Must there be unilateral withdrawal?

There is much to be gained for self-determination if the extraordinary legal and financial resources of the UDC available to Harlem
can be used to carry out the projects that everyone wants. But the
terms being dictated by activist leaders and the inability to unify
community sentiment and representation into a working tool could
weary the patience of God (mentioned by Mr. Innis but would He
be acceptable to all other participants?) if they ever got that far.
It is quite possible that the significance of the building is far less
than whether the state and the community can get an effective
partnership going. Both practically and symbolically, a lot of the
American future rests on that.

How to Kill a City

The Architectural Follies

New York's longest-run show, the Architectural Follies, goes on.
Performances as usual.

First, the comedy act. The New York Bank for Savings announced that it will build a twenty-seven-story apartment house
next to its main office on Third Avenue at 72nd Street, utilizing
the same "Colonial design" as the earlier building. Horace Ginsbern
will be the architect.

Since the earlier building is a Williamsburg-type Governor's
Palace, and a twenty-seven-story apartment building is a high-rise
tower that was not only structurally and stylistically impossible
but also as remote as a spaceship in Colonial times, this will be an
amusing design trick. The "Colonial" label seems to be no more
than a wistful thought, however, because the rendering shows a
typical New York twenty-seven-story apartment house with familiar curtain wall and projecting balconies that might have made
George Washington giddy. Funny? Boffo.

But this kind of joke is something that New York should have

40

outgrown long ago. It is a hangover from the days before modern cities recognized their own magnificence. It doesn't work, as architecture or nostalgia.

Witness the original Bank for Savings building that is to inspire this addition. We banked there, until we were shifted to a newer neighborhood branch that was all "modern," with a wall-length pseudo-Mondrian subsequently painted out so that everything was reduced to safe, washable, plastic-coated middlin' gray and green, including the plants. Call it the Plastic Esthetic.

Saving money—considered a dubious virtue today, anyway—becomes a singularly depressing experience. Dreams die easily at the Bank for Savings. In the main office they die in an inflated, dehydrated, imitation Colonial shell, built with all of the hand-crafted Colonial sincerity of big city commercial construction, housing the unparalleled mechanical impersonality of the modern banking operation. Were banks first to reduce people to numbers? This one has the intimate eighteenth-century charm of its IBM computers. There is nothing sadder or funnier than this kind of misuse, or abuse, of meaningful architectural style.

It's sad and funny to see it done again by the Franklin National Bank at Madison Avenue and 48th Street. Watching this building being transformed from twentieth century to eighteenth century was one of the top midtown acts of last season's Follies. First, there was the steel frame, strong, severe, handsomely rectilinear (the bones are best in most buildings), suggesting the logical shape and design that its covering surface might take, subject only to the architect's talent, imagination and respect for the inspiration of the structure. Painstakingly, brick by brick, the lie was laid up for anyone to observe.

Eighteenth-century arches were hung on the facade like theatrical scrim. Originally, of course, arches like these were carefully built up to wedge-shaped, locking keystones to make openings in a brick wall without having the wall fall down. They were as natural and beautiful for masonry construction as the thin curtain wall is for the metal-framed building today.

Presto change. The hand is quicker than the eye. The arches aren't arches because the masonry is non-supporting. It's all backed by steel. Fooled you. What we have here is a kind of large architectural practical joke. It is tiresome, like most practical jokes.

The Brokaw mansion bites the dust—there's nothing
like a good house-wrecking (THE NEW YORK TIMES BY SAM FALK)

42

But the undertaking was carried out in consistent comic spirit to the end. The opening luncheon, which featured authentic Colonial cooking, was served by waiters in knee breeches. (Authentic Madison Avenue.)

So much for comedy. The tragedy was the razing of the Brokaw mansion. The hoarding went up at the end of the week and major demolition began on Saturday. Saturday, obviously, is not a normal building trades working day and the wrecking crew got double time for its efforts. The Campagna Construction Corporation, the owners and builders of a new apartment house on the site, were taking no chances. It was a dandy way to do enough massive damage at a time when no normal channels are functioning, to assure the building's doom.

No Marquesa de Cuevas had a chance to step forward with $2 million to save it, as with the Pyne house group on Park Avenue. By Monday it was too late. Perhaps the American Institute of Architects, which produced a nice scroll for the Marquesa, could arrange for a suitable trinket for the Campagna Corporation. Something like profit rampant on the seal of the city, upside down.

There is no denying that this is the most dramatic act in the Architectural Follies in a long time. There's nothing quite like a good house-wrecking. Come one, come all. You are cordially invited to a demolition-watching. It's a great performance of a kind being given with increasing frequency in Manhattan, one that could replace the "happening" as the most chic of avant-garde anti-cultural events.

Watch an architectural landmark demolished piece by piece. Be present while a splendid building is reduced to rubble. See the wrecking bars gouge out the fine château-style stonework. Hear the gas-powered saws bite into the great beams and rafters. Thrill to destruction. Take home samples. Hurry to the show.

On second thought, don't hurry. There will be many more performances. Good demolitions could outrun *Abie's Irish Rose.* Free demolition-watchings will be offered in all of New York's best styles and periods: High Victorian, Early Skyscraper, Cast-Iron Commercial in the path of the Lower Manhattan expressway, Greek Revival on the waterfront. If this isn't going to be faced as a public responsibility, it might as well be taken as a public spectacle. Anyone coming from City Hall?

The Urban Scene

The Impoverished Society

The final defeat for Pennsylvania Station was handed down by the City Planning Commission in January, and the crash of ninety-foot columns will be heard this summer.* What was not heard was the bitter and eloquent opposition at the hearings to the demolition of this New York landmark, and the Planning Commission's explanation of its action.

The explanation needs airing. What few realized, and this made all of the impassioned pleas for the cultural and architectural values of the city fruitless, was that however much the commission might be moved in the area of its civic conscience by such arguments, it was totally without power to act on them. As it pointed out in its report, it is permitted only to pass on the *proposed* use of land, not on its *existing* use, and therefore cannot rule on the value of a building that is already on the site, but only on the nature of its replacement.

The matter would not have come before the commission at all except that a zoning variance was necessary to permit an occupancy in excess of 2,500 persons for the new Madison Square Garden, which will replace Penn Station. The decision rested entirely on whether congestion would be increased by issuing the variance. The joker here, and it is a terrifying one, is that the City Planning Commission was unable to judge a case like Penn Station's on the proper and genuine considerations involved.

What this amounts to is carte blanche for demolition of landmarks.† The commission's hands are tied in any interpretation of the public good that rests on evaluation of old versus new or good versus bad. If a giant pizza stand were proposed in an area zoned for such usage, and if studies showed acceptable traffic patterns and building densities, the pizza stand would be "in the public in-

* 1963.

† The situation was somewhat ameliorated by the passage of New York's Landmarks Preservation Law in 1965. This delays demolition on designated landmarks, while salvation is sought, but the building can still be destroyed —contrary to popular impression of the power of the law—if no practical solution is found.

44

terest," even if the Parthenon itself stood on the chosen site. Not that Penn Station is the Parthenon, but it might just as well be because we can never again afford a nine-acre structure of superbly detailed solid travertine any more than we could build one of solid gold. It is a monument to the lost art of magnificent construction, other values aside.

The tragedy is that our own times not only could not produce such a building but cannot even maintain it, so that its fate is as inevitable as the Planning Board's decision. An interesting suggestion, like Robert Zion's in the *Journal of the American Institute of Architects*, that the station's great stone vaults could have sheltered a remarkably handsome and appropriate railroad museum and that its adjoining glass and iron shell could have been converted into a public botanical garden becomes a fairy tale in terms of economic realities. It's time we stopped talking about our affluent society. We are an impoverished society. It is a poor society indeed that can't pay for these amenities, that has no money for anything except expressways to rush people out of our dull and deteriorating cities, and that treats land values as the highest morality.

An even stranger kind of poverty, that of imagination and ideals, is demonstrated by the proposed remodeling of another landmark, the Times Tower, into a modern showcase for the Allied Chemical Corporation. In this case, the old building will not actually be torn down; it will be defaced. But it will be defaced in a morbidly significant way.

When it was designed in 1903 the Times Tower was a blend of progress and romanticism; it stood at the crossroads of the twentieth century. Called "a valuable addition to our short list of artistic skyscrapers" by Montgomery Schuyler at the time, it was an anachronistic solution that combined the radical, still new, forward-looking steel frame with a nostalgic, backward-looking, Victorian-picturesque facade of Gothic and Renaissance details in white (sic) brick and terra cotta.

In what was considered an inspired solution for the city's most important new building on the oddly shaped lot formed by the crossing of Broadway and Seventh Avenue, the architects rather fetchingly inflated Giotto's bell tower in Florence and joined it with the lower office floors in a carefully calculated, but embarrassingly inept, articulation. The result was the building's well-known, and awkward, silhouette. The Times Tower was never a masterpiece; it was ambitious, pedestrian and dull. But it was legitimately conceived for its day, and such buildings, as they embody and preserve historic attitudes and styles, actually improve with age.

The new design is also ambitious, pedestrian and dull, but without the virtue of singularity that marks its predecessor. All exterior detail will be cleaned off and the building "refaced" with a routine, completely faceless contemporary curtain wall. The awkward silhouette, however, will be kept, although it becomes totally meaningless once its *raison d'être* is stripped away. Thus the publicity value of the landmark is retained, while the landmark itself is destroyed.

Surely there could be no more curious confusion of values than this, no clearer evidence of the current emphasis on expedient commercial advantage over all other considerations, no sadder revelation of the architectural standards that prevail today. Anything new is categorically preferred to anything old, no matter how shoddy or undistinguished the new may be. And if the old is wanted occasionally, "reproductions" are preferred to originals, because they are newer and cleaner. It rarely occurs to anyone, as in the case of the 1905 Columbus Tower in San Francisco or the Fidelity Building of the same period, adjoining Charles Center in Baltimore, that an old building can be profitably cleaned, restored and even modernized where necessary for civic enrichment rather than civic loss.

The ultimate curiosity is the willingness, even enthusiasm, of the architectural firms employed by businessmen to wreak the damage; interestingly enough, for the Times Tower, the firm of Voorhees, Walker, Smith, Smith and Haines is successor to the partnership of Eidlitz and MacKenzie, the original designers. Architects' inhumanity to architects surpasses understanding, particularly when the earlier ones are dead. It's a good way to kill off a city, as well.

Legislating Against Quality

Another chapter of the sad saga "How to Kill a City" has been provided by the Appellate Division of the State Supreme Court in the case of the owners of the *Seagram Building* vs. *The Tax Commission of the City of New York*.

This decision, which has established a new, drastically increased tax assessment policy for "prestige" buildings, may turn out to be the worst thing to hit the city, architecturally speaking, short of an atom bomb. Incredible as it seems, New York has chosen to discriminate against good building by imposing a special method of taxing architectural excellence. There is no surer way to outlaw it.

This city has done this, as the saying goes, "strictly from hunger." Its established practice is to tax a commercial building on its "market value," a figure reached on the basis of net income, capitalized at a customary 6 per cent plus 2 per cent for depreciation. (Excursions into finance are not usual Art Page fare, but the art of architecture is compounded of esthetics and economics in a curious and uneasy blend.) By this formula, the Seagram Building comes up with a figure that hovers roughly around $17 million. It is no secret that this beautiful edifice cost $36 million to build. And there, as anyone can clearly see, is more than another $17 million untapped by taxes, in a city starved for revenue. The apple in Eden could not have tempted the tax man more.

It is also no secret that when an investor or speculator constructs a building for profit (as another saying goes, he's not in business for his health), he puts no more into it than will earn him that profit, usually just about enough to hold its minimum-quality, rentable walls together. His construction cost is pretty close to market value. From his point of view, it would be sheer madness to do anything else.

In fact, the one note that keeps recurring throughout the court decision—and we make it clear here that we are in no way commenting on the legal aspects of the case but simply on an attitude relevant to the production of architecture—is that any other procedure can only be considered a form of corporate incompetence. The logical, legal mind holds that no successful businessman with sources of expert advice would ever erect a building at greater cost than practical market value without realizing a specific, measurable profit from his action. This patently foolish behavior must surely be able to be translated into dollars and cents in real estate investment terms, and it is, therefore, taxable.

How, then, does one tax it? How can the city remove Seagram

and other superior structures from the general class of ordinary commercial buildings subject to the blanket rule of "market value" assessment? It is done by declaring these "prestige" structures a "limited specialty," based on the fact that there is a group of buildings in New York called specialties, like the Stock Exchange or Madison Square Garden, that cannot be evaluated by the usual rental-return formula. Taxes on these buildings, because of their particular nature and functions, are figured in replacement terms, using construction or "reproduction" cost, less depreciation.

In a kind of architectural segregation, Seagram and its brothers are now to be evaluated in the same way. Construction cost is to be accepted as the building's "real" value, since it is argued that in most profit-calculated, "prudent" commercial construction the building cost and market value are reasonably close. Whether this is a fair or realistic "real" value for an office building that has not been built primarily as a speculative investment is open to question.

But the effect of the ruling is depressingly clear. Obviously, no one will build a prestige structure if he is to be penalized for doing so. Nor will any builder take advantage of the carefully worked-out voluntary provisions of the new zoning law intended to produce better design and more open space in the city's new construction. He might then have a prestige building on his hands, and that could be an economic disaster. In essence, the city has decreed that there will be no relief from that stultifying spread of lowest-common-denominator mediocrity from now on. There may not even be any new prestige buildings to tax.

The crux of the whole matter seems to be that disturbing (to the city) discrepancy of a building that cost $36 million and is worth, on the market, less than half that amount. The difference, in the judges' concurring opinion, "is never satisfactorily explained, and does not do much credit to the sagacity of the corporate managers."

The difference, of course, is architecture. The difference is a prosperous corporation with a sense of civic responsibility with all-too-rare taste and pride in quality, willing to spend a great deal of money to produce a superb public monument. It is not uncommon theory now that a city should encourage environmental quality by tax incentives. New York has done just the reverse in this case. But this is in the tradition that levies tax increases on "improved" property, a practice that encourages urban deterioration.

48

Seagram Fountains—a penalty for excellence

Certainly Seagram has had business benefits, taxable as income. But it is quite possible to build a large, showy structure of considerably less merit and cost that will do the job of impressing the public and swelling corporate profits just as well. Excellence is always a gratuitous and expensive gesture. Louis XIV would have been hard-pressed to explain Versailles to the City Tax Commis-

49

sion. It was a work of art as well as a "prestige" building and executive headquarters for the French government. Unfortunately, the source of its capital expenditures led to the Revolution, but our corporate kings build their monuments on more solid ground.

Today the large corporation is the only possible patron for the great commissions in art and architecture that will distinguish our time. If the law discourages this, the city, and the century, will suffer. The New York Tax Commission has taken a perilous, extra-legal step into the field of architectural criticism that could turn out to be architectural annihilation.

Abortive Cafes and Redundant Plazas

This chapter of "How to Kill a City" deals with the present rather than the past. It is devoted to the peculiar perversion of noble intentions, or good ideas gone bad. The fact that they are going bad on a monumental scale is not surprising, since that is the way New York does things. It just makes disaster citywide and certain.

We are concerned here, first, with the threat to that lively and lovely focus of the city's spirit and sophistication, the Grand Army Plaza at 59th Street on the southern edge of Central Park, New York's most distinguished, urbane and elegant open space. By extension, we question some unanticipated effects of the new zoning law on the creation and destruction of open space throughout Manhattan.

The Plaza area, a fortuitous combination of a perfectly scaled square and well-related buildings with suitable shopping and social functions, is about to be mutilated as a coherent, justly proportioned element of civic design. This will be done by two undertakings euphemistically known in real estate language as improvements.

The first is a good idea gone very bad, the Huntington Hartford cafe for the southeast corner of Central Park, on the Plaza. The second is a prime example of the perversion of good intentions —in this case the city's new zoning law—by the projected General Motors Building which will replace the Savoy Plaza Hotel. In combination, they will wreak havoc on one of the city's most delightful urban features.

The controversial cafe, which will go ahead as a result of the Court of Appeals decision last week,* will cost Mr. Hartford, who seems to have a gift for backfiring cultural gestures, an extra half million to do the wrong thing.

The vision, of course, is of an idyllic, bucolic, European-style restaurant-cafe, a place to sit and watch the popular parade go by in a pleasant atmosphere of schmaltz and schlag. The reality, alas, will be a perversion of the dream.

The pretty proposal for a pretty building against a sylvan backdrop by Edward Durell Stone does not show additional areas that must be gouged out of the park for deliveries, parking, garbage disposal and assorted ugly, space-consuming services. If the cafe is to be a democratic facility, as the city assures us it will be, hot dogs and ice cream wrappers will be commoner than cappucino and cassis. And the passing parade will consist of more noxious automobiles than ever on a corner where crosstown, uptown and downtown traffic already converge, without still another stopping and parking point.

The worst perversion of all is implied in the court's description of the rustic outcropping of rocks and shrubs as "neglected and misused" land; by implication, expendable. The whole park is neglected and much of it is misused, but the answer is scarcely to eliminate it.

In terms of planning, a factor of which this city remains stubbornly innocent in too many executive decisions, the site is atrocious. It is not only a patent violation of irreplaceable parkland—and it is immaterial whether or not the courts have decided that the city has a legal right or precedent to violate it—but it is also destructive of the plaza itself, by opening its terminating natural boundary to construction and congestion.

As for the General Motors Building,† its contribution to the rape of the plaza is a clear demonstration of how the new zoning, like the old zoning, is to be used exclusively as a tool for profit.

The old zoning law yielded the largest income by permitting the greatest rentable space in a lumpy, ziggurat-shaped mold pushed

---

* It did not go ahead, as a result of a change in administration.
† This one did come to pass; see "The Parthenon Comes to General Motors," p. 92.

51

to the building line. Once it had been worked out in dollars and cents, it became the standard formula.

Reaching for architecture, the new code offers builders bonuses for straight-lined towers, allowing them to rise higher (more rentable space) if plazas and arcades are provided. The intention was admirable. The result is that investors have figured out the new mold for maximum profit, and while it is a better mold, it will be used irrespective of suitability to site. Again, the minimum architectural and maximum economic mold has been established.

General Motors is a perfect example. To achieve the most bulk possible under the new law, it will have an open plaza facing the existing plaza. Ever heard of a redundant plaza? This is it. Something like having two heads. Not only does it provide extra space at the one spot in New York where it is not needed, but it breaks the building line where enclosure is desirable.

It has been suggested that the General Motors plaza belongs on the Madison Avenue side of the building. But opening up Madison Avenue would be an equal mistake, because its best feature, urbanistically, is the intimacy of its small, closely connected, luxurious specialty shops that unroll the treasures of the world for the pedestrian. Why destroy that scale and continuity?*

Obviously General Motors is not interested in a building that makes a public contribution, in spite of official corporate protestations to the contrary. Every creative architectural possibility has been barred, beyond permitting the architect—again Edward Stone —the liberty of making thoughtfully detailed and frequently excellent studies of what can be done within the maximum profit mold.

The handwriting is on the wall. The new code's plaza-tower formula for the greatest investment return has been set. Two forty-five Park Avenue, for example, now under construction, will be set back meaninglessly for still another plaza on Park Avenue, which might have been far more advisable for the congested Lexington Avenue side. As much as we need open space, it can be as destructive of an urban pattern in the wrong place as it can be beneficial in the right one. As usual, it will be calculated not by planners but by profiteers.

* G.M. has also done that; its Madison Avenue front, slightly recessed, is now a lost block of banks and the building's entrance.

Thus the new zoning incentives for a better urban environment are subverted. General Motors, which could have equaled Seagram's handsome municipal gesture with ease, has proved to be no exception to the rule.

Up in Central Park

It would have been nice if the concern about encroachments in Central Park had started a little sooner. It is just about eighty years too late. Even now the belated conservation fever aroused by the project for the police station and stables is unmarked by proper evaluation of the factors involved. These factors are need or desirability firmly balanced against location, size, style, effect on the pastoral qualities of the park and sensitivity to its original philosophy and design.

In the case of the police station and stables, with the exception of the large game ring,* the score adds up in its favor. But to say that an almost total lack of judgment and taste has consistently been the case in the history of park "improvements" is a small, sad understatement of the disastrous facts.

Anyone interested can stroll to the contested site just south of the 85th Street transverse. The approach is through an obstacle course of existing encroachments. If the stroller possesses a trained or innate sensitivity to the picturesque landscape school of the nineteenth century that was the Olmsted-Vaux park style and its priceless hallmark, he will instinctively cringe from metal and concrete intrusions and avert his eyes from blockbuster memorials.

Each one, of course, was proposed and built for the public good. Oh, public good—and that includes philanthropy, patriotism, art, culture, recreation and entertainment—what crimes against the park have been committed in thy name!

Let us suppose that you are taking this walk and that you enter the park at Fifth Avenue and 80th Street. The path goes between an iron-fenced, asphalted play area on the left and a match-

---

* Eliminated in a later version.

ing, but larger iron-fenced, asphalted parking lot for the Metropolitan Museum on the right. It takes a while to actually get into the park, with all that iron and asphalt, and the view is of a pastoral sea of cars, not exactly what Olmsted had in mind. Turn right, now, toward your objective.

You are passing the very plain and unedifying back of the Metropolitan Museum. There is no effort to impress with this rear view, in spite of the monumental classicism of the four-block Fifth Avenue front. This side is obviously meant to be built onto. The museum takes up almost fourteen acres of parkland and remains a discreet cultural threat to more of it. Olmsted recognized the error of putting the museum in the park shortly after the deed was done.

Since there is no greenery to the right, you turn to the left. The obelisk, added in 1881, is a quite properly Victorian picturesque accent. Not so the sterile banality of its "classically" concreted approach, which destroys the pastoral spirit for another few hundred yards. With mixed feelings you cross the drive.

Ahead is the Belvedere Lake. You may walk to its edge on a solid asphalt apron. Beyond is Belvedere Castle, an appropriately romantic landscape image nestling well into the rocks and sprouting weather instruments. Balancing it, with maximum incongruity, is a stark, green-painted mass with towering steel light standards, the Delacorte Shakespeare Theater.

Hold—as the Bard would say—do you not respect free drama on the highest artistic level? Yes, indeed, every greensward-destroying encroachment is well meant and worthwhile. All that this green-destroying eyesore eliminates, permanently, is natural land for rich and poor, in a city where land is the rarest and most expensive of commodities. Only Scrooge would suggest that construction belongs elsewhere.

Eyes right, then, to block the sight of the all-too-solid theater. A looming Polish king prances on bronze horseback, set on an immense, rectangular granite podium. But there is still, flanking and forward, the fifteen-acre Great Lawn.

They are flat, minimally landscaped acres, made of fill from subway excavations dumped into an old Croton reservoir in the 1930's. Less a lawn than an active sports area, wire goal fences are scattered across it. It is a playing field now, not a promenade or pastoral landscape, and like all such, it is useful and rather desolately scrubby.

At the 85th Street transverse end is a stand of trees to the west, and to the east, one of the park's most stolidly ugly play and recreation grounds, iron-fenced, naturally. The backs of shop buildings and the existing Vaux-housed police station on the transverse road terminate the view. This would be the site of the new police station and stables, largely underground and topped by a landscaped rise, which under the circumstances might even qualify for that abused park term, "improvement."

If you are still strolling, you might go north to a point where the wooded vista reveals the massive, jagged roofline of the Lasker pool. Built like a jazzed-up concrete bunker in a sylvan setting, this is an artistic anachronism in the service of social philanthropy, to put it mildly. If you go south, instead, there is the Wollman rink, which replaces a naturalistic arm of an Olmsted pond with brick, canned music, and man-made ice. Any pretense to sensibility in either design was lost, hands down, while Olmsted and Vaux whirled like dervishes in their graves. The results are pastoral sabotage, or parkicide.

At the Mall, there is more wrongheadedness. A cold, classic bandshell permanently anchored in concrete destroys the Mall axis and is the substitute for the gilt-starred, ornate cast-iron bandstand by Jacob Wrey Mould that Olmsted and Vaux put among the trees. At the Lake, the replacement for the original rustic boathouse stands in immutable tiled-lavatory horror. The successors to sylvan summerhouses and refreshment stands that were allowed to rot are asphalt-trimmed, drainpipe-decorated structures in a staunch brick outhouse style. About eighteen acres of the original landscaping have been replaced by misguided memorial "playgrounds" in unsuitable styles. The Parks Department job of landscape architect was accidentally eliminated from the revised 1936 charter.

What all this adds up to is a splendid object lesson in how to destroy a park. The dictionary defines encroachment as advancement "beyond desirable or normal limits." In the absence of any clear understanding of what these limits are, what is probably needed is a handy desirable-and-normal-limit, or DNL quotient, to measure by.

It could be computed of factors of grass removed, planting not replaced and landscape features lost, multiplied by $200 a foot for free prime land and a deficit factor for design unsuitability and donors whose gifts fail to meet costs. This figure could be squared for automobiles and parking lots. Olmsted was not a mathematician, but he certainly would have approved.

Singing the Downtown Blues

Hurry, hurry, hurry, as the pitchmen used to say; last call for anyone who wants to see the wonders of old New York, the real, live, genuine, remaining bits of the old city in Lower Manhattan, sitting at the feet of the most famous skyscrapers in the world. Come see the biggest buildings on the smallest streets, the newest next to the oldest, the soaring present and the small-scaled past. There is no doubt about it, this jam-packed mass of spectacular stone and steel with its dash of historical seasoning is the most spontaneously romantic and shatteringly magnificent cityscape ever known.

But if you can't get there fast, forget it. In a few short years Lower Manhattan will be just another Third or Sixth Avenue.

Good enough, if you fancy the bland, commercial homogenization of postwar Third and Sixth avenues. Their chief fanciers, however, are those builders and investors whose sense of environmental esthetics is limited to the calculable beauties of rentable square footage by the square block and who do more to plan, construct and seal the fate of this city than any combination of officials and municipal agencies theoretically entrusted with the job. A government man on the highest Federal level of urban renewal once remarked to this writer that New York is the only major city in the country that has been planned exclusively for profit and built to that pattern by its businessmen with the city easing the way.

New Yorkers who do not build the city but merely live in it frequently fancy other values. They have a fondness, based on sound instincts of what a great city should be, for the enrichment and contrast of the kind of early buildings and intimate streets that are grist for the speculator's mill.

They esteem the cobbled slips and lanes, the Greek Revival coffee and spice houses just above the Battery that are rapidly disappearing and taking with them the sense of the harbor's historic sailing age; the shabby Georgian-Federal structures redolent of fish in the old Fulton Market; dormered and pitched-roof brick houses against the Gothic stone and spiderweb steel of Brooklyn Bridge; the granite blocks and Greek lintels that still face ropeworks and casual bars and beaneries in the old city; the nineteenth-century breaks in the twentieth-century skyscraper-lined canyons that let in the sleety New York sky and the ghosts of New York history. It is all going, going, gone.

In Lower Manhattan, historic streets have been demapped and eliminated by the City Planning Commission to make profitable superblock parcels for private builders. Historic districts in the path of powerful business interests have been left undesignated by the Landmarks Preservation Commission. What has not already been destroyed or damaged waits resignedly for the speculative developers, who are known to be assembling more superplots.

Until recently, in every possible fashion, city agencies have aided and abetted the process in the biggest urban giveaway of past and future ever negotiated for cash or taxes. What the city has put its stamp of approval on is one of the largest standard-model commercial developments that New York has yet seen. With few exceptions, the names are chillingly familiar—Uris, Rudin, and Rose, Emery Roth—the "stylesetters" of commercial midtown. Downtown, here they come.

It isn't just that New York has had no muscle; it has had no vision. Whatever amateur or archaic attempts it has made to guide redevelopment have been tacitly understood to be totally subservient to commercial prerogatives. Until a very short time ago, it set no standards and made no plans. No other large city can make this statement. Whatever has gone wrong, whatever triumphs or fiascos have resulted, cities such as Boston, Philadelphia and many more have had a framework for some kind of coordinated construction and urban design. That same Federal official quoted earlier found New York's lack of plans and standards unique even in the roster of mediocre urban renewal efforts across the nation.

The problem, now, with an awakening consciousness of the quality of the environment in municipal circles, is that the old pattern is set. In the financial community the old blinders are still on. The old priorities are considered inviolate.

The Urban Scene

With a Lower Manhattan plan belatedly on the city's books, its potential is being eaten away by New York's relentless *force majeure*, the divine right of real estate economics. Said one of the architects involved in a major downtown project, "We only wish that there had been a more cohesive city plan from which to work than the bits and pieces left over by the wheeler-dealers."

Examples? They abound. The investment firm of Atlas-McGrath assembled enough prime Lower Manhattan land not only to frustrate the city's urban renewal designation for the area but to make it possible to create, with ease and art and single ownership, a small-scale

Rockefeller Center on one of the city's most superb waterfront sites. This would have been compensation for historic destruction. It is not being done.

Instead of coordinated planning and design, the *modus operandi* has been simply to milk the most out of each separate, negotiable parcel independently. The architects of the blockbusters for two of the huge plots have no idea what will be on the third, and their relationship is cordial but not collaborative. Actually, it is quite clear what will be on that third site: the biggest deal possible. Community waterfront uses? Parks and plazas united in open-space planning? Human amenities? Urban esthetics? Municipal sense? Public good? None of it balances against private profit.

And so the city closed the streets and handed them over to the developers, moved Jeanette Park and widened Water Street, all in the most pragmatic way possible. There will now be two huge commercial superblocks with oddments of open space that result not from thoughtful urban design but from the bonus provisions of the zoning law, which gives height increases (read rentable floors) for setbacks from the street.

It makes it hard to take the city's talk seriously about using street closings as a negotiating tool with the World Trade Center. As it stands now, the Port Authority is throwing away the remarkable spatial opportunities that this massive project creates, for just another big commercial venture. There will be plazas, yes. But since the Authority seems determined to burrow all circulatory activity underground to concourse level, these plazas promise to be vast, desolate, dull, windswept and empty most of the time. This, where so much could have been done to improve pedestrian functions and pleasures.

It is equally hard to take the Port Authority's gesture of cooperative planning with the city seriously, based on its claim that city officials have sat in on meetings and concurred in decisions from the time of the project's inception. Looking at the record, it is impossible to take past municipal planning efforts seriously at all.

Consider another downtown planning example: Water Street. To provide a broad traffic artery among the narrow, congested

Going, going, gone—historic brick buildings,
center, against soaring skyscrapers
in Lower Manhattan
(THE NEW YORK TIMES BY CARL GOSSETT, JR.)

streets of the old city, all of the buildings on the east side of Water Street were ripped out some years ago, the road enlarged and the gaping wound filled with parking.

Now the entire length of Water Street south from the bridge is a city-made, esthetic slum. It consists of the raw backs of houses revealed mid-block, enhanced by raw parking lots. This is one of New York's best examples of official urban mutilation. The objective now is as obvious as it is insensitive and commercially oriented: clear out whatever old, interesting structures still remain just beyond on Front Street, and bring on the superblock developers.

They will undoubtedly build banks. Most of the new downtown buildings are banks. They are, let it be said, fine and necessary institutions, but en masse they make streetscapes of suffocating dullness. There is, in fact, a kind of creeping bank disease laying a cold, dead hand on New York wherever the shiny new construction appears. Try counting, for example, the new banks from 47th to 59th streets on Park Avenue; add up the number of banks on ground floors of new buildings everywhere. It is as good as counting sheep. Soigné ennui.

Downtown, the days of small shops for fresh-ground coffee or odd electronic gadgets or conviviality in a not-too-pure circa 1827 bar are past or numbered. (It's not very convivial in the personal credit department of a bank and the place smells of computers, not coffee.) If New Yorkers survive the rape of the city, or just crossing the street or breathing the air, there is one last, lethal urban hazard: boredom.

How to Bankrupt a City at $400 a Square Foot

They are worrying out in Kansas City whether Mammon will claim the Villard houses, but they're not worrying very much in New York. Mammon is accepted, with air pollution and traffic jams, as the shaper of the environment here, and when one of the city's finest buildings stands on land currently reputed to be worth $400 a square foot, a sad shrug of the shoulders greets the news that the Villard block is up for grabs. No savvy New Yorker would give any odds on the demolition of this landmark for another Madison Avenue office building.

According to Donald L. Hoffmann, worrying in the *Kansas City Star*, New York's Villard house group—six brownstone mansions of the 1880's in the form of a single Italian Renaissance palace between 50th and 51st streets opposite St. Patrick's Cathedral—is one of the few places in the city that makes sense, visually, architecturally and historically.

Mr. Hoffmann points out that this solidly and beautifully built edifice, once occupied by Mr. Henry Villard, railroad tycoon, and his friends and in recent years the home of the Archdiocese of New York, Random House and the Capital Cities Broadcasting Corporation, ushered in New York's Golden Age. "Precious little of architectural New York can claim that much." It is a qualitative highpoint of the brief and glamorous period from the 1880's through the turn of the century when America's most notorious overachievers lived grandly (or bankruptly, in Mr. Villard's case) in Franco-Italianate chateaux of flamboyant magnificence, superb materials, extravagant detail and sumptuous elegance.

The cut-rate building had not yet been invented. It would not have been tolerated. The architects who built for the barons of steel and rails were men with names like Stanford White and Richard Morris Hunt who had never heard of plastic. It has taken modern corporate taste to produce the cheap monument.

The Villard house block, modeled after the Cancelleria in Rome, is one of the best things the celebrated firm of McKim, Mead and White—purveyors of palaces to nineteenth-century merchant princes —ever did anywhere and one of the best buildings New York could and can claim, then or now.

No one denies that the quality of the city is eroded and ultimately lost by the destruction of such buildings, of which there are so very few to leaven the ordinary commercial Manhattan mix. Not even Mammon denies it. The bankers and real estate men who have conventionally written off any construction approaching the century mark as outmoded and uneconomic have learned to say "Too bad." That somehow makes it worse. To destroy out of ignorance is one thing; to destroy with understanding of the meaning and consequences of the act is a sordid commentary on the values and morality of men.

All that is different or unusual about the Villard houses' story are the expressions of polite regret accompanying the routinely ruthless real estate process. Now Mammon ostensibly has a heart. A few tears are shed. Some poignant comments are made about the past. Then the deal is closed and the wreckers move in.

The Villard houses offer a case history of this more sophisticated method of destruction. First, no one comes right out and says that a landmark is for sale to the highest bidder; the Villard houses are on the market by innuendo. But all the signs of the process, from abandonment to sale to demolition, are clearly indicated; the movements are as prescribed as a Kabuki dance.

The Archdiocese of New York owns all of the Villard block except the north frontage on Madison Avenue that belongs to Random House. The church rents the 51st Street side to the Capital Cities Broadcasting Corporation.

A year ago, when Bennett Cerf announced that Random House would move its still growing and scattered operations to a new skyscraper on Third Avenue, he made the appropriate remarks of ritual regret. He noted that he and Cardinal Spellman, as co-owners, had preserved the mansions and did not want to see them go. Then he opened the door just a little crack to the cold wind of inevitability —the whole process of destruction depends on the doctrine of inevitability—by saying that the buildings would probably be razed when he and the Cardinal were dead.

At about that time, when, overtly, no one was selling at all but Random House had clearly cast the die, one of the city's better-known real estate men approached an equally well-known architect to work on commercial development of the block. Real estate men are not given to throwing their money away. He obviously considered it a realistic investment. The architect, who has built many of the city's blockbusters, but who has a strong professional admiration for the Villard houses, refused the job.

Now Cardinal Spellman is dead and Random House, on its way to conglomerate status after purchase by RCA, has moved out. In the accepted pattern of "inevitability," Mr. Cerf's protestations have shifted slightly. They take the form of a reluctant admission. "We will probably sell," he says, "It's too valuable to keep." No sane conglomerate is going to maintain a landmark. These poor little companies with their backs against the wall know where to find the butter for their bread.

The new Cardinal, Terence J. Cooke, has made no direct statement of intent. His secretary, Monsignor James Rigney, has indicated a shift of an equal number of degrees in the way the wind is blowing. He says that it would be a shame to sell, "but with all our schools and responsibilities, at some point we would have to wonder whether we are justified in keeping property as valuable as this." He has opened the door a bit farther; yes, the church might sell if the price is right.*

The price is obviously going to be right at some time. There is no more prime piece of property in New York. The ritual of "inevitability" goes on as the land value goes up. Capital Cities, which has an eight-year lease, has been receiving steady calls from real estate brokers offering to buy the lease for substantial sums. "We do not want to move," a Capital spokesman says. "We'll do anything we can to preserve the building."

But the process continues inexorably. The feelers are out, the offers are being made, the principals are expressing regretful reluctance, and at some point the purchase will be consummated and the announcement made. Things will not be slowed down by the fact that although hearings have been held on official landmark designation for the block, that designation is still pending by the Landmarks Commission.†

There are several questions to be raised now before the sellers weep all the way to the bank. They concern the church position as leader, upholder and protector of community standards and of those values that have traditionally been called spiritual, beyond Mammon. In New York the temptations of the flesh have long been supplanted by the temptations of money. With its tax-exempt status it can even be argued that the church has an obligation to resist Mammon in the interest of the city's irreplaceable public heritage, or public good. Its human commitments are incontrovertible. But that is not the only kind of community responsibility a religious institution carries.

Still, its real estate people tend to think and operate like real

* The Archdiocese has subsequently assured interested civic groups that it will continue to preserve and maintain the buildings.

† Designation was made after this article appeared.

estate people anywhere. The merchants of cities form a watertight society. If land values ever got too high to keep the Sistine Chapel they would, of course, remove the frescoes first.

The sale of the Villard houses is not the inevitability that the real estate fraternity makes it out to be. The church can keep and use them, as it has in the past. A prestige tenant can be found for the Random House quarters—certainly not impossible for that prime office site—with the help of the parent corporation, the church, the city and its Landmarks Commission and the business community.

It is easier and more profitable, of course, to sell. But it is a serious step to convert the dignity and beauty of the city and its dwindling heritage into cash, even for philanthropic purposes. All New York will be poorer on the profits made.

Strictly from Hunger

It is a well-worn New York cliché that there is no place to go but up. It follows inevitably that after you've built up on all the avenues, there is no place to go but the side streets. Now the peculiarity of New York is that while the avenues are its show, the side streets are its soul.

The boutiques, the specialty shops, the international haute couture and haute cuisine, the offbeat offices and stores, the treasures and services, entertainment and variety that New York spreads out at its accustomed residents' and visitors' feet, are concentrated in the East 50's and 60's, on Manhattan's small, chic side streets.

Hamburg Heaven rubs elbows with La Grenouille and Pop posters coexist with crown jewels in a democracy of sophistication. All of this, with almost uncountable "good little" restaurants, inhabits the converted crannies of four- and five-story Georgian brick town houses, small stone ex-chateaux and remodeled brownstones, on streets of domestic scale with stretches of sky that have the touch of sunlight even on winter days.

Big banking and big business may make New York possible, but what makes New York, New York, are the intimate, multifaceted urban functions and the conspicuous consumption of elegance on those small side streets.

No place for the developer to go
except the side streets—New York's East 54th Street
(LARRY FRIED FOR THE NEW YORK TIMES)

But whatever else this part of town may be, and whatever it may symbolize to New Yorkers and the world of the city's character and style, it is all prime office space. The East 50's and 60's are also the heart of commercial Manhattan.

The demand for business quarters in this area appears to be insatiable. The best corporate addresses, of course, are the avenues, and they have been virtually rebuilt since the war, from First to Broadway. When all the motley old has been replaced by the homogenized new on the avenues, there is, as we said, no place to go but the side streets. And that, now, is exactly where the real estate developers are going.

They are going there, but only strictly from hunger. An avenue or corner property is worth more and can be sold or rented for more than an "inside piece," as it is called in the trade. An inside piece has problems. The space is too confined for a building of conventionally profitable size and layout, and so a major holding must be acquired reaching through the block to both sides—not just a single street facade but back-to-back properties on two streets. There is what the trade calls the "danger and difficulty" of this kind of assembly: the risk of holdups and holdouts with multiple small plots.

But never underestimate the real estate business. It is in there breasting the dangers, assembling.

The Uris Buildings Corporation, experts at an art of assemblage that artists never dreamed of, has put together the north side of 52nd Street and the south side of 53rd Street between Fifth and Madison avenues for a block-through office building site.

On that site there are presently 15,000 square feet of stores. A spokesman for Uris says, with regret ("It's a pity to see something like that disappear"), that there is no chance of creating that kind of store space in the new building.

Most of the ground-floor space will probably be lost to—guess what—as large a plaza as possible surrounding a tower, because the open-space bonus of extra tower height for a plaza given to a builder by the zoning law makes this the most profitable way to build. Since a side street site accommodates a smaller building than a commercial developer considers desirable, he is obviously going to use the zoning law bonus to the maximum.

Adjacent to the Uris operation, a broker has put together a parcel consisting of the north side of 53rd Street and the south side of 54th Street, also from Fifth to Madison avenues. One assumes that any new structure would wrap itself around Paley Park on 53rd.

These two contiguous projects will replace four prime East Side streets with a four-block desert of two more office buildings of completely predictable stamp.

Probably the last thing in the world that New York needs on its small side streets is plazas. An occasional vest-pocket park, like Mr. Paley's golden gesture of sheer delight, cannot be faulted; it is a beautiful change of pace, not a disruption of the neighborhood. In urban and human if not real estate terms, the return on the money is sensational.

New York's side streets are a human-scale, pedestrian environment. Their measure is that of the foot and the eye. Their feature is their fascinating continuity. One is drawn along by the unflagging interest of their uninterrupted. highly personal pleasures and uses in an endlessly varied architectural context. To destroy this, you could bomb the streets or build office tower plazas. The effect would be just about the same.

Wherever the lively side streets exist, there is vitality in a city. This is where the action is. Farther uptown, for example, where the developers' glazed brick, look-alike apartments stop on Second Avenue in the 80's, the fun begins. Here are the shops and restaurants and bars that make a kind of weekend Tivoli in the warm weather for in-towners, drawing neighborhood residents like a magnet. Here is life.

The buildings here are the old five-story low-rent tenement type that developers demolished so easily along Third and Second avenues for the characterless conformity of the new apartments.

Turn into the side streets in the East 70's and 80's and you will find some of those fine, rummagy antique shops and bookstores and specialty enterprises that have been forced out of Third Avenue by the high rents of the bland glass boutiques and expensive dry cleaners in the new brick boxes. Not all have migrated; these are only survivors. The squeeze is on, the attrition continues, and after the side streets there is no place to go.

Midtown, however, is the heart of the matter in every way. Unquestionably, these side streets are one of New York's great urban assets. They cannot disappear. New Yorkers simply assume that it can't happen here. These enterprises are prosperous and popular. But their prosperity is only a relative thing when pressured by spiraling land values.

A sort of glassy death is already creeping along Madison Avenue and around the corners, sped by those values; there is a foretaste of the future even in Union Carbide's handsome, moribund plaza and in the blank stare of banks that occupy increasingly boring amounts of ground-floor space, killing the streets. Architectural quality or distinguished building has nothing to do with this. It is a matter of urban function and character, and that is what a city is largely about, whatever the transactions in its board rooms.

The time may have come when certain functions that give New York its services and style may need to be protected, either by zoning amendment or some kind of administrative or planning action. The real estate community does not believe that the city should stop building new quarters for business and their contention is beyond argument. The new construction can be designed and located, however, in a more constructive context than the present planless pattern of destruction.

Zoning bonuses are allowed for arcades, for example, a far better answer to pedestrian shopping streets than plazas, as long as they shelter something more than banks. The City Planning Commission is working with the use of the bonus formula for amenities other than open space. High on the list would be those enterprises and neighborhoods that provide so much of New York's vitality, useful delight and characteristic sophistication.

At any rate, the handwriting is on the wall, or the street. One need not be clairvoyant to spot a trend or an alarmist to see the future.

Side Street Sabotage

Neither planning nor preservation nor people nor consideration of style, function or livability can stay the profit-motivated speculator's hand. And no wonder. With the "leverage," as it is called in business parlance, of tax advantages and borrowed money peculiar to the real estate world, leading to returns, generally, of 15 to 35 per cent on investments requiring little of the operator's own money as opposed to a median return of 11.3 per cent for the country's largest corporations where equity runs much higher, real estate is the closest thing to the proverbial pot of gold. (Argue this with *Fortune*, please, not with us, from which these unblushing facts of business come.) And who pays income tax?

Any city that invites destruction at a return of 15 to 35 per cent plus a few depreciation benefits and capital gains bonuses and tax shelters can hardly be saved. Interestingly, when real estate men turn to philanthropy, they always do so outside of the building or land buying fields. That would be *too* philanthropic.

And so those who care about what happens to New York—and

its future as a city of civilized amenities balances on a surprisingly thin line—put their hopes in those institutions, corporations, foundations and educational organizations that supposedly· support noncommercial standards and will balance them against purely economic factors. Again, in business terms, one looks for the "trade-off" between profit and the urban humanities. These institutions, one assumes, will help keep some kind of desirable urban balance. They will preserve. They will build better buildings. They will consider the city's design, function and esthetics, if the speculator will not. And on occasion, they do all of this conspicuously well.

This brings us to the depressing fact that one notable case of serious side street sabotage is the work of an educational institution theoretically committed to an understanding of urban and cultural values—Syracuse University. Obviously, a 15 to 35 per cent return looks good to a university endowment fund, too.

Since last spring, Syracuse University has purchased 12, 14, 16 and 18 East 62nd Street. It is currently negotiating for the houses

Houses on 62nd Street bought by Syracuse University
(LARRY FRIED FOR THE NEW YORK TIMES)

at 4 and 6 East 62nd. The school already owned 11 East 61st Street, which is operated as an in-town admissions office and cultural center named for its donor, real estate man and philanthropist Joseph I. Lubin. Mr. Lubin, a Syracuse trustee, has been the university's prime mover for the purchases.

Syracuse has now assembled most of the block between Fifth and Madison avenues on both 61st and 62nd streets, from the Fifth Avenue frontage to the Carlton House apartments on Madison. On Fifth Avenue the Knickerbocker Club is at 62nd Street and the Hartley Marcellus Dodge House is at 61st Street. This building, closed and shuttered since the death of Mr. Dodge by his elderly widow, Geraldine Rockefeller Dodge, is clearly destined to complete a large, extremely valuable and negotiable parcel of land.

The houses at 4 and 6 East 62nd Street, presently being negotiated for as part of that parcel, belong to the York Club, one of the city's private women's clubs. Because Syracuse University is known to be involved in the purchase, some club members feel that they should sell for a vaguely altruistic reason suggested by the fact that the buildings are being sought by an educational institution. Others feel that they are simply being subjected to a rather familiar and unpleasant kind of commercial real estate pressure to give up and get out.

The offer for these two houses has gone up from $1.7 million to $2.7 million in a few months, although the five houses purchased earlier were bought for a total of $1,245,000. That, of course, should be the tipoff that nothing else is involved here than the completion of an investment purchase that will be worth a fantastic amount on the real estate market. Yet there has been a strange reluctance on the part of club members who favor selling to entertain open or competitive bids. Ladies, you are being had. Speculation, and only speculation, is what Syracuse University has in mind.

That fact was confirmed to this reporter by Francis A. Wingate, the university's treasurer. Except for the house that Syracuse now operates at 11 East 61st Street, he made it clear that there is no question of using any of this property for educational purposes. Even if such a use were being considered, which it is not, it would be debatable in that area.

What Syracuse intends to do, after having assembled the land by paying no more than it must and hopefully not on the open market, is to eventually resell the properties at the highest possible profit for demolition and development. "This is simply an endowment fund investment," Mr. Wingate says. "We have no intention of keeping these properties. We will carry them until such time as we get a good offer."

The doomed 62nd Street block is an unusually handsome and characteristic example of a well-preserved row of elegant five-story stone town houses in the French Renaissance or Beaux Arts style popular after the turn of the century. Their landmark quality is enhanced by the completeness of the block. Nothing like them will be built again. Greetings, New York City, from Syracuse University.

Still another case of side street sabotage is taking place on West 78th Street between Columbus and Amsterdam avenues behind the Museum of Natural History. Here a row of brownstones has been patiently and privately restored by their owners. They have been renovated with loving care and architectural sensitivity and not much encouragement from the city or its lending institutions, which tend to consider the individual New Yorker's attempt to stay in the city and maintain its human and architectural character as some kind of deterrent to economic progress.

Now the work of these owner-residents is being destroyed by an owner-investor who has begun remodeling two of the houses, at 120 and 122 West 78th Street, in a manner that will ruin the scrupulously preserved block. He will extend the frontages of his property beyond the present building line, making damaging, out-of-character "improvements." Evidently banks are rather good about giving loans for this kind of thing, called modernization, which is supposed to jack up values, rather than for sympathetic restoration, which retains values not in bankers' books. Ultimately, of course, proper historic restoration sends property values way up.

Advice and help offered by block residents—including an architect—on ways that would do the job and still save the street architecturally and urbanistically have been summarily rejected. Perhaps the city should make the gentleman a gift of an anti-landmark plaque, engraved "owner-saboteur." One more way to kill a city.

New York Architecture
Stumbles On

The Dilemma of Housing

No political battles are being fought over urban design; it is not, in politicians' words, an issue with "sex appeal." They are being fought, understandably, for the immediate problems of the poor and the minorities. There are two reasons why this is so. First, the misery is real and the ghetto is hideous, and housing is one of the city's hottest political issues. Second, there is little recognition of urban or housing design and how it affects the environment, beyond the specialized professional level.

This necessary perspective is easy to lose when confronted with housing costs. Middle-income housing that went up from $18 to $21 to $22 a room in New York in the early 1960's reached $50 a room in 1969. Increased costs of money, construction, materials, labor, maintenance and interest rates are sending that figure spiraling. Middle-income housing can no longer be delivered without massive land write-down and tax abatement.

Construction costs, usually up 3 to 5 per cent a year, sky-rocketed 8 to 10 per cent in New York in the mid-1960's, where the expense of building is the highest and sometimes the most eccentric in the nation. By 1969 the figure was 12 per cent, and rising.

The tool that has been most effective for middle-income housing, called 221(d)3 for the section of the Federal housing bill that authorizes it, keeps costs and rents low by a fixed, below-market 3 per cent interest rate. The Federal Housing Act of 1968 would provide money at a one per cent rate, but it has yet to be adequately funded. At the low-income level, public housing is far behind schedule and new government tools, such as rent subsidies and turnkey housing, seem to be unworkable in New York due to expenses and legal complexities. With these costs and complications, plus the greater profitability of commercial construction in the city, housing for all income groups came to a virtual standstill in New York City by 1969.

Even if this were all to change, housing is torn apart by dissident groups, bottlenecked by bureaucracy, delayed by politics, confused by champions of the poor, sabotaged by planners without perspective, lost by inertia and incomprehension. If it can be built at all, it must be much more than an exercise in sliding rent scales. There must be variety and human scale, services and pleasures, in a multi-level complex of dwellings, commercial, recreational and open-space functions. There must be new neighborhoods created through design.

Much of the so-called crisis of cities, many of its racial, social and human problems, rise from the lack of urban design. The architecture of housing grows out of the concept of housing and the concept of the community. This is a basic cause-and-effect relationship that those responsible for housing have been tragically slow to grasp. New York is first in the size of its problems and the magnitude of its incomprehension.

Riverbend Houses: It Can Happen Here

Imagine, if you can in New York, duplex apartments designed like town houses, each with its own front door reached through a small, walled terrace from an outside gallery that runs the length of the building or from a "sky street" for duplexes stacked above. Each duplex is floor-through, with windows on both sides. There are spectacular river views or an outlook on a landscaped plaza connecting the buildings like a private park for tenant use. Picture

Improvements and economies,
as well as distinguished architecture at Riverbend Houses
(DAVID HIRSCH FOR THE NEW YORK TIMES)

eight of these structures attached to two towers with simplex apartments; each of these has sliding doors to its own terrace and city views.

We are not putting you on. That would be cruel in a city where housing is as critical as it is in New York. Nor are we indulging in Utopian housing dreams, an easy thing to do when rentals in "good" neighborhoods are an unabashed $125 a room and a modest co-op is an unblushing $50,000.

This housing exists. But it is not for the Rolls-Royce trade. It

74

is in Harlem. This is Riverbend, built under the Mitchell-Lama limited profit housing program and through the city's Housing and Development Administration. It is a $14 million, 624-family moderate-income cooperative on a triangular 3.7-acre site bounded by Fifth Avenue, the Harlem River Drive and 138th Street. Apartment purchase costs are less than $500 a room, with an average $32 a room carrying charge.

What Riverbend proves is that well-designed housing at a rational price can be built in New York. But it cannot be done without subsidy. This is a fact of New York real estate known by all but faced by few.

Design, however, is independent of subsidy. The point here is that Riverbend, with or without subsidy, would be handsome, imaginative and desirable and offer alternative options for living to the stereotyped minimum formulas provided by New York's apartment house builders, who may well give the least for the money in any major American city, even taking into account New York's extraordinary land and construction costs. The exterior design and materials of one of the city's most expensive and visible new cooperatives are so crudely detailed that one wonders if the affluent are blind. Amenities deal in gilded faucets.

The HRH Construction Corporation, which sponsored and built Riverbend, says that commercial developers can reproduce Riverbend's standards of housing design at competitive private sector prices. But they don't. The same old brick boxes are flung in the public's face whether the money market is tight or loose and regardless of rate or cost of construction. And when costs are too high, nothing is built. When New York builders do build, you know what you are going to get for that ever-increasing slice of that ever-diminishing take-home dollar. It is a sure, standardized profit-formula thing.

What makes the difference at Riverbend? The builder, the architects and the sponsoring city agency. They were a determined triumvirate, slogging through a six-year obstacle course, since everything in American society and municipal bureaucracy seems stacked against doing something different. Richard Ravitch of HRH, Davis, Brody and Associates, the architects, and Samuel Ratensky of the Housing and Development Administration all share a knowledge of

75

what good housing design is. It was a matter of principle and standards to them to produce it.

It can probably be fairly said that a lot of New York builders have absolutely no idea of what good housing design is. What they don't know certainly hasn't hurt them financially. Nor has good housing design ever been understood or encouraged by some of the city's largest non-profit housing sponsors, who keep both rents and standards low. You don't quarrel in New York with what you can afford. Even the best-intentioned housing "experts" fail to grasp the idea that design is the concept, not a bit of trim.

The firm of Davis, Brody is one of the more talented in the city. You will not find any speculative apartment houses by this office, and, except for a rarity or two, by any other firm of comparable creative stature. New York apartment houses are not designed; they are punched out to meet the standard formula.

There is no standard formula at Riverbend. The results are not even recognizable as Mitchell-Lama housing, which carries its rigidly specified trademarks and economies from project to project. From hardware to graphics, from special brick to sprayed wall and ceiling finishes, better answers have been sought. These buildings are a notable demonstration of how creativity and taste can lead to improvements and economies, as well as to distinguished architectural results.

Examples: that handsome, rugged, oversize brick that gives character to the brick and concrete structures was much cheaper to lay than the conventional kind that carries an institutional stamp. With careful site planning and building relationships, the higher floors of the duplex blocks are served by elevators in the two towers through connecting corridors, eliminating the expense of elevators in a large number of the ten buildings.

The particularly attractive lighting fixtures designed by the architects to illuminate the duplex front doors serve two at once and ultimately proved cheaper than available standard fixtures. Those raised community plazas between the buildings in place of bleak, open space conceal required parking underneath at the same time that they turn the space into a social amenity.

The architects lost money at Riverbend, in the time spent on special design, specification and supervision, but it was a calculated risk that has paid off in experience and other jobs. They are also the architects for city-sponsored houses in construction in the Bellevue South renewal area, and for Waterside, another breakthrough in design and urban land use. City fees are higher now, but city contract problems remain.

Waterside, the city's pioneering attempt at mixed-income housing that is yet to be built, has drawn blood from proponents of low-income housing as offering too many apartments to those who are not poor and whose lives are not infested with rats. The argument is strong. Riverbend will probably provoke the same criticism, although its beneficiaries are not white. They are middle income, middle class and black. Most of the people buying the apartments want it just this way. Black or white, this is a group essential to the city's support.

The idea that the city might purchase some units for subsidized low-income housing was outspokenly opposed. Even a liquor store was vetoed as a commercial rental because it might attract trouble. The black middle class making it now is too close to misery to want any part of it. The polemics of integration and housing priorities interest these people less than questions of security, from the alarms installed on doors during construction that many will keep, to the inviolability of their new neighborhood. Riverbend is part of a growing black middle-class enclave. Anyone interested in the other side of the coin of Harlem sociology would do well to study it.

The significance of Riverbend, however, is beyond controversy. It is simply that the same thoughtful standards of design can be brought to bear on every kind of housing, from low to high income, in ghettos and out. The dignity of the environment has a lot to do with the dignity of man.

Co-op City: A Singularly New York Product

It is hard to grasp the size, importance and impact of Co-op City. In New York, superlatives bore. This is a city that swallows cities; not, however, without serious urban indigestion. But the simple facts of Co-op City stun those trained to think in urban terms. The world's largest cooperative community. The largest single apartment development in the United States. A city of 50,000 to 60,000 people in 15,382 apartments piled onto 300 acres—instant new town.

A community of 60,000 was the standard starting point of almost all of the British government-planned, postwar new towns. It was the initial population of those famous Scandinavian planning models, Vallingby and Farsta in Sweden and Tapiola in Finland. But the similarity ends right there.

Co-op City is an example of a singularly American, or New York, product. Its size and scale are monumental; its environmental and social planning is minimal. The British and Scandinavian new towns are total town-planning concepts. Major preliminary investment in both design and money has been concentrated on providing and integrating those important services and amenities and land-use features that turn houses into real places to live.

Construction of Co-op City—
some large buildings that raise some large questions
(THE NEW YORK TIMES BY PATRICK A. BURNS)

In Scandinavia, for example, a great deal of the investment goes into attractive town centers, always a large, focally located and frequently attractive group of buildings, plazas, stores, fountains and recreation spaces that are much more than the shopping centers considered adequate at Co-op City. The true town center, through its architectural style and quality, creates a community core, a way of life and a special kind of shared environment.

The overwhelming consideration of Co-op City's non-profit sponsors and builders, the United Housing Foundation, has been to provide livable apartments at an exceptionally low cost, period. This is an unassailable objective in a city that can use all the housing it can get. The United Housing Foundation's philosophy and practice has been to buy relatively inexpensive land and put up uniform, large buildings at high density in a standard cookie-cutter pattern for maximum cost benefits. Beyond the provision of some basic shopping facilities and the space allotment for necessary public services that the city must follow along and provide, everything else is expected to fall into place. Foundation partisans say this pattern, repeated in all their projects, makes the low-cost formula possible. Certainly, success is on their side. They build good apartments at unbeatable prices.

The foundation has provided this kind of housing in at least a dozen cooperatives to the tune of about half a billion dollars, or half of New York State's investment in low-interest mortgage financing for housing low- and middle-income families.

Why, then, is there any debate about the virtues of Co-op City? Why has the UHF been under constant professional attack for sterile site-planning and uninspired architectural design, for communities that are not communities in the urban expert's sense or according to the standards of the more urbanistically enlightened countries of the world? With so much government financing, are greater sociological and environmental planning the luxuries that the foundation stubbornly contends them to be?

The story of how Co-op City got built provides answers. It reveals the mutually serious faults and failures of the UHF's planning and design limitations and of the city's sticky machinery for assisting such an undertaking.

The city argues that the full implications of the huge scale of Co-op City were not acknowledged by any significant change in

UHF building or planning attitudes. There was no planner involved —only the architect, Herman J. Jessor, who had been producing standard UHF housing since the forties. The process that made Co-op City what it is today—a somewhat improved version of the foundation formula, if far short of a planner's dream—can be called only planning fence-mending, or a posteriori planning by negotiation.

What the city used for persuasion was its tax abatement powers under the State Mitchell-Lama Law, which provided Co-op City's financing, and necessary mapping and zoning changes. What the foundation used was the promise of all that housing.

"They came in with the usual stereotype that they always build," a city spokesman says. They went out with the density cut from 17,000 to 15,382 units; a revised plan and street system; consultant site planners and landscape architects—Zion and Breen of Paley Park fame, recommended by the city—tower and V-form variations of their standard buildings, grouped where possible; changes in material and color from endless institutional red brick and 236 town houses for human scale. While the results will set no world standards and are considered largely cosmetic by the profession, they could have been a great deal worse.

Protracted negotiations have determined public facilities, transportation, institutional sites for religious and social agencies, garages, schools, open-area treatment and parks and the relationship of the huge project to its surroundings, including provision for industrial development and jobs. There are 100 pages of street agreements alone. "I can't remember all the gruesome details," one of the city's planning staff says. It took four bitter years.

A city coordinator had to be appointed to pull a dozen bureaucratically mixed city departments into coordinated action, much of it too late. Roads are going in after building occupancy. Schools will be built by the UHF and repurchased by the city, to get them built at all. The crippling city zoning that locks big buildings into those desolately spread site plans is yet to be changed to make better planning possible. It will be years before subway lines are extended. Architectural design possibilities, including prefabrication and standardized parts, remain unexplored.

"Design innovation is not permitted to drive up costs," the foundation insists. That means that New York's most important producer of housing closes the door that might ultimately drive costs down and house more New Yorkers in unaccustomed style. The greatest city in the world stumbles on.

Pan Am: The Big, the Expedient and the Deathlessly Ordinary

The city's most monumental addition since the Empire State Building—the $100 million Pan Am Building—made its official debut with brass-band ceremonies worthy of a Presidential inauguration.

In other development news at the same time, announcement was made of the sixty-acre plan for New York's Civic Center in the City Hall-Foley Square area. Federal and city agencies have been engaged since in a deadlocked vendetta—to borrow James R. Hoffa's useful word—over changes that New York has requested in the Federal Government's previously designed structures to fit into the city's belated plan. Federal resistance, backed by irrefutable arguments of money and time, is nibbling away at the original concept with predictable bureaucratic compromises. ("We went to Washington to ask for a banquet," said New York Public Works Commissioner Peter Reidy, "and they gave us a bag of peanuts.")*

The Avenue of the Americas continues its transformation with some of the most glossily impersonal facades of the city. On Columbus Circle, Edward Durell Stone's little seraglio for Huntington Hartford's Gallery of Modern Art is more suggestive of houris behind its pierced marble screen than art. This is a provocatively misplaced pleasure pavilion transplanted from some Shalimar garden to a Manhattan traffic island.

Of these new buildings, Pan Am has by far the greatest impact on the city scene. Criticism, which has been plentiful since the building's inception, is directed largely at its physical and sociological implications: the effect of 17,000 new tenants and 250,000 daily transients on the already overcrowded Grand Central area and its services, and the unresolved conflicts and responsibilities of the city and private enterprise in the control of urban densities and master planning.

* For the results, see "The Federal Goverment Lays a Colossal Architectural Egg," p. 105.

But now that the building is functioning, something else becomes distressingly apparent. Bigness is blinding. A $100 million building cannot really be called cheap. But Pan Am is a colossal collection of minimums. Its exterior and its public spaces, in particular, use minimum good materials of minimum acceptable quality executed with a minimum of imagination (always an expensive commodity), or distinction (which comes high), or finesse (which costs more). Pan Am is gigantically second-rate.

This is no Michelangelesque masterwork from the late and latter-day Medici, promoter Erwin Wolfson, but a super economy package with the usual face-saving gimmick: painting and sculpture in the lobby. In its new role as an architectural cover-up, the builders of New York are turning good art into a bad joke. Pan Am's one effective esthetic feature is its brutality. In afternoon sun, from lower Park Avenue, its patterned mass rises with striking power behind the dwarfed familiarity of Grand Central's proper academic facade. Its one functional plus is the pedestrian throughway that its lobby and connections provide from Grand Central Terminal to 45th Street.

At best, Pan Am is an impressive demonstration of the number of square feet (2.4 million) of completely standard rentable office space that can be packed into one income-producing structure, a lesson in how to be mediocre without really trying. For its bulk, its importance, its effect and its ballyhoo, it had an obligation to be much better. Size is not nobility; a monumental deal does not make a monument. This is a prime example of a New York specialty: the big, the expedient and the deathlessly ordinary. Build we must, but on the record it is questionable if we are building for a better New York.

Grand Central Tower Grotesquerie

In the classic verbal shorthand by which New Yorkers communicate, the man-in-the-street response to the projected $100 million tower above Grand Central is "Who needs it?"

The Penn Central says it needs it; the English developer Morris Saady says he wants it; and the architect Marcel Breuer says he'll

A cut-rate monument

do it. The railroad wants it to help make ends meet and Mr. Saady frankly wants a profitable New York monument.

The Landmarks Commission wishes it would go away quietly and the City Planning Commission would like to wake up to find that it had dreamed the whole fantastic concept because it can't do a thing about it. The building is completely within the limits of the zoning law and needs no commission-controlled variances or approvals. Therefore New York may very likely get it.

What the city will get, if it goes ahead, is another Pan Am Building only 221 feet from the first one and at least 150 feet higher. It will get some improved underground circulation and an architectural curiosity that could make a perverse kind of esthetic and urban history. It would be a monument less to Mr. Saady than to the awesome value of New York air rights.

The value of polluted Manhattan air is another curiosity that will go down in history. If the air over Grand Central Terminal were not worth several hundred million dollars in building rights and income over the next fifty years there would be no Grand Central tower project. That solid gold air is there to stay, and if its superheated values continue to rise as anticipated in the coming half century Manhattan could someday replace Fort Knox.

The terminal, whatever its spacious turn-of-the-century graces, would obviously not be there to stay, measuring its land and air utilization in terms of these values, if there were no city landmarks law to protect it. And the law only protects the exterior, not the Grand Concourse.

The railroad understandably is going to persist in finding a way to tap its air rights treasure, landmark or not. The realities of this situation are not going to change. What the situation has produced is a truly remarkable shotgun wedding between sentiment and speculative economics. The result is a colossal modern office building surrealistically astride a mansarded French palace. The trick is pulled off with striking technical élan and much more suaveness than at the Pan Am, but it has inevitably created a grotesquerie. The result is no less grotesque, however, than those midtown real estate values.

Give a grotesquerie to a good architect and you are going to get a better grotesquerie, like a better mousetrap. Mr. Breuer has done an excellent job with a dubious undertaking, which is like

84

saying it would be great if it weren't awful. Even definitions of "awful" vary today, and the awful has its advocates; to some this could be a Pop masterpiece. Incongruity is the essence of Pop art and architecture.

Entrusting such a job to a genuinely creative talent assures that ways and means will be found of doing the impossible or undesirable that would not occur to more humdrum minds. It also guarantees a thoughtful refinement of detail beyond the call of commerce.

The building, though still an oddity, is dazzlingly better than tentative proposals circulated earlier to developers by the railroad's real estate department. This improvement is chiefly in the originality of the structural system that permits the insinuation of the tower's core through the station waiting room for maximum preservation of the old structure.

Inside, the south mezzanine of the concourse would be destroyed and the dramatic shafts of natural light that still stream hazily through the unwashed high south windows would be permanently blocked.

The solution is ingenious, technically daring and very expensive. According to Mr. Breuer, going to these costly extremes to save a landmark is a romantic whim that he finds stranger than the architectural results. He would frankly prefer to demolish the terminal.

Assuming that this expensive, unorthodox construction is economically feasible for a speculative building, and Mr. Saady does not seem like a man who would risk losing his custom-made shirt, the project still raises serious questions.

There is the question of whether this spectacular construction trick within a building could be carried out without damage to the building itself. Is Breuer's stylistic trademark of cast stone, which he handles with sensitivity and skill, the most appropriate answer here, if there is any appropriate answer at all?

Would more bravura and less Breuer be better? If you are dealing in esthetic effrontery, why not go all the way with the contrast of a sheer glass, sky-reflecting tower for maximum theatrics? For this is essentially a theatrical architecture of the absurd.

To make his superproject palatable, Mr. Saady has used a top architect, and he has taken responsibility for at least the part of public circulation with which his building is involved. Builders who do these things in New York can be counted on slightly more than one thumb. As almost irresistible bait, he has offered to rescue the concourse from its present condition as an esthetic slum.

More important than any of this, however, is the question of whether the city has anything to say about a project that so critically affects planning and construction in one of Manhattan's most congested, focal areas.

Will those improved underground pedestrian patterns to be contributed to the city by the builder merely dump several thousand more people daily on the dead end of inadequate subway platforms and service? Is the promise of relief from new subway lines in the future enough to justify the solidification of chaos now? At what point, and by what means, can the city control its destiny? In New York only Solomon could know for sure.

The Ford Foundation Flies High

The Ford Foundation building is twelve stories of subtle splendor half a block west of the United Nations. The building on the 200 by 200 foot site reaching from 42nd to 43rd streets, designed by Kevin Roche, John Dinkeloo and Associates, has achieved instant fame as a New York landmark and one of the most important and beautiful new structures anywhere.

By now most people know that the glass box anchored by granite piers and partially embraced by granite side walls contains a giant indoor garden—a twelve-story, 160-foot-high, skylit, air-conditioned, third-of-an-acre terraced park.

The seventeen full-grown trees include acacia, magnolia and eucalyptus; there are 999 shrubs, for anyone who wants to count, 148 vines, 21,954 ground-cover plants and eighteen aquatic plants in a still-water pool. The seasons will bring bloomings of rhododendron, gardenia, camellia, azalea and bougainvillea, special plantings of tulips in spring, begonias in summer, chrysanthemums in fall and poinsettias in winter. The landscaping, by Dan Kiley, is carried up the projecting top surfaces of the first five floors.

New York Architecture Stumbles On

This huge greenhouse is illuminated by seventy-six spotlights from the eleventh floor and forty-three ground lights, as well as by the changing moods and colors of natural sky and weather through the glass roof and walls. It is a horticultural spectacular and probably one of the most romantic environments ever devised by corporate man.

It is also an architectural spectacular. The garden is wrapped on two sides and part of a third by a glass-walled office block that opens visually and physically to the planted court with sliding glass panels. This luminous, transparent interior structure soars to the top in a complex counterpoint of the modular geometry of

Consideration of a building's place
in the existing city
(THE NEW YORK TIMES BY SAM FALK)

visible, stacked work floors bathed with golden light played against the huge open court with its illuminated greenery. This is an even more rich, complex and subtle esthetic when viewed from the outside through the ten-story-high glass walls, or from inside, through the court, to the street.

The building reveals itself totally from the street; the Ford Foundation has built itself a splendid, shimmering Crystal Palace. More important, it has built a significant addition to the New York scene. It is one of the small handful of buildings released from the exigencies of commercial construction to rank as architecture at all. The excellence of this building is not just in its original, highly romantic beauty, or the effective way it opens up a closed corporate group into a communicating organization focused on that great garden court. It is more than superb and special standards of design in which every uncompromising detail is a lavish custom solution. Its great lesson is in its extraordinarily sensitive consideration of its place in the existing city.*

The conventional way to build a "status" structure in New York today is to erect a tower set well back on a landscaped plaza. This solution, aided by the new zoning law, repeatedly and senselessly breaks the continuity of the street line, New York's only coherent urban design feature in a city of constantly competitive structural chaos.

Here the architect chose to preserve the street rather than to disrupt it and to relate sympathetically to a curious set of neighbors rather than to ignore them: a commercial building, some small town houses, a park at the edge of Tudor City and some radical changes in ground level across the site. In a virtual reversal of current practice, he put the building around the plaza instead of the plaza around the building. The glass-enclosed court is open to the passing public from 42nd to 43rd streets. The design offers sensitive transitions to every part of the environment. It is that rarity, a building aware of its world, as well as a work of art.

The building is too well-mannered to make its neighbors look cheap or shabby. The granite is a blending taupe-gray warmed with

---

* There is an increasing tendency to dismiss this building as a less-than-lovable symbol of Establishment Foundation. I believe this is a confusion of values that might be called the socio-esthetic fallacy, and that monumentally and urbanistically, the structure works well.

The Ford Foundation's crystal palace
(THE NEW YORK TIMES BY SAM FALK)

rose laid up without mortared joints; the glass walls are steel-framed. The granite sheathes the vertical structure, consisting of piers and walls, which is of reinforced concrete. The piers contain stairs and mechanical shafts.

The horizontal structure is steel, faced with a second steel that weathers a rusty bronze, because exposed structural steel is against the city's fire laws. The top two floors, which ring the building completely above the ten-story-high glass window wall, are suspended over that non-load-bearing wall from large spandrel girders. These are the two special executive floors in an all-executive building. At skylight height, a promenade surrounds the court.

All materials are natural. The plastic esthetic, the "hot modern" spectrum of colors, have not been permitted here, in this most modern of buildings. Golden-beige wool rugs are set into oak parquet floors so that deep pile is level with wood, a discreet study in expensive non-ostentation. There are natural linen covered modular walls, English wool upholstery, real leather and Honduras mahogany furniture of contemporary style and a satiny, traditional nineteenth-century finish. All furnishings are by Warren Platner, of the architectural firm, for a totally unified, interior-exterior design. Grants will be made and programs pursued in a virtual hothouse of standardized, suave elegance.

The price for understated magnificence for 287,400 square feet, of which 83.3 per cent is "net" working space, is approximately $16 million. Of this cost, the landscaping, surprisingly, is under one per cent. It is, in every sense, a luxury building.

It is quite obvious that in the structure and buildings of corporate democracy the United States has found a natural replacement for nobility and its monuments. (One of the great debates during the design process, whether the offices should be uniformly furnished as the architect wished, was resolved on the basis of democracy. The best is good enough for all.)

The large American foundation, with royal resources, has consequently become a kind of corporate Medici. Considerably less colorful and more cautious than the Medici, however, its super-organization men are frequently more committed to bland altruism than to courageous creative acts. Occasionally they come across with a smashing gesture in proper Florentine fashion. Ford has given New York a superlative work of architecture.

There will be two arguments about this building. One will be based on standards of speculative commercial construction, under which the building will be explained away as unrealistically extravagant due to design emphasis on "waste space." There is a gold mine of "lost" square footage in that open court, as builders have demonstrated by tearing down the great open court buildings of the nineteenth century to jam standard rental floors onto the same sites.

To judge the building on these grounds is not only tiresome nonsense but unfair to both the Ford Foundation, which could build non-commercially to the city's benefit, and to the commercial builder, who cannot. The two kinds of building bear no comparison at all.

Space, and the handling of that space, are the essence of all great architecture. Every monument from the Baths of Caracalla through St. Peter's is filled with "waste space." Every inch of the Ford building's "waste" space works in terms of design, function and corporate or urban purpose. It is a humanistic rather than an economic environment. In the twentieth-century city, space and humanism are luxuries that we can no longer afford. Therefore architecture is something that we can no longer afford.

It is equally ridiculous to argue as to whether the Ford Foundation has built a monument to itself or whether the money might not be better spent on the problems of the world. Certainly the building could come under the heading of one of the foundation's more valid contributions to the arts. It is a significant contribution to the quality of the city. It is also certain that Ford will never give most New Yorkers anything except this civic gesture of beauty and excellence, and that is a grant of some importance in a world where spirit and soul are deadened by the speculative cheapness of the environment. The loss is measurable not in square footage, that favorite yardstick, but in the quality of life. That so few seem capable of making the distinction between art and profit is one of the serious failures of our cities and a notable cultural tragedy of our time. And it is a social and urban tragedy that those who recognize the urgency of our human problems see their solution only in terms of the total sacrifice of style.

The Urban Scene

The Parthenon Comes to General Motors

The General Motors Building opened to huge crowds and what might be called mixed reviews. To the public at large, it's a smash. Some professional responses are less enthusiastic. The gap between the two is the difference between I-know-what-I-like and serious judgment of the building's form and functions, and its impact on the New York scene.

Any structure that rises fifty conspicuous stories on one of the city's prime sites with a make-or-break urban relationship to the elegant and focal small plaza that sets the tone of Fifth Avenue must be looked at as more than just a building. General Motors, its associated developers, the Savoy Fifth Avenue Corporation, and the architects Edward Durell Stone and Emery Roth and Sons consider it more than just a building. It must, therefore, be judged as architecture and urban design.

Behind the marble cladding and bay windows, architecture, like the proverbial thin man in the fat man's body, is signaling wildly to get out.

Under their seven-eighths-inch marble veneer those fifty-story hexagonal piers are actually hollow, bearing concrete columns carrying service ducts, a functional design solution that frees the building's periphery of columns behind the windows and integrates services with structure. The rest of the structure is steel. The silhouette, head on, is a slim, soaring shaft.

Beneath the curious mixture of small-town department store and styling section décor is the kind of breath-taking skyscraper shell balanced in space that modern technology makes possible. You could wrap it in brown paper, instead of Georgia marble, and it would still be impressive. General Motors, however, prefers marble.

Without the screens, gimmick lights and revolving and stationary automobiles, the high-ceilinged, glass-walled lobby would have striking architectural scale. Liberated of looped gold "drapes" that cover the thirty-foot windows and obscure the unparalleled view for a kind of G.M.-Hilton look, and without the carved-border gold area rugs that even amateur decorators gave up years ago, the main floor would be a handsome architectural space.

Marble does not a Parthenon make
(THE NEW YORK TIMES BY DON HOGAN CHARLES)

In other words, relieved of all the schmaltz that both client and architect seem to feel is necessary to disguise and diminish one of the great art forms of our age—they fight the natural elegance of the contemporary skyscraper with overlays of low-level corn and pseudo-grandeur all the way—a building of clear, contemporary beauty might have emerged.

Indications of those elements of structure, space and light that are basically and essentially architecture are still there. Inside Edward Durell Stone there is an architect signaling to get out.

Inside the building there is wall-to-wall marble. The Parthenon has come to General Motors. Pentelic marble by the ton from the same Greek quarries that supplied the Acropolis lathers the lobby walls; the rejects are upstairs. It is good to keep thinking of the Parthenon or one begins to think of luxury lavatories. Here and there, on the high walls and around elevators, the marble is chamfered and incised.

In the General Motors offices above the ground floor, architecture and interiors part company completely. (G.M. has the first twenty-six floors and the rest is rental space at the city's highest rates.) The architects did not design these work areas; they are the product of the G.M. staff, headed by Ervine Klein, and the interiors firm of J. Gordon Carr and Associates. The ground-floor showrooms and the executive offices have been done by LeRoy Kiefer of the Detroit styling staff.

The building's twenty-foot interior column module is ignored by the module set for the office space. The columns, therefore, appear strangely and frequently in the corners of reception areas and just beyond corridor walls.

One of the basic battles of skyscraper design has been to develop systems that integrate the column into modular office schemes, and when one sees these offices one understands why. It is a matter of esthetics and logic. But G.M. gains some square footage this way, even if it looks as if it had to make the best of a building over which it had no structural or design control.

The twenty-fifth, or executive, floor simply abdicates the twentieth century. The top executive offices are furnished in conventional Grand Rapids-type reproductions of "traditional" pieces. No antiques have been purchased and there has been no art program.

Smoothly illustrative oils of geese flying and barns in snow with a few mistily impressionistic landscapes have been fetched in by staff on a trial and error basis. One recalls the Chase Manhattan Bank's art program for its headquarters building, which set up a museum-caliber advisory board to select a fine collection.

Which brings us to the question of style, that stamp of individual or corporate taste that makes waves in its surroundings, for better or worse. In its early days, automotive taste was touchingly buckeye. Measured by the General Motors Building, it is now pretentiously ordinary. One wonders if this taste should have been turned into a monument.

The style might be called Throwback Classicism or Furniture Store Posh. Mr. Stone has been called a classicist *manqué*. In spite of much propaganda to that effect, he is really a modernist *manqué* and a good one, who simply fruits it up.

General Motors states proudly that the building cost (unspecified) was 20 to 25 per cent less than that of comparable luxury structures in New York.

Asked whether that meant that G.M. was poorer than Union Carbide or other corporate builders, the response was stunned silence. Asked why it was good to build a monument cheap, the reply was that the pressing of economies was "sound business practice." It does not look as if any money was saved on marble.

The sunken Fifth Avenue shopping plaza is a promising urban device. But here its lower level only partly ameliorates the disruption of previously perfectly scaled open space of singular sophisticated graciousness. This and the influx of crowds—both factors considered when the Hartford cafe was vetoed for the south end of Central Park—have effected the dissolution of one of the last of the city's quality environments.

The lady of the Fountain of Abundance and her dwarfed parklet look shabby genteel. General Motors has brought a new style and a new kind of abundance to Fifth Avenue. What it lacks, unfortunately, is class. It has the best address in town. It has not given the city its best building.

The Urban Scene

The Met's Design Muddle

The architect of the new Metropolitan Opera House, Wallace K. Harrison, has been designing it for approximately forty years. It began with the original scheme for Rockefeller Center in the late 1920's that was to focus on a new opera house in its earliest version and has continued in one or another frustrated form for four decades. The trail of yellowed sketches, studies and blueprints and crumbling models has led finally to the opening of the $47.5 million building that is New York's glittering claim to cultural fame.

Forty years is a long time to have a dream. The dream, of both the architect and the client, was for the finest modern opera house in the world. The result, technically, is apparently just that. Architecturally, however, in the sense of the exhilarating and beautiful synthesis of structure and style that produces the great buildings of our age, it is not a modern opera house at all.

Nor is it the realization of the dream. The architect's concept for the new house was for structurally independent stage and seating enclosed within an arcaded shell, the two separated by an insulating cushion of space. Services were to be in a tower at the rear. The possibilities existed for logic, clarity, exciting contemporaneity and strong visual drama. Reams of drawings testify to the effort put into seating design and imaginative interior treatment.

But the estimates came in too high. (This is the dirgelike refrain to which design quality and architectural excellence are being buried all over the United States.) Structurally, the cantilevered seating remains, although there is no visible indication, and the auditorium no longer stands free.

The offices, workshops and services of the tower have been placed between the auditorium and the outer shell, muddling the design concept, filling the open area and creating two huge walls high on either side, facing the glass facade, where there was to have been clear, soaring space. These walls were awkwardly placed and blank. The solution of the Opera Committee—a reflex that seems to be automatic with any cultural group today—was to commission the Chagall murals.

Inside the house the Metropolitan Opera made it clear that it

96

knew what it wanted. And what it wanted were the gilded trappings of tradition and all the comforts of home. "We couldn't have a modern house," Mr. Harrison says with a gentle sadness. "I finally got hammered down by the opera people. I personally would have liked to have found some way around it, but my client wouldn't have liked that at all."

The client liked, and got, crystal glitter, gold leaf, which goes only to the Grand Tier and is replaced by a Dutch metal substitute from there up, a concrete grand staircase and uncounted kilometers of red carpet. It got a house whose general shapes, dimensions, forms and curves were resolved by acoustic requirements that leaned heavily on successful formulas of the past. It got a good plan that works well in terms of circulation, bars, restaurants and general social movement, and then proceeded to have it embellished in a style that is most notable as a curiously unresolved collision of past and present of which the best that can be said is that it is consistently cautious in décor, art and atmosphere. It is a sterile and often tasteless throwback rather than creative twentieth-century design.

There are swags and tassels at the top of the boxes ("the opera people wanted those," says Mr. Harrison) and textured fans at the bottom ("that was for the acoustics people," he explains), a gilded cheesestraw pattern around the proscenium and a ceiling of flying saucers. There is also a strong temptation to close the eyes.

The design *coup de grâce* is in the clubs executed by opera-selected decorators. These clubs range from overstuffed Georgian to Prohibition-nightclub Empire. By contrast, in some of the back-stage areas where tradition was a less oppressive factor, the architect's office provided handsome furniture, color and finishes.

Behind the dubious décor are a million mechanical marvels. Like the rich man who has been a hungry child and keeps three refrigerators full of food, the Metropolitan can now gorge itself on turntables, elevators, raked, raised and lowered stages, moving footlights and scenery and a computer-style lighting system, all to make up for its deprivations in the old house. It is now possible, as the Met demonstrated immediately, to overproduce, overmechanize and overdesign.

The exterior of the building conforms to the ground rules set down for Lincoln Center. Like its neighbors, the opera house is classically arcaded and travertine-faced. At night, the movement on the grand stair and promenades, seen through the lighted glass facade, defines the building's scale impressively and suggests a sparkling, gala party.

Since the new opera promises to be an excellent performing house, with satisfactory acoustics, it may not matter that the architecture sets no high-water mark for the city; that it is average, rather than adventurous or avant-garde. Performance, after all, was the primary objective. It is secondary, but no less disappointing, to have a monument *manqué*.

CBS: Eero Saarinen's Somber Skyscraper

The first observation that one must make about the new CBS headquarters that rises somberly from its sunken plaza at Sixth Avenue and 52nd Street is that it is a building. It is not, like so much of today's large-scale construction, a handy commercial package, a shiny wraparound envelope, a packing case, a box of cards, a trick with mirrors.

It does not look like a cigar lighter, a vending machine, a nutmeg grater. It is a building in the true, classic sense: a complete design in which technology, function and esthetics are conceived and executed integrally for its purpose. As its architect, Eero Saarinen, wanted, this is a building to be looked at above the bottom fifty feet, to be comprehended as a whole.

CBS is Saarinen's only skyscraper and only work in New York. It is the first of the city's landmark skyscrapers to be executed in reinforced concrete and one of the first to use an exterior bearing wall rather than the usual skeleton frame-curtain wall formula. It served as a demonstration model for the new zoning when it was being formulated in 1960–61, with the Saarinen office helping to develop realistic land coverage ratios to permit the plaza-surrounded sheer tower. As such, CBS set the shape and standard for New York building today, for better or worse.

It does all of this with distinction for a figure estimated at not too far above the speculative norm of about $24 a square foot and

well below the luxury building price of $40 upward. Like ABC next door, CBS could simply have taken space offered to it in a conventional investor's building, which would then have been named for it, but the company was seeking something special. It got good value and good looks.

And yet the reaction to the building is extremely mixed. The dark dignity that appeals to architectural sophisticates puts off the public, which tends to reject it as funereal. There is certainly nothing seductive about CBS. But its sober solidity is in a noble architectural tradition. The Strozzi Palace, as a historic example, is an awesome masterpiece of forbidding, stony strength. It is doubtful, of course, whether Renaissance princes were as friendly as Chase Manhattan, and today people want friendly banks and friendly buildings. Quality and presence are more usual requisites for great architecture; there are few friendly buildings on the list.

The first fault, therefore, is in the public eye. Thoroughly corrupted by what might be called the American Product Esthetic—applied equally to buildings and possessions—it takes bright and shiny as synonymous with new and good. Surrounded by tinsel and tinfoil, it finds CBS's somber restraint gloomy, and gloom is not part of the admired American way of life. The spurious glitter of much of the new Sixth Avenue surrounding CBS eclipses Saarinen's sober subtleties.

The second fault is in the building. The failure to carry through its distinctive style and concept consistently into all of its major interior spaces, which are done in stultifyingly familiar luxe corporate formulas, accounts for a curious deadness. Deadness and darkness are easily equated. The result is a first-rate work of architecture that just misses coming alive as a unified work of art.

But it is still an extraordinarily impressive structure. The strong, straight shaft is sheathed in dull Canadian black granite and gray glass and set back twenty-five feet from the building line to take up 50.8 per cent of the block-long, 200-foot-deep site. It rises severely from its depressed plaza for thirty-eight stories and 491 feet. On winter days, the wind whips around it with extra force and chill. No frills, no nonsense, no tricks; no pretty come-on with art and flowers.

Approached from outside, the granite-faced, triangular poured-concrete columns appear first as overlapping, faceted fins of solid stone. As one's perspective changes, they open to reveal glass, then close slowly, massively again. Their module is five feet; five feet of wall or column and five of glass, for a particularly felicitous scale. The relationship inside offers superbly calculated framing of the inexhaustible miracle of New York views.

These columns are neither as simple nor as solid as they seem. Rising uninterrupted from ground to top, they have a dual purpose: as a bearing wall and as conduits for services. From the second-floor level they are hollow for ducts and sheared flat on the interior. At the ground floor, they are solid and fully diamond-shaped inside and out and almost as impressive as Greek columns.

What is involved here is the complexity of structure and service of the modern high-rise building and its relationship to visual esthetics, a problem that separates the men from the boys and good buildings from bad. CBS solves it with maximum logic and minimum ambiguity. The difference between CBS and its neighbors, however, is the basic difference between building and architecture. It is in the fact that most of New York's mammoth commercial structures are no more than weatherproof containers of rentable square footage or candy-wrapped bulk space.

In contrast, CBS is all one architectonic piece. The outside perimeter of columns and an interior service core support it. Between, there is a thirty-five-foot ring, or "square doughnut," in Saarinen's words, of flexible, totally open office space, uninterrupted by columns or corridors. It all fits together in an economical scheme that unifies structure, planning and esthetics. It makes the "whole thing" that Saarinen envisioned.

But in New York buildings are rarely whole things and CBS, unfortunately, is no exception. This can be blamed partly on the untimeliness of Saarinen's death just before construction, which led to a double switch of firms for interiors, and partly on the accepted practice of separating container from contained in the design of the city's business quarters.

Credits list Carson, Lundin and Shaw as "interior architect" (sic) and Florence Knoll Bassett as interior designer. The inside of CBS is a solid gold corporate cliché; a lavish cocoon, complete to standardized concealed wastebaskets and accredited and almost as equally standardized abstract art—interchangeable from Sixth to Third avenues. The building has been turned into the anonymous, vacuum-packed commercial shell that it was never meant to be. And CBS does not become, as Saarinen had hoped, a whole and "soaring thing." It is a great building, grounded.

Schizophrenia at the New York Hilton

American hotel design is suffering from a bad case of esthetic schizophrenia. The cold war is being fought at the New York Hilton at Rockefeller Center, with skirmishes in every corridor and on every floor. Battle lines are drawn between architecture and decoration, between modern automated efficiency and nostalgia for elaborately ersatz things past.

At a distance, there is no evidence of conflict. The Hilton on the Avenue of the Americas from 53rd to 54th streets, a forty-six-story structure designed by William B. Tabler, is an uncompromisingly contemporary container for 2,153 guest rooms and fifty-nine suites that fill a tall slab tower. The tower rests on a squat base, which accommodates the public areas and convention facilities. Designed to be strictly functional, the architecture makes its functions clear.

The flat tower is faced in blue-tinted glass framed by gray-anodized aluminum, the flatness relieved by the repeated short, sharp bays of angled windows. These bays permit the placing of heating and air conditioning ducts outside of the structure, add pleasurably to the size of the rooms and offer interest to what might otherwise be a starkly mechanical facade. The base, or podium, and the tower's end walls are faced in contrasting precast stone, with vertical ribs on the north and south sides of the base to temper the light and unify a variety of functions.*

Aimed at the convention trade, the Hilton is laid out with a competence that would make a computer blush. (Computers are its heart; automated hospitality keeps its guest bills relentlessly up

---

* Another tower is to be added to the New York Hilton, making it the world's largest hotel, even surpassing Moscow's Rossiya. Economic-esthetic attrition will now eliminate the bay windows. Hilton sets a better architectural and environmental standard abroad, notably in Istanbul and Tel Aviv.

Aimed at the convention trade
(AL LEVINE)

to the second.) If the building has a look that suggests that one
might put change in at the top and get something out of the bottom,
this is only because today's slickly designed commercial structures
more and more frequently resemble a product, a machine or a
package.

In a sense, of course, it is a package, since the functions are
neatly wrapped in curtain wall components figured according to
cost-accounting procedures to produce an international hotel formula.
This differs from the native, or Miami modern, formula, which is
easily recognized because it is always built on the bias.

103

The Urban Scene

From the outside this is clearly the world of tomorrow, as promised by Messrs. Conrad Hilton, Laurance Rockefeller and Percy Uris, principals of Rock-Hil-Uris, Inc., the owning company. Within its businesslike limits, the directness of the concept, the expertness of the plan and the quality of execution are acceptable. Inside, the world of tomorrow gives way to never-never land, and it would be better if it never had. Beyond the door the designers of the interiors have figuratively and esthetically thumbed their noses at the architect and vertigo sets in.

Only the registration facilities and the 54th Street lobby show any relationship to the architecture or any acknowledgment of the modern world, although the superfluous curtains that needlessly cover glass walls would give Salome a lifetime supply of veils. This "fringe" area has a collection of specially commissioned and assembled painting and sculpture. (A group of prints chosen for the rooms is defeated by the level of the decor and the department store manner in which they are hung.) The entering visitor is briefly promised the sophisticated, exhilarating experience of contemporary New York.

But conflict waits around the corner. A turn to the left and the promise is broken. Here lurk stone walls made of plastered aluminum, paneled doors made of painted plywood, parodies of antiquity without authenticity; all of the farcical paraphernalia that deride and camouflage. This, too, is formula, repeated in hotels and restaurants from coast to coast with a suffocating sameness.

The Rue des Gourmets, as this corridor is called, is the entrance to the restaurants, and it will please a large number of people who equate pretentious confusion and cheap tricks with charm. It will give others heartburn. But it is sufficient preparation for all except the Kismet Lounge, for which no less than a few years in an MGM harem or a fortification of preliminary cocktails will do. Downstairs, there is the busy banality of the Taveerne Coffee Shop, decorated with Dutch tiles and cloth tulips.

Banquet customers have a choice of a surprising period piece of 1930's *salon moderne* decoration in the Grand Ballroom, which sets hotel design back thirty years, a stage-set in the "French" manner in the Trianon Ballroom, or the unclassifiable Mercury Ballroom.

A certain amount of make-believe is acceptable in restaurants and ballrooms, although there is no law that says that the designer must turn his back on the present or plumb the depths of corn. But there is even less excuse for the damage done to the guest rooms, which increases in violence as they rise in importance and price. The architect has produced a better room, with nine-foot ceilings and bay-window walls, than most new New York hotels or apartments can boast. On the lower floors they are defaced by motel modern colors that assault the senses. (For headaches, there are handy automatic ice cubes in the bathrooms.) In the top-echelon suites the rejection of the architecture is total.

Every decorating trick is used to disguise and destroy the possibility of a legitimate dramatic beauty within the framework of our own time, suggesting the magnificence of mid-twentieth-century New York. This is not just an opportunity missed; it is a design disaster. The $75 million question (the cost of hotel and furnishings) is how an expert group of investors, which obviously took care to select one of the most experienced hotel architects in the profession and put together an ambitious art collection, could have failed to set the same standard for the building's interiors. The Hilton is the loser, and so is the American public, which must accept this kind of design cross-country along with equally grotesque room service—bagless jugs of cold tea and foil-wrapped cold toast—both symptomatic of the standards of our time.

The Federal Government Lays a Colossal Architectural Egg

A funny thing happened on the way to a Civic Center. While New York backed and filled and studied and restudied plans for the environs of City Hall, the Federal Government went ahead and built a forty-one-story office building and connected courthouse in City Hall's backyard that dominate and destroy the entire Civic Center area.

The new blockbuster can scarcely be called a surprise. It has been rising in solemn, outsize non-splendor for about three years and is quite impossible to miss from anywhere around. Just look for the biggest checkerboard in the world. The office tower is attached to a smaller building with structural paranoia; hung by

What is it?
Only its architects know for sure
(THE NEW YORK TIMES BY ERNEST SISTO)

trusses, supported by columns and cantilevered at the edges behind a standard glass skin. Is it a suspended structure or isn't it? Only its architects know for sure.

Together, the buildings are about as funny as a bad Joe Miller joke. Architecturally, the Federal Government has laid a colossal egg. What has been going on in planning and design terms for at least the last four years, however, is not so much funny as it is pure farce. As a case study of how New York got one of the most monumentally mediocre Federal buildings in history, it is edifying. It could be called a classic performance in bureaucratic inflexibility.

In the fall of 1963 New York City released the results of a Civic Center study that attempted to pull together the chaos around Foley Square, including bridge approaches, highway spaghetti, fragmented open space and new building needs. The design of the Federal building and courthouse, by Kahn and Jacobs, Alfred Easton Poor, and Eggers and Higgins, was complete, but construction had not yet begun.

In the interests of sense and symmetry, the city asked Washington (the General Services Administration, which builds Federal structures throughout the country) to move the building toward Broadway to conform with New York's plan. The answer, apparently based on the fact that while the wheels of government grind slowly they cannot reverse or change direction, was no. End of Act One.

Act Two: During excavation for the office tower, foundations of several older office buildings on the Broadway side gave way. The Federal Government was forced to demolish them. This extended the site to exactly the location that had been requested by the city. Asked again by the city for relocation and redesign, Washington again said no.

Act Three: The buildings went up as planned, with an immense, blank, featureless concrete wall facing Broadway. This civic embellishment will remain, as well as the vacant Broadway frontage, until more space is needed, and then the Federal building will double its size. Considering its size now, and what can only be called its belligerent banality, this might be called Washington's gift of double disaster to New York.

Just across Broadway are two matching Victorian buildings fronted in cast iron on the corner of Thomas Street, framing the vista of the huge, blank wall and mammoth checkerboard beyond. Called the Thomas twins by the Landmarks Preservation Commission, their "Renaissance palace" facades of cast columns and repeated arches, rich in plasticity, style and scale, offer a mute, visual lesson in esthetic and cultural aspirations. They are the nineteenth-century city; the Federal building is the twentieth-century city. In the hundred-year trip across Broadway someone mislaid or lost the art of architecture.

The Urban Scene

Of Art and Genocide

There have been several disastrous proposals for a New York memorial to the six million Jews killed in concentration camps in World War II made over the past years in which the agony and the art were almost too much to bear. A memorial to genocide is a crushing problem, emotionally and esthetically. The Committee to Commemorate the Six Million Jewish Martyrs, an affiliation of Jewish groups created for the purpose of commissioning and constructing the monument, has been aided by an Art Advisory Committee, which recommended Louis Kahn, the architect.

In an age of violence that has made a flat mockery of conventional memorial values and platitudes, Mr. Kahn's solution is a cool, abstract, poetic, powerful and absolute statement of unspeakable tragedy. It could rank with the great works of commemorative art in which man has attempted to capture spirit, in symbol, for the ages. All the wrenching angst of earlier proposals is noticeably absent.

The memorial consists of a flat gray granite base, sixty-six feet square and high enough to sit on, with seven glass near-cubes placed on it. Each "cube" is ten feet square and eleven feet high, constructed of tightly laid and jointed elongated glass blocks. In Mr. Kahn's words, "the sun could come through and leave a shadow filled with light." It is a concept expressive of death and hope. Six of the rectangles represent the six million dead. The seventh, in the center, is open, so that people may enter. Inscribed, it would serve as a chapel. Again, in Mr. Kahn's words. "The one, the chapel, speaks; the other six are silent."

The design is beautiful and chilling. There is about it a silent, almost frozen formality, a crystalline sense of the eternal emptiness of death. The glass rectangles reflect another kind of eternity, the changes of weather, light and season. This is architecture and, at the same time, sculpture, and it is symbolism of the highest order, timeless and contemporary. Mr. Kahn weds poetry and philosophy to form.

The question to be raised is not about the monument but about the site. It is meant for Battery Park, just behind the paved area and

Model of the Monument to the Six Million Jewish Martyrs
(MUSEUM OF MODERN ART)

promenade facing the water. The Parks Department has approved the monument in principle. But the quality of the design and tragic importance of the cause do not cancel out the basic question that still must be faced: whether monuments belong in parks at all. New York's parks are an eroded testament to the popular tradition that puts them there.

Moreover, Battery Park, a green miracle at the base of Manhattan with a theatrical skyline backdrop, offers a surprisingly unsympathetic setting. It is a most curiously landscaped park, with a blank, featureless grand allée leading to Castle Clinton, that marvelous circular red sandstone relic of New York history that has housed everything from guns to Jenny Lind to fish and is now being restored to its first incarnation as a fort. The rest of the park is scalloped off into curves or ovals dotted with a chaotic accretion of things: in addition to the fort, there is an occasional statue, a Coast Guard building and a tomblike structure that contains either the remains of a Salvation Army official, commemorated by a nearby stone slab, or an air intake for the Brooklyn-Battery tunnel. It is, essentially, a Pop landscape.

What this memorial needs is its own site, walled in, functioning much as Paley Park does on 53rd Street near Fifth Avenue. It deserves nothing less and will be compromised by anything less, because there is, potentially, overwhelming art and symbolism here. It is a suitable memorial if a suitable site can be found.

The generation that lived through the time and events the monument proposes to commemorate will never forget them. We have that memorial seared in our souls. The generations that are innocent of this kind of totalitarianism and ultimate tragedy will find no monument meaningful. That is one of the anachronisms of art and history in an age of violence.

This memorial could work, as art and as history, and as a lasting expression of the human spirit. In a nihilistic, value-destroying society, that is no mean artistic accomplishment.

Other Places, Other Problems

Manchester, N.H.: Lessons in Urbicide

THE story of the destruction of the Amoskeag mill complex that has formed the heart of Manchester, N.H., for over a hundred years has a terrible pertinence for the numberless cities committing blind mutilation in the name of urban renewal.

Demolition is under way of one of the most remarkable manifestations of our urban and industrial culture. The historic, but still functioning, planned mill community of Manchester, faced with adjusting to changing economics, is being indiscriminately bulldozed for a researched, consultant-approved and officially adopted urban renewal scheme consisting almost totally of parking lots that mocks the quality of vision and design now being ruthlessly effaced.

The Amoskeag plan, conceived and started in the 1830's by the Amoskeag Company's nineteen-year-old engineer, Ezekial Straw (later governor of New Hampshire), united factories, waterways, public buildings and public commons, housing and commerce in an integrated design. The famous mill town's simple, handsome, ver-

Mutilation in the name of urban renewal at Manchester, N. H.
(RANDOLPH LANGENBACH FOR SMITHSONIAN INSTITUTION)

nacular red brick buildings, constructed for the textile industry from 1838 to 1915, stretched for more than a mile along the Merrimac River, flanking canals and mill yards. The excellence of the complex has made it an acknowledged monument of American industrial history and urban design.

"Monuments don't pay," says Manchester's urban renewal director, Cary P. Davis, quoted in *Time,* as he handed them over to the bulldozer. Still, the tragedy of Manchester has not gone unremarked. *Time, Fortune* and *The Architectural Forum,* representing the professional press, have added their voices to the usual ones of the historians. Maybe that is a good sign. By slow drops and trickles in the pool of public information and opinion, a force that exerts considerable political leverage, an awareness of our losses might hopefully develop before the country is stripped bare of its urban art and history.

It is significant in this context that the term "industrial archeology," a phrase employed by historians, is beginning to break into more popular usage. Industrial archeology is the study of the buildings, plans and structural and social complexes developed by the forces of commerce and industry that have conspicuously shaped this country in the nineteenth and twentieth centuries. Manchester is, or was, a prime example. The term covers a large, important and varied body of building that makes special technological, functional and esthetic contributions to the American environment. But its monuments are largely ignored. We have a way of sweeping under the rug art and history that do not conform to accepted, preconceived notions of cultural achievement. We tear down those genuine and often strikingly handsome monuments while we build meaningless reproductions of the domestic and official eighteenth century. There is a game, for example, that could be called "Who's got the real Independence Hall?" played cross-country.

Industrial archeology is concerned with a great deal of the American scene—significant, strong, tradition-shattering structures and plans that tell more about American civilization than many of the conventional touchstones.

Randolph Langenbach, a Harvard graduate who has spent several years documenting the Amoskeag-Manchester story for the Smithsonian archives and on his own, writes that Manchester's "role in the growth of American society is really more important and symbolic than the role of Williamsburg. Although much venerated, Williamsburg was more English than American in style, and its significance did not last through the greatest period of America's industrial and social growth, as did Manchester's." This was written in an article for the Harvard Alumni Bulletin. (Harvard grads, community leaders all, supporters of culture, read and remember.) But in the preservation script as it is written today, Williamsburg and its imitators get all the lines. And all the money. They are rebuilt and refurnished to expensive, improbable perfection, while the wrecker's ball swings freely in the country's Manchesters. What a splendid $75 million Rockefeller restoration and re-use demonstration project this could have made. Development problems of this magnitude and of this historic importance probably cannot be solved by any city without foundation aid.

The tragedy cannot be blamed on lack of information. John Coolidge's book on the Utopian nineteenth-century planning of Lowell, Mass., *Mill and Mansion,* has become a classic in the field. The Lowell buildings no longer exist. William Pierson's studies of New England mill towns are standard literature. Between this competent scholarship and the politically appointed agencies that run urban renewal there is an unconscionable communications gap that could most kindly be called ignorance. The results of ignorance are urbicide.

Mr. Langenbach is now documenting Manchester's self-destruction. Ninety of the buildings will go for parking lots and access to still-functioning factories. The canals, now polluted, will be filled in for sewers. What is being destroyed for some of the most limited and discredited aims of urban renewal, he points out, is the "unity and impact of one of the most powerful urban scenes anywhere in the world."

How did it happen? The same way that the heart and soul are being cut out of uncounted American cities to be replaced by faceless clichés. First, an outside research firm is called in to analyze the community's problems and make recommendations. The extremely respected, internationally known firm of Arthur D. Little, Inc. produced such a consultant survey for Manchester in 1961. While making numerous economic suggestions, the report offered the information that "even with extensive improvements and upgrading, the millyard will never be an asset from the esthetic point of view."

Well. The blind telling the blind what to do. Say that to any architectural historian or urban designer worthy of the name and watch the fireworks. The real catastrophe, however, is that it is exactly this kind of seriously inadequate, damaging nonsense that is being sold successfully to municipalities countrywide. The researchers, the planners and the surveys themselves are close to identical, ignoring any indigenous character for formulas of repetitive, profitable sterility.

The conclusions thus offered and received as gospel are much like the grotesque solutions of incompletely programed computers. They are wretchedly wrong. No one has remembered to put in the factor of environmental design sensitivity based on recognition of its characteristics through knowledge of its forms and appreciation of its history. On those well-known research and planning teams collecting fat fees for a depressingly standard product ground out in town after town, there is rarely a contributor of this essential expertise. The tragically faulty recommendations that result from this basic omission are then translated into action by renewal agencies, most of whom are urbanistic amateurs. Surgery is carried on by plumbers.

What is being produced is a kind of urban Pablum. We are making a dull porridge of parking lots and cheap commercialism, to replace the forms and evidence of American civilization. The buildings despised and sacrificed today are, or would have been, tomorrow's heritage. We have forgotten, to quote Mr. Langenbach again, that "economics is a social science." We wonder why the economic formulas produce inhuman cities.

This is the certain way to the blight of the future. In Manchester where the memory of the mills as a poor and oppressive way of life is still alive, nobody really cares. And that is the most tragic indictment of all.

Syracuse, N.Y.: Ugly Cities and How They Grow

The crisis of our cities can be stated in very simple terms: they are becoming insupportably hideous. Underneath the ugliness and often causing it are many real ills brought on by overwhelming social and economic changes and population pressures since the war. The cities are sick, and urban renewal is government-applied first aid.

One suspects that the doctor's cures may be killing the patient. Visit almost any city in the United States and its most striking aspect is apt to be a bulldozed wasteland in its heart. Out of the wasteland, more often than not, rises another dreary wasteland of new construction.

The story is the same for private redevelopment. Only one sure fact emerges—the new is replacing the old indiscriminately, as a kind of sanitary cure-all, often without satisfactory rationale or results. All too frequently, good is replaced by bad.

These remarks could apply to almost any American city, since most share the same ills and cures, but they are prompted by a visit to Syracuse, N.Y., a community of approximately 216,000 afflicted with all of the symptoms of a city this size, at this particular time.

In spite of a general effect of spotty disorder, Syracuse is rich in good architecture of all periods. In addition to a range from great Greek Revival to high style High Victorian, it has the most magnificent "modernistic" fruitcake that this observer has ever seen, in the Niagara Mohawk Power Building of the 1930's. What is happening to all of it, however, is so typical and so deplorable that Syracuse can stand as a case history.

Clinton Square, the former downtown center from which business has now moved southward, is, or was, a well-scaled public space surrounded by fine vintage buildings. The Syracuse Savings Bank of 1876 by Joseph Lyman Silsbee, who later trained Frank Lloyd Wright in Chicago, ranked as a Victorian Gothic masterpiece. Flanking it is, or was, a splendid Second Empire structure, the Gridley Building of 1867, and the third Onondaga County Courthouse of 1856, a landmark of high quality by Horatio White. Opposite is a competent Classic Revival post office of 1928. Each is a top example of its style.

Between them are more recent structures, dull beyond credulity, but still not destructive of the complex. The old buildings relate perfectly in size and scale to the square; they offer rich stylistic variety to the city. The rub, of course, is that most of them are obsolete.

This is the tragedy and the problem of urban "progress." The

116

savings bank has existed by grace of a previous owner who prized it. The courthouse, which has had "temporary" government uses for fifty years, faces demolition with the removal of the adjoining Police Headquarters to a new building in Syracuse's chief urban renewal area, where a combined civic and cultural center is rising. This area has produced at least one structure of special interest— the Everson Museum by I. M. Pei.

Syracuse is wearing those peculiar renewal blinders that make it fail to see the possibility of the present conversion of a historic structure for a concert hall, for example, rather than marking a nebulous future X in the new cultural center.

The city wears blinders in many ways. It fails to appreciate the superb cut granite mass and steeple of St. Paul's Church. It ignores the numbing object lesson of the contrast between its strong, rusticated, nineteenth-century Richardsonian City Hall and the flat, pusillanimous, twentieth-century state office building next to it that wins some kind of booby prize for totally undistinguished design.

In cities like Syracuse, new and old coexist as bellicose, resentful strangers. There is a curious, Martian mixture of almost surrealist strangeness; Queen Anne gingerbread next to cantilevered steel. The old waits grotesquely for the new to sweep it to destruction, and the all-important lesson of urban design is still unlearned. You don't wish the old city away; you work with its assets, allying them to the best new building for strengthening relationships for both.

As long as architects reject the past and fail to deal in continuity, cities like Syracuse are doomed to self-destruction.

St. Louis, Mo.: Success and Blues

The success of Powell Symphony Hall in St. Louis is probably going to lead a lot of people to a lot of wrong conclusions. In a kind of architectural Gresham's law, the right thing wrongly interpreted usually has more bad than good results.

The first wrong conclusion is that Powell Hall represents the triumph of traditional over modern architecture. False. The correct conclusion here is that a good old building is better than a bad new one. Powell Hall represents the triumph simply of suitable preservation. And, one might add, of rare good sense.

This conversion of a 1925 movie palace represents the intelligent re-use of an old structure that was, and is, a stagily handsome theatrical setting. It has the added advantage of having started with conventionally satisfactory conditions for good acoustics. It is quite fair to conclude that this involves less of a gamble than a new design solution.

The building's elaborate, unreproducible, Silver Screen Versailles features are a fortuitous "architecture *trouvé.*" The result is a concert hall of suave elegance, beautiful sound and stunning economy (about $2½ million total cost instead of the $10 to $20 million required for a new building) with a maximum of glamor and glitter. As St. Louisans danced to Strauss waltzes on the stage and in the Grand Foyer after the opening concert under eleven-foot chandeliers in a cream-white, crimson and gold-leaf setting, leaders in other cities were crying quietly over their multi-million-dollar, superstatus, superbuilding plans.

Most of those cities are engaged in the absurd cycle of tearing down irreplaceable old structures while they promote expensive new projects of depressing vacuity. Perhaps the sheer rationality and taste of the St. Louis venture may set some kind of badly needed example.

A pertinent conclusion that is being systematically evaded would be that we are putting up a lot of bad new buildings in the name of the arts. Somehow cultural centers turn into camels. (A camel, it will be remembered, is a committee-designed horse.)

The well-meant efforts of community groups lead to few artistic triumphs or architectural masterpieces. They lead, instead, to those big, miserably ordinary new houses tricked up with depressing applied art that fall flat on the eye and ear. They lead to compromise and caution (Lincoln Center), and great art is never cautious. They lead to pretty mediocrity on a colossal scale (the Kennedy Center) and pratfall bows to tradition (the Metropolitan Opera House). They produce a comfortable, conservative culture, without a single *frisson,* in both package and product. Most depressing of all is the fact that so much power and prestige stand behind these failures of nerve and style.

Chamber of Commerce renewal in St. Louis's downtown,
with housing, hotels, stadium and parking garages

The Urban Scene

It is not that modern architecture has failed. It is that we have yet to use the dramatic beauty or unparalleled design and structural potential of our age. It is not that we are already tired of contemporary halls. We have hardly experienced one, in the proper creative sense of the word.

Any discussion of success or failure in St. Louis leads inevitably to the city's major downtown renewal program. (The decision not to put Powell Hall downtown was motivated partly by the fact that the new Busch Stadium preempts all parking and traffic facilities —a curious shutout for a new plan.)

The completed St. Louis Arch, soaring 630 feet at the river's edge, is magnificent. Its superscaled, stainless steel curve soars grandly enough to justify any questionable engineering rationale. It offers surprising attitudes of contemporary abstract grandeur from almost every angle, and if you must share in the great American tourist compulsion to get to the top of everything big, you can be shot up in a purple capsule, like one of five peas in a pod, to see the view from its gently swaying apex.

This may be the only way you will see the Mississippi and its historic levee. They are lost to the eye and to the ordinary pedestrian, although it is possible to get to the river if you know how. The stunning, slow rise of textured rose-gray granite that once provided a working slope for riverboat cargo is, as a prominent St. Louisan pointed out, as handsome as a city-size Nagare sculpture. The level of the park created for the arch when the old waterfront with its priceless cast-iron architectural heritage was bulldozed, hides river and levee. The park is still desolately unlandscaped.

The arch stands in a curious kind of limbo called urban redevelopment. It has no setting, and this is meant less in terms of planting or vistas than in its relationship to the city at its feet.

Waterfront St. Louis was a case history of a dying downtown. It can now be judged as a case history of commercially sponsored renewal.

Except for the arch and the old courthouse, which form some genuinely provocative urban views, downtown St. Louis is a monument to Chamber of Commerce planning and design. It is a businessman's dream of redevelopment come true.

There are all of the faceless, characterless, scaleless symbols of economic regeneration—luxury apartments, hotels, a 50,000-seat

120

stadium and multiple parking garages for 7,400 cars. Sleek, new, prosperous, stolid and dull, well-served by superhighways, the buildings are a collection of familiar profit formulas, uninspired in concept, unvarying in scale, unrelated by any standards, principles or subtleties of planning or urban design. They just stand there. They come round, rectangular, singly and in pairs. Pick your standard commercial cliché. The centerpiece is the Busch Stadium, big and banal, smoothed up by the esthetic ministrations of Edward Durell Stone.

There are none of the traditional values of vitality, variety and humanity that make cities challenging and great. Sensing something lacking, St. Louisans thought the answer might be to add a kind of Disneyland for those whose interests are not bounded by baseball and football, an idea that was fortunately abandoned.

There was a competition for a mall leading to courthouse and arch, won by Sasaki, Dawson, De May Associates, but no one sees much point in building it, since malls are for people involved in pleasurable urban activities and what is pleasurable or interesting about a promenade bounded on one full side by a parking garage? This will not be helped environmentally by the re-erection of the Spanish Pavilion from the New York World's Fair, a building more meaningful for its interior display than its exterior architecture.

The new St. Louis is a success economically and a failure urbanistically. It has the impersonal gloss of a promotional brochure. A prime example of the modern landscape of urban alienation, it has gained a lot of real estate and lost a historic city.

Saratoga, N.Y.: Losing Race

Saratoga, N.Y., is a community known for horse racing, a historic Victorian heritage and its new cultural center.

The city's past is firmly linked with hotels—some of the most luxurious of the Gilded Age. This is a community still rich in fine late nineteenth-century houses, and those who look can find the celebrated Canfield Casino, now shabby-elegant, a semi-museum and a preservation problem. Not much more remains of Saratoga's vanishing record of high Victorian society, a historical and esthetic phenomenon that few cities anywhere could match.

The extravagant hotels, with their baroque opulence, elaborate gingerbread and eleven-course dinners, have gone the way of the dinosaurs that they grew to resemble. It is not without significance that on the site of one of the greatest hostelries, the Grand Union, there are now a Grand Union supermarket and parking lot that have stamped Saratoga's once-great main street with a back-alley look. It is impossible to get more environmentally ordinary than that.

Ironies abound in the Saratoga saga. As the old hotels were bulldozed and the new cultural center was built, a shortage of hotel space developed. The timing was bad in more ways than one. Now that it no longer seems impossible to restore and modernize old buildings—we are seeing a small, swelling groundwave of striking preservation successes in several cities that would have been called pie-in-the-sky projects ten years ago—it is probable that not everything of the past had to be sacrificed. The supermarket-motel image doesn't do a thing for Saratoga except downgrade it. Some of its unique heritage could have been fitted into the city's cultural renaissance by sensitive, civilized planning.

It has been touch and go since 1957 for Saratoga's park and casino that still stands in it, when a referendum was passed approving the leasing of park space for a hotel, which did not materialize at the time. Instead, a hotel was built just outside of the park. But the authorization is still on the books.

Unfortunately, there is no such thing as an appropriate design for the destruction of a public park. And in front of the hotel that was built instead of the one in the park, as beacon, focus and image of the new Saratoga, is the Holiday Inn sign, the granddaddy horror of them all.

This visual monstrosity poisons the environment wherever it is, and it is everywhere because the Holiday Inn corporation insists on it as identification all over the country. The sign seems to be a prime clause of the franchise. A coast-to-coast atrocity, it could undo a dozen natural-beauty programs. It would have been a hole-in-one triumph for Mrs. Johnson's campaign if all Holiday Inn signs had disappeared, outlawed in the public interest.

This does not mean that all signs everywhere are bad, or that

122

they must be in discreet or quaint eighteenth-century script to be O.K. Public graphics is another environmental subject that needs clarification.

Subway advertising, for example, is generally excellent. It gives brightness and scale and an emotional and visual lift as well as waiting-time distraction to a dreary setting, and it seems rather sad that the new Washington subway, in an excess of architectural purity, will have none. The ads on New York's buses, also bitterly fought by the purists, add a flash of moving color and wit to the city's tense, gray streets.

What one of the professional magazines, *Progressive Architecture*, calls Supergraphics, a highly imaginative public use of bold lettering, image and color, can be an environmental pickup. Even those telephoto shots of highway vulgarization with their shoulder-to-shoulder neon and plastic, used as arguments for beautification, become quite smashing graphic compositions in their own right—the photo result, curiously, is an art form in itself.

There is a thin line everywhere today between art and accident, or even art and atrocity; it is a characteristic of our time. Current architectural theory calls for complexity and disorder (in a kind of tastefully arranged, properly evocative counterpoint of esthetic experiences, of course), using the happy accidents of unplanned construction as examples. The unhappy accidents don't count. There is a perfectly good case to be made for subtleties and variations of design outside of Cartesian order, but the idea is already being carried to extremes of heady intellectual irrelevance.

Billboard blight is fought by concerned citizens in a losing battle against a powerful business lobby, and yet billboard art, as sophisticated abstraction and out of environmental context, becomes Pop Art, translating the punch-in-the-stomach assault of the highway into the esthetic punch in the eye of the gallery. The line grows steadily thinner.

But even with this precarious balance of values, there is still simple environmental malpractice—and the theorists of the new chaos be hanged. When an Indianapolis-based store chain called Vonnegut's (to take a typical, all-American example) gets a pat on the back from a trade publication for its "new look"—one of those totem pole accretions of towering mix-matched and mismatched humdrum graphics to lure the helpless driver—it is archetypal bad. It is really bad because it isn't even bad enough to be good enough for the new chaos.

Certainly Saratoga is no more confused or much worse off than any other community today; its "new look" is national. It is only that Saratoga's unique architectural history makes its transgressions a special study of environmental abuse. What the next abuse will be is always a gamble, although the outrages and odds are reasonably predictable. But that's what makes horse racing, anywhere.

London: Skyscraper Asparagus

The postwar crop of highly controversial skyscrapers in this city has been almost universally undistinguished—or worse. They stand like lonely stalks of asparagus against the sky.

The reasons that Londoners dislike them have less to do with their conspicuous lack of architectural quality than with their disruption of tradition and the skyline.

London has finally been promised a top-grade skyscraper by one of the world's most celebrated architects, Mies van der Rohe, and the project has become one of the city's most controversial subjects. The proposed building, a distinguished 290-foot office tower, is to be the new headquarters of Lloyds Bank. It will be in the City, the financial district, adjacent to Mansion House, the Lord Mayor's residence, and close to that fortress of financial and architectural probity, the Bank of England.

The building, to be carried out in collaboration with the English architect Lord Holford, will be one of Mies's characteristically chaste, elegant, meticulously detailed and superbly proportioned sheer shafts, richly finished in bronze and faced with bronze-tinted glass. It is similar to his Seagram Building in New York, done in association with Philip Johnson.

It's big, it's new, it's questionable—
London's 30-story National Provincial Bank
(MARVIN LICHTNER)

124

The Urban Scene

The site, a triangular open plaza to be made by the staged demolition of existing Victorian structures, is bounded by Poultry, Victoria and Queen streets. These structures include the large Mappin and Webb jewelry store and many small shops.

The argument about the Mies building has been entered full tilt by the public, which was invited to comment at an official exhibition of the project, and the press, which does not lack for architecture critics. The debate focuses on the height and style of the tower and the creation of the proposed plaza.

As is not the case in New York, no new office building can go up in any part of London without permission of the appropriate planning body. This is a requirement of an extremely strong set of town and country planning acts that have controlled national development since 1947. The public exhibition is a recent addition to this planning process meant to insure public knowledge of and participation in the planning procedure.

Incredibly, 26,000 Londoners attended the exhibition of this project put on by the Corporation of the City of London.

The city's architects and intellectuals have made the point that London's eighteenth- and nineteenth-century building achievements are matched by nothing of comparable quality in the twentieth century, and they have voted heavily in favor of the Mies tower. The more visceral and traditional public clings to its fear of heights, new materials and change. Lloyds and the architects have submitted their official application to build and are waiting for the city's decision.

The Corporation of the City of London's planners and architects have worked out the project with the bank—the customary procedure for any astute developer intent on getting the city's permission to build. They clearly hope to avoid Royal Art Commission involvement; the commission has been quite consistent in lopping off the tops of buildings too tall for its taste.

Height must be understood as a relative thing in London. Even the word "skyscraper" is a comparative term. Twenty stories seems high in this solid, horizontal city, and tall buildings range from 250 to 400 feet. The popular idea of a tall building is eight stories. Until the end of World War II, no London building had gone higher than 150 feet. That had been the limit since Queen Victoria was displeased by the intrusion on her view of a rapidly rising develop-

126

ment called Queen Anne's Mansions and the height lid was clamped on by the first London Building Act of 1894.

As postwar buildings have grown bigger, their architecture has gotten meaner. In this stronghold of tradition, architectural excellence is one tradition that seems to have been forgotten. The new large-scale London construction, with few exceptions, can be listed in two categories.

One is the apogee of the nadir—an implausible but necessary term—of the most completely ordinary and disruptive kind of routine speculative building. It could be called, kindly, international commercial, and it sits with particularly bad grace in London. The other is a British commercial mutant best described as Miami mod, or Pop Architecture with an English accent.

Some of London's most conspicuous big buildings are the following:

The British Petroleum Building, 1967, thirty-five stories and 395 feet high, bordering the Barbican area, near a row of nondescript little Lever Houses along London Wall and three soaring, close-to-400-foot apartment towers in the Barbican area developments; Joseph and F. Milton Cashmore and Partners, architects. An overly familiar, uninspired exercise in the glass curtain wall.

The Shell Building, constructed in the late 1950's, twenty-six stories and about 350 feet high; Easton and Robertson, Cusdin, Preston and Smith, architects. Lumpen-skyscraper style, this one looms squarely, in every sense of the word, on the horizon, dwarfing the South Bank Arts Center beside it.

The London Hilton, 1963, twenty-eight stories and 328 feet high; Sidney Kaye, architect. This slick commercial tower not only broke Mayfair's uniformly scaled domestic and discreet business gentility but also peered into Buckingham Palace's yard. That was a double affront, to propriety and to urban sensibility.

Centre Point, 1964, thirty-five stories and 385 feet high, at St. Giles Circus; built by London's mysterious millionaire-developer, Harry Hyams, and R. Seifert and Partners, the city's leading commercial architects. London planners got a road under this building, now useless because of changed traffic patterns. The developer got an immensely valuable site and London got the architectural Jazz Age.

The National Provincial Bank headquarters, 1967, thirty stories and 335 feet high, at Drapers Gardens, near the Stock Exchange. An outstanding Hyams-Seifert speculative, if not architectural, triumph, its flashy commercialism is singularly unsuited to the financial area's substantial, classical style.

The twenty-story, 322-foot high Stock Exchange on Throgmorton Street; Llewelyn Davies, Weeks and Partners, architects. This promises to be an overdesigned, precast facade in Concrete Wishful Think, meant to offer a dubious bulky blend with its stone neighbors.

The twenty-three-story speculative building at 20 and 24 Fenchurch Street, also in the financial district. A blatantly average commercial building.

The Commercial Union Assurance Building, twenty-three stories and 389 feet high, near Leadenhall Street, in the same area; Gollins, Melvin Ward, Architects and Partners. A clearly Mies-inspired tower of considerable, cool style, by far the best of the lot. It belatedly demonstrates the kind of contemporary dignity and presence that London requires and rarely gets in its new construction.

London needs its new Mies building badly. It is going to get the twentieth century whether it wants it or not, and the question is how much architectural quality will come with it. The plaza for the building is another matter. One boundary of the proposed triangular site is taken up by a huge and typical structure of the mid-1950's called Bucklersbury House. To deliberately expose the full expanse of Bucklersbury House, which is the epitome of the apogee of the nadir, would be a disaster. Moreover, because of the peculiarly pointless way that Bucklersbury House is set back from the street line, the essential sense of containment for one whole side of the new plaza has already been lost.

Unlike New York, which is a massed, concentrated city, London is a low, scattered city with an even, spreading horizon marked by Christopher Wren's church spires and a large and often lowering sky. Its magnificence is due to the kind of great architecture that can make men seem great and invests their acts with a sense of nobility.

It is not the big buildings that damage this city. It is the big, bad buildings that are a London catastrophe.

128

London: Renewing Covent Garden

English plans, unlike American plans, which tend to remain in the blue-sky category, have a way of becoming reality. They are assisted by strong government legislation and participation. The Covent Garden plan, with the famous Covent Garden market at its heart, is considered one of the most important and far-reaching of the proposals for London's future. If it goes ahead, Eliza Doolittle would never recognize her old neighborhood.

Fifteen acres of the center-city site are devoted now to London's colorful fruit, vegetable and flower market. It is in what is left of Inigo Jones's celebrated seventeenth-century design for the city's first great residential square.

The market is scheduled to leave for a South Bank location in 1972, just over 300 years after the Duke of Bedford obtained the first market charter when produce became more profitable than the handsome houses, since demolished, that he had built. St. Paul's Church, Jones's Tuscan masterpiece, still stands amid stacks of Brussels sprouts at the west end of the square.

The redevelopment program is a multi-use, multi-level scheme to re-use the market buildings and add a new convention center, drama and recreation centers, hotels and commercial buildings, change traffic patterns and double the amount of existing housing. Financing would be carried out with public and private funds in a three-phase construction program that would continue over the next twenty years. The project area is bounded by the Strand on the south, Charing Cross Road on the west, Shaftesbury Avenue and High Holborn on the north, and a line following Newton, Great Queen, Wild, Kean and Tavistock streets on the east. This is a substantial section of central London.

The proposal is part of a continuing, official replanning and reconstruction program that is changing the face of this city's most famous sites and squares in the name of modern functional needs and urban problems.

New plans and construction in London include the war-damaged environs of St. Paul's Cathedral and the high-rise Barbican district, both already rebuilt. There are schemes in the study stage for Piccadilly Circus and Regent Street, Trafalgar Square, Whitehall and Parliament Square. The South Bank development presents a massive new cultural center. Most of London's historic core is on the boards of the city's planners.

The ninety-three acres centered on the market form an important "downtown" area where the economic return on old buildings has not kept pace with rising land values. There are almost uniform five-story structures dated from eighteenth-century Georgian to nineteenth-century Victorian. The most historic will be preserved.

The land is considered ripe for redevelopment. Prices range from $50 to $100 a square foot, close to London's highest. For comparison, the most superinflated prices anywhere, in midtown Manhattan, are $200 to $400 a square foot. In the classic pattern of all cities, small enterprises and low-cost housing are threatened. With the removal of the market, speculative opportunities will skyrocket.

Private development has been deliberately held off by the government for the last ten years, pending the completion of a comprehensive Covent Garden area plan. This can be done under the British Planning Act by not issuing development permits to private builders.

The area under study contains the market, sixteen of the thirty-three West End theaters, the Royal Opera House and an assortment of one-man, small-scale businesses and shops of spectacular variety and interest. It is a literary center, for publishers, printers, engravers and bookstores. The low-rent loft space accommodates art and theater services and its stores range from take-out Chinese food to dealers in antiques, hardware and stamps. Londoners speak warmly of "bananas and ballerinas cheek to jowl." It is one of the most successful mixed-use neighborhoods in the world.

The Covent Garden plan is a sophisticated proposal, containing much new theory that has been learned by trial, error and catastrophe in the last twenty years. It claims to recognize the special character of the area and to update it to modern city needs. Whether the two objectives are not mutually exclusive is something the planners have not really faced.

It also raises serious questions about the degree and extent of master-planning control that is desirable or necessary for problem solving in a city whose distinctive character and appeal have been created by scattered, organic growth. As the Danish planner Steen Eiler Rasmussen has pointed out, the best thing that ever happened to London was the city's failure to adopt Christopher Wren's master plan after the fire of 1666.

The Covent Garden scheme is for a continued mixed-use neighborhood, with even greater emphasis on entertainment and tourist attractions. The vacated market hall would become a kind of galleria with shops and commercial enterprises. The square, freed of Brussels sprouts, would be an open pedestrian plaza. The Royal Opera would expand to form a new southern boundary. Between Covent Garden and the Strand would be a "spine" of tall new buildings replacing small, old ones. The chief feature would be a 4,000-seat convention center and one or more 2,000-room hotels.

Covent Garden Market, London (MARVIN LICHTNER)

Another "spine" along the northern edge would be the site of new housing. An open green would be created where commercial buildings now stand just north of the market square. New traffic and service roads would be below ground, with pedestrian walkways above to separate people and cars. The walkways would be determined in part by present landmarks and small, paved courts that thread the area.

There are no firm designs yet; the plan is schematic, pending acceptance by the collaborating local and Greater London governments.

There would be massive demolition in the phased stages of construction. Listed landmarks, such as the Royal Opera House, the Theater Royal, Drury Lane and St. Paul's Church, would be kept. So would what is called a "character route" through the center of the site. But the area is dotted with historic buildings that could not be saved; old streets such as Henrietta Street and Maiden Lane would go, and so would Rule's Restaurant, a London landmark since the eighteenth century.

The "trade-off," to use a business rather than a planning term, is the picturesque and problematic past for possible solution for the equally problematic present. Much of the new construction already in the area or in rebuilt precincts such as that of St. Paul's Cathedral is so appallingly characterless that one fears for both past and future.

There are questions raised by the plan that its authors have undoubtedly considered carefully but that will haunt any London-lover.

Is this the place for a convention center at all? Should this ever be the site of concentrated, large-scale building? Does it make sense to remove the market and its trucking congestion to replace them with the congestion of conventions and tourist hotels? At what point does urban sensibility bow to the need for foreign exchange?

Are those "spines" of housing, culture and commerce, and particularly the convention center, not totally destructive of indigenous characteristics? What will happen to the rich mixture of small enterprises and the cohesive community of elderly residents on small incomes when this construction, with its inevitable inflation of land values, moves in? Is this plan not certain doom rather than salvation, even if it is of the ordered instead of the speculative variety?

If there is blight here, it is minimal. This is a neighborhood rich in comfortable, historic continuity. It is sociologically and urbanistically sound, in spite of the fact that private bath counts make a negative statistic and modern traffic, here as everywhere else in London, has paralyzed old streets. Its character is bound to change some when the market goes, but it need not be willfully mutilated. The incentive seems to be rising land value, not urbanism or sociology.

To all except planners it is blindingly obvious that as little should be done here as possible beyond the appropriate conversion and re-use of the market buildings. Covent Garden's distinctive kind of urbanity and history is an irreplaceable asset, as cities have learned when they have destroyed such qualities for "improvements."

It is both fashionable and necessary in these days of exploding urban problems to think ahead and to think big. The Covent Garden plan is conscientiously, professionally, comprehensive, and that is its danger as well as its value. As the vision grows large in planners' eyes, existing values and buildings tend to fade and disappear long before the bulldozer arrives. For that vision, fifty-five of the ninety-three acres of the Covent Garden district would be destroyed. Come and get your London while it lasts. Even Christopher Wren could make a mistake.

London: Putting the Brakes on "Progress"

What is popularly called progress in American cities is being stopped dead in its tracks, or at least slowed to a stumbling halt in London. A strong government brake is being put on the private development of large parts of this city's older, historic areas, the kind of places and names that form a litany of London history, character and beauty for both residents and visitors.

Under the Civic Amenities Act of 1967, a law just getting into high gear, these districts can be protected as officially designated conservation areas. Town-planning authorities, who select such conservation areas, have the right either to prohibit any demolition or

Nonconforming construction in London's Montagu Square
(MARVIN LICHTNER)

new construction or to control development through necessary permissions to owners and builders.

At least eight sizable London districts have been designated as conservation areas this year. They are the major parts of Mayfair, Belgravia, Bloomsbury and St. John's Wood and sections of Paddington, Pimlico, Bayswater and Kensington. A considerable part of Soho is in the process of designation now, and areas around St. James's Place, Whitehall, Parliament and Westminster Abbey are being studied for future action.

There is no lack of desire among private developers in London to rip down whole blocks for profitable new commercial construction. The urge is international and the need of such construction is real. It is not so easy to do in London as in New York, because permission is needed from the planning authorities here for the erection of office buildings.

But as blankly depressing expanses of new office blocks have gone up in older neighborhoods, bringing with them a singular absence of style, Londoners have become angrily aware of the erosion of the past. Even with planning control, damage to the traditional fabric of the city is obvious.

The building that blew the fuse was the London Hilton's twenty-eight-story tower, which disrupted the traditional, five-story serenity of Mayfair in 1963. In the subsequent five years there has been strong public agitation for preservation of the traditional character of special neighborhoods. Popular sentiment against change is backed by the more sophisticated preservation objectives of the Georgian and Victorian societies, which enjoy a remarkable status in Britain.

Under the leadership of Duncan Sandys, a Minister of Housing from 1954 to 1957, the Civic Amenities Act was passed last year, adding powers of architecture and urban preservation to the functions of the earlier town-planning acts.

The process of creating conservation areas is not so high-handed as it sounds. There are inquiries and hearings, and appeal of decision is possible. Under the town and country planning acts enacted since 1947, British cities have immense planning powers and responsibilities. Land is bought and sold privately and freely. But permission for commercial development of the land, which has been generally programed under London's master plan now being revised, must be gotten from the planning authorities. The process is frequently a compromise between the desires of the developers willing to invest hard cash and the objectives of the city.

According to Frank West, director of architecture and planning for the City of Westminster, which has been designating many of London's conservation areas, the individual whose property rights are involved cannot bring suit as he does in the United States. The matter is dealt with in London administratively, not judicially, by public inquiry, with decision made by the local planning authorities. These decisions can be appealed to the Minister of Housing, whose action is final. The matter does not go through the courts at all.

There are some forms of "permitted" development that do not require government approval, such as the extension of an existing building by 10 per cent of its floor space.

Under the town and country planning acts, compensation must be paid to the owner who is refused his development rights. These sums come from grants made to planning bodies by the government.

The key word to the whole preservation program is the word "amenities" in the Civic Amenities Act. As understood in England, amenities in this sense covers a civilized concept of total environmental excellence. The term refers to the complete effect of an attractive or pleasurable neighborhood, or of an architecturally or historically important district, whether its quality is due to planning or design excellence, the stamp of the past or simply to a style of life.

What is involved in these criteria is what is sacrificed constantly in New York while preservationists look for "landmarks"; as they look, a street or neighborhood of less than landmark importance, but of genuine urban value, is demolished. These losses are irreparable in any city. The British concept of preservation as an act that is involved with, not isolated from, the living fabric of the city leaves United States policy on the subject in the dark ages.

London's examples of conservation areas range from a striking series of uniform, cool, clean, white streetscapes built at the same time and offering a single style, such as Belgravia's nineteenth-century classical facades, to the frequently architecturally undistinguished but lively streets of Soho that house equally irreplaceable small shops and services. The amenity standard can include just the grouping of compatible buildings around one of London's lush, green squares.

Under the Civic Amenities Act a builder can no longer get approval for such development as the kind of undistinguished, unrelated apartment houses with a luxury label at the south end of Montagu Square in the Portman Estates, which have shattered the square's period style and scale.

Under the act a new Soho hotel is being designed with the collaboration of the developer and his architect and the architects and planners of the City of Westminster, not only to avoid disruption of existing character, but also to reinforce the area's intimate, diversified humanity.

The big hurdle ahead will be financial compensation to those whose development plans are refused. It will take Solomon-like decisions to determine where the funds are to be given in the light of the massive designation of conservation areas, and on those decisions historic London will stand or fall.

Dutch Planning: Cities in a Box

If the Dutch did not invent the ruler and T-square, they were invented for them. The rigid geometry of rectangular Dutch fields and the measured straight lines of canals, roads, trees and dykes leading to endless flat horizons make one of the most oddly romantic landscapes in the world.

With a huge red sun suspended low in a hazy sky behind bat-winged windmills and the eye reaching to infinity, the Dutch landscape is pure surrealism. In the cities and towns, where rows of new houses are as unrelentingly straight and horizontal as the landscape, it is pure pragmatism.

The Dutch are a notoriously practical people and they have painstakingly created their strangely exotic landscape from the sea. The hard-won land has been regulated into a totally "planned" country of carefully decentralized cities. Now controls are so rigid, bureaucracy so complex, labor so short and social change so great in the postwar years that the Dutch are in a straight-edged box.

It is a situation, and a country, with strong Alice-in-Wonderland overtones. Even with comprehensive government controls and a record amount of construction, the Dutch housing shortage remains as critical as ever. In this through-the-looking-glass country where the fields are lower than the sea, planners are running as fast as they can just to stay in one place.

Since 1945 approximately 1.3 million new dwellings have been built. But as many dwellings are needed today as were needed after the war. With reduction of the family unit through earlier marriages, separation of generations, rising birthrate and falling deathrate, the same number of dwellings today house proportionately fewer people. About 320 dwelling units per 1,000 are required now, as against 272 in 1939. This is looking-glass mathematics.

Current building activity is concentrated on the planned exten-

Housing and superhighway west of Amsterdam
(KLM AEROCARTO, N.V. AMSTERDAM)

sion of towns and villages and the construction of new districts and suburbs. The areas southwest of The Hague, south and west of Amsterdam and south of Rotterdam are a totally new Dutch landscape, closer to the De Stijl architectural pioneering of the 1920's and to the principle of the English garden city laid out with the Dutch straight edge, than to Ruisdael's celebrated and familiar seventeenth-century pastorals. The result is a tidier Dutch landscape than ever.

If it is neat, it is not gaudy. In the words of the Ministry of Housing, an effort has been made to produce "well thought out plans in which efficiency and beauty are soundly balanced. It must unfortunately be admitted that efficiency is apt to predominate." The Dutch are not only neat and efficient; they are also honest.

With the greatest concentration of population to land in the world, the low density garden city has been the module of postwar development. This is looking-glass logic.

Endless straight rows of widely spaced, rigidly arranged, pleasantly enough designed low apartment blocks with squared-off open green plots are neither gardens nor cities. The flat blankets of grass often do little more than spread the houses at too great a distance for unity or use. Now high-rise towers are appearing in the newest developments on the edges of cities, rupturing the small, low scale of Dutch tradition, but promising a giant step into the future.

The uniformity of Dutch housing grows largely out of the rigid controls of government regulation, reaching even to room sizes and construction costs. Every plan for anything larger than a small garage must be approved by the Ministry of Housing at The Hague. It is argued in Holland that less centralized control and more competitive building could provide a greater amount of housing of more varied design. Since free competition usually produces equivalent conformity according to economic rather than government rules, the point is moot. But without government control, the limited Dutch land would be in hopeless chaos.

Another factor in the strong state role in all construction is the technically complex and extremely costly process of preparing the land for building, which must be undertaken by the government before anything else can be done. The cost of filling and preparing the boggy land for the postwar expansion west of Amsterdam alone was over $100 million. The construction that follows

139

is largely by non-profit building companies, building societies or the municipality, all heavily government subsidized.

Balancing the housing monotony is some relatively superior planning. The most notable example is the heart of Rotterdam, almost 100 per cent destroyed in the 1940 bombings, replanned in 1946 and 1948 and rebuilt in the early 1950's.

The city's commercial and shopping center, the Lijnbaan, designed by van den Broek and Bakema, is the prototype for all of the handsome Swedish centers after 1952, as well as the direct ancestor of the various versions of pedestrian malls currently appearing in Germany and the United States. An equally attractive example by the same architects has been carried out at Amstelveen, a new community for 100,000 just outside of Amsterdam.

The relationship of housing to Rotterdam's commercial center is particularly satisfactory. High-rise apartments by Maaskant, Krijgsman and Bakker are placed at right angles to the mall of shops, with their backs to service streets and their fronts to open courts of grass and flowers. The arrangement offers community closeness and residential serenity in the midst of lively urban activity.

The consistent impression made by the best Dutch building is that architecture is approached primarily as a social art. This is equally true throughout Europe and is perhaps the most striking difference between today's building here and abroad. European architecture is part of a social pattern; this is rarely the case in the United States.

The European work, in the mass, is low-key building of very acceptable quality, short on theatrical esthetics and long on contributions to environment. These commendable effects have been consistently upstaged by American architectural exhibitionism and the European product is beginning to be corrupted by its influence.

In general, European architecture is far less photogenic than its American counterparts. But it is often far more felicitous for human purposes.

Part II / Architecture

The Art of Expediency

THERE used to be a newspaper game called "What's wrong with this picture?" It was a cartoon in which there were a number of things wrong, from doors without handles and upside-down windows to pictures with mismatched halves hidden in the wallpaper. It was a world of cockeyed domesticity, antimacassared and cozily askew. The game was to find and list all the errors, or deviations from the norm.

What's wrong with the pictures on pages 144 and 145? The ruins of Penn Station in the Secaucus Meadows and a new subway entrance in its replacement building are not quite so simple. To begin with, what they show is the norm, in a world far from cozy and quite askew. They pose disturbing questions and touch problems that go to the core of a culture in which destruction and regeneration, art and nihilism, are becoming indistinguishable. But they say a great deal about how things are, and why, in the world that man is building for himself today.

The picture of what remains of Penn Station in its burial ground in the Secaucus Meadows shows a fragment of a classical figure and shards of columns in a setting of macabre surrealist *vérité*.*

---

* Since then, the classical fragments have been pulverized and buried as "fill," and the "prepared" site offered for commercial development. No trace remains.

The subway entrance is part of the vast Madison Square Garden-Penn Station complex.

Superficially, the message is terribly clear. Tossed into the Secaucus graveyard are about twenty-five centuries of classical culture and the standards of style, elegance and grandeur that it gave to the dreams and constructions of Western man. That turns the Jersey wasteland into a pretty classy dump.

As for the subway entrance, you could say, in abstract, clinical design terms, that there is nothing very much wrong with it at all: clean tilework, acceptable good graphics, a direct, non-flashy solution to a routine functional problem. And yet—it is a singularly grim picture. It speaks volumes on alienation through architecture. Kafka or Sartre never said it better. That single human figure, equally isolated in a crowd, proceeds through the chill, bleak anonymity of the twentieth-century transit catacombs (ancient catacombs softened even death with frescoes) in a setting of impersonal, ordinary sterility that could just as well be a clean, functional gas chamber. The human spirit and human environment have reached absolute zero.

New subway entrance at Penn Station
(THE NEW YORK TIMES BY WILLIAM E. SAURO)

Penn Station wreckage in Secaucus Meadows
(THE NEW YORK TIMES BY EDWARD HAUSNER)

Architecture

The easiest indictment to make is that this is a failure of modern architecture. That we have exchanged caryatids and columns for a mess of functional pottage and that Secaucus is the final resting place of our culture.

It would be simple, and false. It is the nostalgic argument of those who believe that re-creating the appearance of the past will bring back the reality of the past or the values of the past. Nothing could be farther from the truth. It is the kind of reasoning that makes well-intentioned people think it is a good idea, for example, to build Benjamin Latrobe's unrealized eighteenth-century theater for Richmond now, because all the drawings still exist.

At the least, that is begging the twentieth century; at the worst, it is the denial and corruption of creativity in our own time. No number of archeological constructions or caryatids can put that world back together again. There is something terribly pathetic in the self-delusory belief that it can be done.

Today's architecture is the highest dramatic revelation of changes in technology, structure, style and need in a revolutionary age. It is one of the genuine revolutions in our revolution-high times. Its monuments are superb; its potential develops constantly.

What that subway picture represents is simply the esthetics of economics. The results are, as much as possible, vandal proof, dirt proof, extravagance proof and delight proof—a kind of penitentiary style. The esthetics of economics characterize not only our common commercial construction but also the institutions and public buildings that were once meant to symbolize the shaky nobility of man. The economic standard is as accepted today as the four orders were in Rome.

Take, for example, the old and new Jersey City courthouses built side by side as if to deliberately make the point. The old courthouse—a solid, turn-of-the-century Beaux Arts monument of marble, murals and soaring rotunda space—has been in and out of the news in its battle for existence. Its replacement, the new courthouse, says nothing about the majesty of the law (the passion for breaking it right now simply underlines its importance) and a great deal about the society that built it. It says that society is mean and cheap and that it considers excellence a gratuitous commodity.

But the real point is that it is a dead match to Jersey City. This is the kind of city that the esthetics of economics makes; a tawdry, formless limbo of hamburger joints, discount stores, parking lots, matchbox houses, cheap office buildings, automobile salesrooms, jarring signs and disruptive highway spaghetti. It is the environment of expediency.

Today we have politics that preach destruction and art that acts out destruction; perhaps this is the architecture of destruction. As we said about something else, society gets the cities it deserves. The courthouse only underlines the process.

Curiously, it is not the Establishment or the older generation that sees old buildings in contemporary urban terms. It is the young people, the architects and city-oriented intellectuals who have rejected the Utopian idea of an artificially imposed new order of the last professional generation and who believe in change, complexity, contrast and a multi-dimensional urban scene. They are not antiquarians. But they are the ones who lead visitors to Victorian monuments, early Chicago skyscrapers, cast-iron buildings in New York, old Texas houses. These are the young professionals who are testing architecture in the shifting values of a world in crisis.

"Values" is a word they avoid, but the commitment to values is there. They are not the values handed down by society or the past. They are often the denial of values as conventionally understood. Realists and futurists, the present generation finds some of its values even in the environment of expediency. Art and life always coexist.

If the wreckage of the nineteenth century is in the Secaucus Meadows, and the failure of the twentieth century is in the landscape of alienation, the promise of the art of building is very much alive. It is not in the individual structure as traditionally designed, but in the relationships of people, land and buildings for life and use— it is in the esthetic and human ferment that is currently called architecture.

The Decline and Fall
of Public Building

Hudson County Courthouse: Whatever Happened to the
Majesty of The Law?

THE closing of the doors of the stately Hudson County Courthouse
in Jersey City echoed across the country. When the judges left their
marble-colonnaded courtrooms for functional modern quarters in
a new building next door, they made a move that is being made,
in one form or another, in almost every American city. They left
behind offices of solid oak and mahogany and moved into quarters
lined with flexwood.

If county officials had deliberately placed the two buildings in
their side-by-side position as an object lesson in the decline and
fall of American public architecture, they could not have provided
a better example. Never has the deterioration of style and standards
been so clearly and devastatingly illustrated.

By the pragmatic measurement of population growth and space
needs, the old courthouse is obsolete. No one wants a circa 1910,
solid Maine granite building with bronze lanterns and crestings and
a four-story interior rotunda of pearl-gray marble, opening through
all floors to a central dome, embellished by murals and surrounded
by polished Italian green marble Ionic columns.

New Hudson County Courthouse and Administration
Building, 1966, catalogue components
and paste-on sculpture
(THE NEW YORK TIMES BY MEYER LIEBOWITZ)

Old Hudson County Courthouse, 1910, art, solidity and style
(THE NEW YORK TIMES BY MEYER LIEBOWITZ)

Architecture

Its style was "Modern Renaissance," or Beaux Arts, after the name of the school in France where this country's best architects studied at the beginning of the century. Its designer was Hugh Roberts. The buildings that the French-trained American architects came back to create, the critic and historian Fiske Kimball has pointed out, "had no equal anywhere at the time, not even in France itself."

Offered the courthouse for one dollar as a substitute for the dingy Victorian structure which has the singular historical asset of having housed the Hague administration, Jersey City Mayor Thomas Whelan replied that the city is in the process of "liquidating its unnecessary real estate holdings" and "has no need for a ceremonial city hall."

There is no nonsense about ceremony in the new Hudson County Administration and Courthouse Building that now stands next to the old one. It has been characterized as "strictly functional from top to bottom and from inside out." As the architects of the new building have observed, the rotunda of the old building is "waste space."

Instead of a soaring central well, in which the entire space of the building is caught and celebrated, there is a low-ceilinged, businesslike lobby with flat granite panel walls, standard fluorescent lighting and a terrazzo floor. Instead of four figures of Fame in the dome's pendentives by the celebrated turn-of-the-century painter Edwin Blashfield and murals of New Jersey history by Howard Pyle, Frank D. Millet and Charles Y. Turner, there is a freeform squiggle in the ordinary terrazzo floor. Plastic plants and recorded music take care of esthetic and spiritual requirements.

Above ground level, walls are penitentiary-style structural glazed tile. In the old building there are marble railings and wainscoting for every floor and corridor. The new walls are plaster. The new courtrooms are finished with paper-thin wood applied like wallpaper. There is vestigial marble trim. So much for the dignity of the institutions of man.

On the outside of the new building a stolid attachment of Indiana limestone makes a mock-formal entrance to a Catalogue Commercial structure with a middling green, stock glass curtain wall. It is ornamented with a handy paste-on figure of Justice.

150

Murals and marble in rotunda of the old building
(THE NEW YORK TIMES BY BARTON SILVERMAN)

Terrazzo and plastic plants
in the lobby of the new building
(THE NEW YORK TIMES BY BARTON SILVERMAN)

Exterior extruded aluminum mullion sections holding the glass panels have unsightly connections; glass and window sash come together sloppily and abruptly; joints are casual inside and out. The side porte-cochere that now faces a weedy field surrounding the old courthouse, with the obvious purpose of serving future parking on its site, rests on lumpily welded and painted steel beams. The noted architect Mies van der Rohe once said of building, "God is in the details." Not in New Jersey.

The materials and details of the old courthouse, according to contemporary accounts, were selected for "grace, dignity and vigor."

The Decline and Fall of Public Building

It was meant to convey "a feeling of strength and durability." Descriptions of the new building focus on the splendors of its heating, cooling and elevator systems.

Built in two stages, from 1954 to 1957 and from 1963 to 1966, the new building cost $14 million. Its architects are Comparetto and Kenny of Jersey City. The old courthouse, one-third the size, was built for $3 million. Its replacement price would be untouchable. An additional $3 million, estimated by the architects of the new building as the cost of necessary mechanical renovation, would bring the old structure to $6 million.

Today its classical splendor looms as some surrealist vision in the peculiarly formless esthetic squalor that is the Jersey City environment. Its gray grandeur stands aloof on a grassy rise. Children slide down the dry slope on corrugated cardboard.

The story is repeated over and over. The landmark invites the wreckers and its replacement reduces the public image to the lowest possible common denominator. Architecture has ceased to be a noble art. But it only serves man's needs and aspirations, and men and cities get what they deserve.

The Federal Image: Everyone Back into the Old Rut

In a country that has demonstrated a peculiar propensity for tragic violence, the political mortality rate for men and dreams is particularly high.

When John F. Kennedy was President, he issued a directive to government departments ordering the elevation of architectural standards in Federal building programs. That was in 1962, and there was heaving and hauling in the General Services Administration, the agency in charge of all Federal construction, which then brought forth a kind of stumbling revolution.

First, Lafayette Square was redesigned under the Presidential eye. Even too much red brick and some unavoidably dubious scale wins hands down over the deadly scheme the President scrapped.

Next, Federal office building commissions went to architectural leaders like Marcel Breuer in Washington and Mies van der Rohe

153

in Chicago, something that had not happened in government building in the living memory of man. Those projects were completed under the Johnson administration.

But there is a traditional political attitude toward architecture that these buildings flouted. In politics and government it has always been understood that architecture is a prime, accepted source of pork barrel and patronage, from design contracts to building materials. Esthetic results are irrelevant and predictable.

Unfortunately, not only men are assassinated; so are their dreams and programs. The death of a program in the world of government occurs not by rifle or pistol shot but by a sort of turgid torture in which the dream is gradually destroyed by the relentless, enveloping tentacles of the Federal bureaucracy and its inflexible procedures and standards, which have never changed at all. Under the bright surface of reform is the vested interest status quo, calculatedly, surpassingly ordinary in everything it produces. Like death itself, this standard always wins in the end. It is the only thing that is immortal.

All this is prelude to the fact that you can probably write off the Federal building revolution. The lumbering Federal pace has finally produced the Mies and Breuer buildings and a few others of merit that went into the pipeline under, or shortly after, the Kennedy prodding.

The Hellmuth, Obata and Kassabaum Air Museum, the Roche and Dinkeloo Aquarium and the Lundy tax court are all waiting for Congressional appropriations which may or may not ever come. But in the mass of Federal office construction in the Capital and across the country, projects coming out of the pipeline and probably being fed into it are right back in the prereform pattern of official sub-architecture.

The tentative tremors at GSA are settling into the same old comfortable ruts to the apparent satisfaction of everyone there, with the exception, perhaps, of a skillfully demoted design director brought in by the Kennedy administration to nurse the reforms through, who fought the system valiantly and produced those few good buildings until the system did him in.

That took several tries over the last few years, including those curious shifts of title and classification that are the weapons of civil service institutional assassination. But once the pressure from above for better building was off, there could be no doubt about the final outcome.

The point that we wish to make here is that under the Federal system these results are as inevitable as rain and only incidental to the honesty or expertise, or lack of either, in staff and administrators. What comes out of GSA generally is an entrenched mediocrity committed to a rigid, standardized system of codified values and rules. This system is not going to support revolution.

GSA is essentially a managerial, or housekeeping, organization. Among other things, it runs and maintains massive inventories of government buildings from coast to coast and disposes of them when surplus, as it does with stockpiles of nuts and bolts. It also gets the building built. The obvious question, in the light of results, is whether GSA should be the commissioning agency or whether the design function, if it cannot be improved, should be removed.

The single objective of GSA's huge design and building program is quite clear. It is to get the most square feet for the money appropriated. This is a measurable standard of economy and efficiency. It is a standard that can be understood by anyone, including a Congressman, and it never gets into trouble except with those whose professional expertise includes architectural values, which are not easily analyzed.

The whole Federal program is tailored to this formula. Every architect's plans are checked on this square footage-cost principle, and deviations are blue-penciled out by GSA space cadet examiners labeled architects, engineers and cost accountants. These variations are, of course, what architectural style, symbolism and creativity are made of. They may actually lead to better functions and better plans and ways of building. To see them x-ed out as "waste space," as this observer has, is a soul-shrinking experience.

In the end, every building is fitted to the process. But the killing of creative design goes further. Any architect dealing with GSA soon learns the way he must work. The building must fit the mold. The procedure breeds the product. Then out of the warehouses and order books come the stultifying, preordained fittings, selected and specified, again, for economy and efficiency, that include some of the most banal and hideous artifacts known to man.

You can see the battles in some of the better buildings. The quality of the wood-faced courtrooms in John Carl Warnecke's new

Court of Claims on Lafayette Square, for example, is totally destroyed by the lighting. That is because GSA orders a singularly passé cold fluorescent tube and installs it universally, in the interests, naturally, of efficiency and economy. A little architectural assassination is incidental.

In Mies's Federal courts and office building in Chicago, the Federal taste-breakers have been insinuating some kind of greenish long-life spot into the lobby ceiling instead of the architect's incandescents. It is ruinous, as is the curious ticker-tape-type moving electric sign inexplicably added to the reception desk, and the plastic wall covering that GSA prefers for maintenance which is already enveloping the painted plaster walls.

Close by, Chicago's Civic Center, housing the same functions, has no problems with plaster walls, well-designed fittings and handsome graphics. If there is a symbol for GSA design, it is that wretched little wood-framed sign with the badly lettered occupant's name that is affixed outside of every standard GSA office door.

What is lost in this ossified process, all the way down the line, is quality. The product gets cheaper and duller and more tastelessly homogenized. There is not the ghost of a chance for innovation or excellence. That is too bad in a country with stunning reserves of talent and technical expertise that will never serve the national image or the national good.

The Rayburn Building: A National Disaster

The 169 occupants of the Rayburn Office Building on Capitol Hill, completed in 1965, may have a view of the Capitol dome or an interior court, depending on seniority. Even seniority, however, does not give any legislator a door leading from his office, or his aide's office, to his working staff without passage through a waiting room full of constituents and special pleaders. To correct this small planning error would add $200,000 to costs already estimated at anywhere from $86 million to $122 million for the expensive and controversial building.

The professional architectural press was bitterly critical as con-

Washington's Rayburn Building,
the biggest star-spangled blunder of them all
(FRED WARD)

struction progressed. (The building took seven years and $22 million more to complete than originally estimated, largely as the result of expensive miscalculations. Change orders reached 300 per cent over government average; bid estimates on contracts were as much as $4.5 million off.)

There were accusations of secret planning, pork barrel commissions and possible misuse of public funds. The fact that the general contractor was Matthew J. McCloskey, Democratic party stalwart of Philadelphia, did not escape notice. But the storm swirled uselessly around a behemoth that is obviously here to stay.

Architecture

Architecturally, the Rayburn Building is a national disaster. Its defects range from profligate mishandling of fifty acres of space to elephantine esthetic banality at record costs. The costs have been investigated by the General Accounting Office.

Equal to the question of costs, however, is the question of what Congress and the capital have received for the investment. It is quite possible that this is the worst building for the most money in the history of the construction art. It stuns by sheer mass and boring bulk. Only 15 per cent of its space is devoted to the offices and hearing rooms for which it was erected.

Forty-two per cent of the floor area is used for parking. Endless corridors have been likened to "Last Year at Marienbad." Stylistically, it is the apotheosis of humdrum.

It is hard to label the building, but it might be called Corrupt Classic. Its empty aridity and degraded classical details are vulgarization without drama, and to be both dull and vulgar may be an achievement of sorts.

The structure's chief "design features" are hollow exercises in sham grandeur. A supercolossal exterior expanse of stolid, Mussolini-style pomp is embellished with sculpture that would be the apogee of art in the Soviet Union, where overscaled muscles and expressions of empty solemnity are still admired.

A monumental entrance at second-floor level is reached by pretentious steps that will never be used. The real entrance, on the ground floor just below, abandons false dignity for no dignity at all.

The formal marble front with its blank, machine-stamped look sits on a gargantuan base of informal, random-cut granite of obviously miscalculated proportions, an effect comparable to combining a top hat with blue jeans. Groups of columns meant to dress up the drab, flat facade not only fail to suggest that columns are traditionally supporting members, but they also terminate incongruously on balconies that appear to support the columns—a neat combination of structural illogic and stylistic flimflam.

Inside, a pedestrian statue of Sam Rayburn presents the seat of its pants to entering visitors.* It faces a huge landscaped central court that is an artless cliché. Embracing Mr. Sam is another cliché,

* Turned around after this article—the rewards of architectural criticism.

158

a two-story curved double stair fated to be not only useless but graceless.

In the hearing rooms coarse, lifeless classical cornices and moldings are joined to stock modern acoustic ceilings and panel lighting for a state of esthetic warfare tempered only by their matching mediocrity. This model comes in red, green, gold and blue.

Behind the scenes the classic false front is abandoned and working subcommittee rooms use ordinary partitions and fittings of the lowest commercial common denominator. Throughout the building the design level is consistent: whatever is not hack is heavy-handed.

For $100 million, give or take a few million (the cost of New York's mammoth Pan Am Building), the gentlemen of the House have got a sterile, stock plan of singularly insensitive design and detailing that was moribund more than half a century ago. Even the basic functional requirements have been insufficiently studied. The making of useful and beautiful public spaces with the power to inspire and symbolize as well as to serve—the timeless aim of architecture and one that is mandatory for Washington—is conspicuously absent.

The Rayburn Building is the third solid gold turkey in a row to come out of the office of the Architect of the Capitol, J. George Stewart, who is not an architect, but who picks them for Congress. For this one he selected Harbeson, Hough, Livingston and Larson of Philadelphia. He is also responsible for the ill-advised remodeling of the Capitol's East Front and the construction of the new Senate Office Building.

There are no controls or reviews for Mr. Stewart's work, and none for the House committee that authorized the Rayburn Building's construction and appropriations, generally behind closed doors.

An old architectural saying has it that there's no point in crying over spilled marble. Seven million pounds of it have been poured onto Capitol Hill in this latest Congressional building venture, and there is nothing quite as invulnerable as a really monumental mistake. The Rayburn Building's ultimate claim to fame may well be that it is the biggest star-spangled architectural blunder of our time.

Architecture

The Madison Memorial Library: Full Speed Backward

It has come, and it is just what everyone expected: the new, $75 million Madison Memorial Library for Capitol Hill in Washington is to be another mammoth mock-classical cookie from the Architect of the Capitol's well-known cookie cutter for gargantuan architectural disasters.

It follows, as day follows night, the notorious Rayburn Building, the new Senate Office Building and the remodeled East Front of the Capitol, a compendium of matched errors in moribund academic clichés that Congress has been building for itself on a blockbuster scale, at extravagant expense and with unabashed architectural know-nothingness.

The list at least has consistency. As an example of legislative Establishment taste it is as expected and American as that increasingly celebrated yardstick, cherry pie. No other country in the world produces this kind of ponderous, passé official architecture. Even the Russians gave it up ten years ago.

The design of the library was prefigured and preshadowed in a decade of political and architectural maneuvering in the halls of Congress and on Capitol Hill.

To review the workings of that office, the Architect of the Capitol, J. George Stewart, a seventy-seven-year-old engineer and political pro who is absolute esthetic monarch of the Capitol environs, builds without review or approval from the Fine Arts Commission, the National Capitol Planning Commission or any of the advisory bodies that function for official Washington. Their jurisdiction stops dead at the foot of Capitol Hill. His immense building schemes are developed behind closed doors and accepted in closed hearings; plans and commissions are shrouded in secrecy, known only to the committees for which he builds and from which he receives money. This is, of course, taxpayers' money, for public buildings of national importance.

For a rough idea of the bundle of Congressional red tape through which such buildings must pass, with predictable design attrition, the Madison Memorial Library is a product of the Senate Office Building Commission, the House Office Building Commission,

Drawing of Madison Memorial Building
for the Library of Congress

the Joint Commission of the Library and the James Madison Memorial Commission, with a Coordinating Committee composed of members of the three Congressional bodies and the Madison Memorial Commission. Not one of these groups has been put together on the basis of professional competence in matters of architecture, construction or design.

In addition, Public Law 89-260, passed in 1965 to authorize construction of the building, set up a series of stipulations that created an insoluble dilemma of conflicting and self-defeating directives. These included a budget, floor area and a design philosophy, by amateur design philosophers, for a building "in keeping with the prevailing architecture of the Federal buildings on Capitol Hill," a statement guaranteed to open a Pandora's box of conflicting interpretation.

As a result of outcries against the monumental ugliness of the Rayburn Building and in response to some concerned members of Congress, the law also set up an advisory committee of the American Institute of Architects, which was meant to be insurance against another $100 million plus Rayburn Building debacle.

The A.I.A. committee was duly appointed and immediately presented with another dead-end dilemma by a suave Stewart maneuver in which some of his favorite architects were commissioned for the library without the knowledge of the A.I.A. consultants. Most of these architects have been connected in one way or another with all of the Architect of the Capitol's important buildings. They are known informally to the profession as "The Club." For the Madison Library, they are Roscoe DeWitt of Dallas, Alfred Easton Poor and Albert Homer Swanke of New York, and Jesse M. Shelton and A. Pearson Almond of Atlanta.

This left the A.I.A. committee powerless to guide program, philosophy or commissions, with only the sticky job of criticizing members of its own organization in what remained of its "advisory" role. The A.I.A. doesn't like the library, and it has said so in a report. (Unfortunately, the Fine Arts Commission did not like the A.I.A.-approved addition for its own Washington headquarters, and this is tossed back at the A.I.A. by everyone who, in turn, does not like the criticism of the library.)

Still with me? Take a deep breath and look at the building that Congress hath wrought. The Madison Library is a badly needed extension of the handsome Victorian Library of Congress, which already has one annex and rents all over town. The Madison Memorial, originally planned as a separate, small, temple-type monument, has been combined with the library.

Inside, the building is thoughtfully programed, packing maximum library facilities into a minimum site, plus a Memorial Hall. The plan is a tight, efficient, functional response to overdue and urgent needs.

There are three floors below grade, the full size of the site, and six floors plus mechanical equipment above grade, with varying setbacks. These interior floors are huge work areas, broken by one small, token, skyless court requested by the A.I.A. consultants as breathing space for the unrelieved floor mass, which rises only three of the six stories and is topped by more solid work floors. Except for the Memorial Hall, there will be endless 9½-foot ceilings. This is basically a bulk, business building.

The practical, monolithic structure, a whopping 514 feet by 414 feet and 101.5 feet high, is stuffed into a pompous marble shroud. Wrapped around the no-nonsense plan is that weary dodge, a rigidly symmetrical, so-called "classical" design of central, stripped-down columns and solid end walls that is supposed to be a wedding of traditional and modern modes. This is a compromise that never works; it is a redundant Washington disaster. Yet here it is again, in all of its familiar, failed, heavy-handed, stagnant lifelessness, proving once more that the formula produces nothing but hollow and meaningless results. The library is the latest misalliance.

Even the A.I.A. committee, which was strongly critical of the library in urban planning terms, backed discreetly away from design criticism that would have been an esthetic slap at its colleagues while murmuring something off the record about wishing that a "fresher" solution had been found.

Whether this solution represents the last gasp of what all indications point to as Mr. Stewart's almost surrealistically reactionary taste, or if it is the taste of less-than-swinging senior Congressmen convinced of their Olympian omniscience, or the taste of the architects who did the job, is hard to determine. It is probably an interplay of all three. This reviewer, for one, is willing to bet that those architects' offices contain enough up-to-date talent and sensibility to produce less tragi-comic results. Research has suggested that at least one progressive alternative produced during study sessions was scuttled.

One hears constant defenses from Mr. Stewart's office of the "suitability" of his buildings and how few men can produce the genre any more. That is fortunately true. And one reads pages of debate in the Congressional Record, with sinking heart, in which grown men with distinguished names display the wilful ignorance of stubborn children. They may not know if it's architecture, but they know what they like and they are building about half-a-billion-dollars' worth of it.

The new library, with its abortive gestures to debased and worn-out classical formulas, is neither suitable nor compatible to its surroundings or to the twentieth century. It is "in keeping" with nothing. In spite of its wishful esthetic rationale, it is totally and tragically out of character with its neighbors and its times.

In fairness, the limitations forced on the architects by the legislation, the site and the program have been instrumental in producing a design that is esthetically, urbanistically and environmentally unsatisfactory. But it is also unsatisfactory because the design process is wrong, the method of architect selection is wrong, the autonomy, powers and procedures of the office of the Architect of the Capitol are wrong, the lack of a master plan for Capitol Hill is wrong and the perpetuation of such a system is wrong. The building is wrong.

But the Library of Congress needs it and the Architect of the Capitol and his Congressional cronies love and have approved it and the James Madison Memorial Library will join the Rayburn Building as another monument to the bottom end of American architecture. How sad for Mr. Madison and the nation.

Washington Tax Court: Full Speed Forward

The design for the United States Tax Court Building, to occupy a site not far from the Capitol on 2nd Street N.W. between D and E streets, represents everything that the Madison Library does not: a progressive, sensitive, contemporary solution fully responsive to Washington's classical tradition and yet fully part of the mid-twentieth century—a period of exceptional vigor and beauty in the history of structure and design.

The Madison Library, as we have pointed out, is a product of the office of the Architect of the Capitol, devoted for the past fifteen years to the laying of monstrous marble eggs on Capitol Hill.

This process is carried on by a favored and familiar syndicate of practitioners who specialize in a kind of consummate conventionality that the Architect of the Capitol and his Congressional sponsors consider "suitable" and "in keeping" with the Washington spirit and style. Contemplating the awesome awfulness of the results, one can only conclude that the country has run out of spirit and style.

The design for the Tax Court Building is evidence that we have not. This building is a product of the General Services Administration, the Federal agency responsible for all Federal construction—except on Capitol Hill, which is the fiefdom of the Architect of the Capitol—anywhere in the country, including Washington.

Working drawings for the court building have just been completed, to be followed by bids and construction. The architects are Victor A. Lundy and Lyles, Bissett, Carlisle and Wolff. Approval

Drawing of project
for United States Tax Court Building

of the design by the Fine Arts Commission after rejection of an earlier scheme has been enthusiastic.

For many years the GSA building program projected an image of the Federal Government that could have made any loyal but sensitive citizen defect. (Where to, in this world of esthetic and environmental blunders, is hard to say.) The difference between the monumentally mediocre products of GSA and the banal behemoths of the Architect of the Capitol was largely a matter of pomposity and pretensions. GSA did not aspire to any pretensions beyond applying the yardstick of ultimate economy to art, life, government, symbolism and the American ideal. All were reduced to a kind of pragmatic stylistic sludge.

In recent years, under the guidance of Karel Yasko, Special Assistant to the Commissioner, Public Buildings Service, that picture changed for a while. With a marvelous, ham-handed persuasion and an unbureaucratic willingness to stick his neck out, Mr. Yasko helped bring a new quality to government work. Still hung up by rules, regulations, reviews and curious internal pressures, he nevertheless managed to nurse through a series of designs in which government standards were elevated temporarily.

Architecture

It should be noted immediately that no comparisons can be made between the functional needs and plans of the Madison Library and the Tax Court beyond the fact that each requires a considerable amount of routine office space. The programs are totally different.

They are both big buildings, but the library is bigger. The library is a nearly square 514-by-414-foot blockbuster; the court is a rectangle of 405 by 120 feet. (That is still big; the standard New York blockfront is 250 feet.) The library has three floors below ground and six floors above. The Tax Court is six stories, with two of the floors forming a podium base. The court will be built for approximately one-tenth the library's cost.

Each building, interestingly, is actually organized in four parts, in spite of different requirements. The library is described as being, in effect, four buildings, each with its own service core. All are enclosed in an unrevealing semi-classical slipcover. The Tax Court, in contrast, is four clearly articulated volumes tied together with a soaring central public hall in an obvious and extremely handsome organization of the building's working parts.

In this case, the mass has been opened up to show how it works, to allow space to flow through and to give it division and scale, heart and humanity. Space moves under and around the courts cantilevered visibly over the entrance and the end and rear blocks for judges' offices and chambers, through bronze-framed, bronze-tinted glass connecting the four granite-faced blocks with the skylit central hall.

"Inside this building," Mr. Lundy explains, "you will always have a sense of where you are, and of the sky outside." Sky is one of Washington's most agreeable urban assets. This is not a skyless, monolithic mass, as the library is, with an exterior that camouflages an interior or gives promise of an interior that is never fulfilled. Light flows through, with space.

Behind the bold design is equally bold engineering. The court block will be suspended as a "floating" box of prestressed concrete, joined to the rear block by a "compression" bridge at the third, or ceremonial, floor level and a tension link at the roof level. Continuous vertical concrete shear walls will support precast tees for forty-foot interior divisions.

The difference between the court and library, however, goes

even beyond structure and design. It is a matter of approach. It is in the architects' response to the program. Architecture is the way in which a program is given form. This is at the bottom of the disparate qualitative results of the two buildings and of an architectural success or failure in any age.

It would have been easy to box in the judges' quarters and bury the courtrooms and wrap it all up in an "appropriate" false front. That, however, is begging a creative responsibility and a responsibility to the nation's capital. If Washington still pretends to urban greatness, it needs a much tougher definition of architectural "suitability."

The Tax Court is a "suitable" and "classical" contemporary building; the library is not. The Tax Court Building deals in the generalized and timeless sense of balance, order and serenity that is genuine classicism, not in substitutes of vestigial ornament or stylized recall. It meets the challenge of today's expression and technology as a prime creative objective. It is heart, hand and mind working together for man's most durable testament. It is "truth for today and tomorrow," in Mr. Lundy's words, and truth, or reality, is something that Washington and its architecture badly need.*

Boston City Hall: A Winner

"Whatever it is, it's not beautiful," said the Boston cab driver taking the visitor to the new City Hall. "What would you call it, Gothic?" asked another. Which about sums up the architectural gap, or abyss, as it exists between those who design and those who use the twentieth-century's buildings.

The new $26.3 million Boston City Hall has been an object of international attention and debate since the architects Kallmann, McKinnell and Knowles won the competition for its design in 1962. A week of festivities marked its opening seven years later.

---

* Expenses of the Vietnam war stopped almost all government building appropriations. The Tax Court, at the time this book was prepared, was still unfunded, Washington was still short of architectural reality, and construction costs were rising 12 per cent a year.

Continuity and contrast: Boston's successful City Hall
(THE NEW YORK TIMES BY WILLIAM E. SAURO)

Boston can celebrate with the knowledge that it has produced a superior public building in an age that values cheapness over quality as a form of public virtue. It also has one of the handsomest buildings around, and thus far, one of the least understood. It is not Gothic. ("No kiddin'," said the cab driver.) It is a product of this moment and these times—something that can be said of successful art of any period. And it is a winner in more ways than one.

Not only cab drivers are puzzled by the unconventional structure. Cultural and community leaders who are also society's decision makers and a public with more and higher education than at any time in history also draw a blank. Too bad about that architecture gap. It has a lot to do with the meanness of our cities.

Boston's new City Hall is a solid, impressive demonstration of creativity and quality—uncommon currencies in today's environment. A powerful focus for the new Government Center that has replaced the sordid charms of the old Scollay Square, it makes a

South entrance of the lobby of Boston's City Hall
(THE NEW YORK TIMES BY WILLIAM E. SAURO)

motley collection of very large, very average new buildings around it look good. It confers, in a kind of architectural status transferral, an instant image of progressive excellence on a city government traditionally known for something less than creativity and quality. That is an old trick of architecture called symbolism.

They call it the new Boston, but inside the new structure Councilors Saltonstall and Timilty work side by side at old desks moved from the old City Hall that suggest the old politics. The City Council gave itself a raise but voted down the $24,000, room-size horseshoe installation that would have completed the Council Chamber and accommodated all its members in the new style. Tradition dies hard in Boston.

The building will survive the councilors' objections and the Mayor's ideas of decoration. Its rugged cast-in-place and precast concrete and brick construction inside and out (the New Brutalism, for those who like stylistic labels) is meant to be impervious to the vicissitudes of changing tastes and administrations.

The monumentality of this public building—and it is magnificently monumental without a single one of those pompous pratfalls to the classical past that building committees clutch like Linus's blanket—is neither forbidding nor austere.

It is an "open" City Hall. At ground level it is meant to serve as a concourse to other parts of the city, and there are views of the city from every part of the structure. The visitor is made aware of the city in a very special way—of its history in the architects' sensitively glass-framed vistas through deep concrete modular window reveals of adjoining Federal brick buildings and Faneuil Hall and the granite Quincy Market and waterfront to the east, and of its burgeoning growth in new construction to west, north and south.

This appropriate and finely calculated sense of historic continuity is no small architectural achievement.

Today's buildings rupture historic scale and this one was placed in the heart of historic Boston. But there is no "style-dropping" here. The architects have neatly disposed of Preservation Fallacy Number One. There are none of the overblown vestigial traditional details or "recalls" considered "appropriate" in such situations, milked of architectural meaning and offered as pious ligaments between old and new to create caricatures of both. This is subtle, dramatic, respectful homage to the past by an uncompromising present. It is a lesson in proper preservation philosophy and esthetics.

There is also a lesson in that basic element of building, the use of space. The entire structure is conceived as a progression of functional and hierarchical spaces. Its striking exterior reflects this arrangement.

This is not space as a container. See any office building for that. It is space molded to function, form and expressive purpose. The striking irregular shapes and surfaces that show the functions and mechanical services, all of which are more commonly hidden behind flat walls and ceiling slabs, are part of the visual and sensuous impact.

The building is a hollow rectangle around a court. Its focus is the lobby, which rises a dramatic six of the building's nine stories on two sides to skylights, and centers on a platform of ascending brick steps. This is a space equally satisfactory to connoisseurs of the art of architecture and the art of sit-ins, and that is exactly what the designers had in mind as public architecture.

Above the lobby are the Council Chamber and offices and the Mayor's quarters. These large, ceremonial rooms are visible outside as rugged projections on the building's east and west facades and as strong, broken wall planes inside, within the soaring skylight shafts. The upper levels are office space. This also shows clearly on the outside as a massive, stepped "cornice" at the top.

The building stands, not in isolation, but on a still unfinished fan-shaped brick plaza of stepped levels that will embrace the neighboring structures.

It is as certain as politics and taxes that without the national competition that was held for this building nothing like it would have been designed or constructed. Mr. Kallmann and Mr. McKinnell were young and unknown as architects when they won. The usual route of public building commissions is through political patronage or to familiar, established names.

The architects have worked with the Boston firm of Campbell, Aldrich and Nulty, and Le Messurier Associates, structural engineers. Virtually no changes were made in the prize-winning design. The result is a tough and complex building for a tough and complex age, a structure of dignity, humanism and power. It mixes strengths with subtleties. It will outlast the last hurrah.

The State of the Art

Pop Architecture: Here to Stay*

THERE has been a lot of pseudo-profound theorizing about the democratization of the arts in our time, but the only art in which the process has actually taken place is architecture. What has happened in painting and sculpture is, more properly, popularization. The product itself still follows the standards of a small group that might be called the creative elite, although it is merchandised to the masses.

The public, in the case of these arts, is merely the consumer, and it is presently consuming at a record rate; but it sets no standards for what is produced. And if it chooses to consume the products of, say, a Washington Square outdoor show, this work, in turn, has little effect on "art." The real thing continues to be produced by a cultural and creative aristocracy, if aristocracy is defined as that portion of the trend-setting minority that operates on accepted traditions of knowledge, talent and taste. Today it is called the Establishment and it is no longer the traditional social aristocracy. Nor are its standards like the traditional standards. They are often a deliberate reversal of those standards, but their criterion is basically the same: acceptability by the taste-making elite.

The situation used to be particularly true in architecture, where

* This comment has been revised slightly since publication, reflecting increased analytical interest in the functional phenomena of the Pop scene.

172

the style and standards of past periods have been established consistently by the creative elite. Today, however, the situation is virtually reversed.

Except for a pathetically small showing, the cultural aristocracy is no longer responsible for most building styles. It is barely holding its own, with those isolated examples that represent structural and design excellence, against the tide, or better, flood, or what we propose to call Pop Architecture.

Pop Architecture is the true democratization of the art of architecture in that it represents not just mass consumption but mass taste.

Its standards are set not by those with an informed and knowledgeable judgment, but by those with little knowledge or judgment at all. It is the indisputable creation of the lower rather than of the upper classes. As such, it is a significant first: probably the only architectural style in history to be formed at the bottom rather than at the top.

Even more significantly, it consists of the vast, inescapable, depressingly omnipresent and all-too-typical bulk of American building. This includes the greatest part of today's construction and capital investment.

In Pop Architecture the timeless determinants of comparative knowledge and trained evaluation have been supplanted by the typical parvenu love of the novel, the flashy and the bizarre.

The characteristics of Pop Architecture are gaudy misuses of structural effects for aggressive and often meaningless eccentricities of form, the garish misapplication of color and material for jazzed-up facades of fluorescent brilliance and busy metal and enamel panel patterns unrelated to underlying structure, with glittering grilles and appendages that conceal the most pedestrian plans.

It is, of course, Miami with its uninhibited monuments to lavish pretentious ignorance like the prototypal Fontainebleau. It is every Miracle Mile in suburbia, offering every new effect in the architect's sample book and a frankly phony, but eye-catching version of every new structural technique. It is dazzling glamor to the optically naive; consummate vulgarity to the conventionally visually educated; and a new kick to the avant-garde, which discerns—often correctly—some underlying basics of contemporary function and life-style in the drive-in and the architecture of the road. Some of the architectural facts of contemporary life undoubtedly deserve critical analysis, since they serve modern society legitimately and are equally obviously not going to be wished away. Dismissal is too simplistic an attitude.

However, like Pop Art, Pop Architecture shows mass taste at its most cruelly self-revealing. Unlike Pop Art, it is the real thing rather than a sophisticated, detached commentary. Pop Art is the ironical statement of those who know, being outrageous. Pop Architecture is the straight-faced product of those who don't know, just being themselves.

Pop Architecture may be derided, but it cannot be dismissed. While the Washington Square canvases and all of their kind may not make a ripple on art's surface, the hotels, motels, stores, shopping centers, bowling alleys, restaurants, office buildings and commercial complexes of Pop Architecture and those churches, community centers, speculative buildings and civic and other structures that ape their style stack up as the country's major building effort in quantity, size and expense.

This is architectural reality, and an esthetic and historical phenomenon not to be dismissed just as "bad design." It is frequently atrocious design, of course, but it is obviously here to stay in appalling amounts unless its characteristic look of transient tinniness indicates a fortuitous built-in obsolescence. It is determining the face of America and it is, inescapably, our architecture, whether we like it or not.

And whether we like it or not, it will have its place in history as well, as an awesome demonstration of the first truly democratic style and popular art on a scale that the twentieth century only promised until now, but has finally delivered. It may go down in the record with bad generals, decadent states and corrupt societies when submitted to the cool, objective scrutiny of future scholars or it may be taken as a serious departure point to a new kind of world.

But it is pointed, legitimate commentary on our current cultural condition and the general level of architectural practice, even among qualified professionals. And where Pop Art shocks the laymen, Pop Architecture does not—perhaps the most terrifying comment of all.

The End of the Line?

The plans and proposals bursting into print today vie with each other for size, novelty and status. Architecture has never been more important; it is the stuff with which our cities are being built and rebuilt for unprecedented sums on an unprecedented scale. What is being built represents the culmination of a twentieth-century revolution in structure and design based on profound philosophical considerations and technical miracles that should have produced, by any reasoning, one of the greatest periods in the history of the building art.

But a look around shows a distorted dream, a travesty of purpose, an abandonment of principles, a jazzy slide down the primrose path of fads, publicity, structural sensationalism, muzzy romanticism and dubious art for art's sake that has led to a vicious decline in architectural values and a corruption of architectural purpose. It has also led to some of the worst and most offensive building ever produced.

A serious indictment? It is long overdue. The evidence is inescapable. A Stamford, Conn., office center is an architectural fun fair of corporate flying saucers and ramped, battlemented research centers. A Manhattan branch bank in early Howard Johnson pseudo-Georgian style offers a classic cupola, computers and infrared comfort for outdoor customers at eighteenth-century-type deposit windows, and, we assume, twentieth-century money. The banklet is in a landscaped parklet.

The buildings would be funny, if they were not typical and tragic indications of the depth to which the great revolution has sunk. These examples represent two extremes of the current malaise.

The first, the Stamford headquarters for the General Time Corporation and a laboratory for the Columbia Broadcasting System (oh, shades of Eero Saarinen!), might be called the space-age-fly-with-the-future trend. The second, Franklin National's "bank in the park" for a corner lot at Broadway and Howard Street, is the stop-the-world-I-want-to-get-off school, or time-turn-backward-in-your-flight-with-all-modern-conveniences.

Given the choice between hot modern and cold Colonial, one

hardly blames Franklin National for settling for ersatz nostalgia. At least Franklin has the dubious distinction of pursuing ersatz all-out.

Billing itself as "the country bank in New York" since it started on Long Island, bucolic paradise of subdivisions, Franklin settled on the country Colonial image executed by the firm of Eggers and Higgins, even when it meant disguising a nine-story steel-frame structure as an inflated five-story Georgian mansion on Madison Avenue. Its officers are far from farmers. They have also devised "La Banque," the Franklin National branch at Fifth Avenue and 60th Street. This is solid Louis Seize for a clientele of non-rural sophisticates with a mandatory balance of $25,000, in dollars, not francs.

The Pop Architecture at Stamford causes distress of a different kind. The architect, Victor Bisharat, describes the battered, striated walls of the CBS laboratory as "symbolizing the upsurge of the creative force in research, reaching for the sky with questing fingers." The effect seems more like sticky fingers reaching for Wright and Saarinen.

This kind of architectural whizz-bang was originally restricted to the spangled sunglasses set. It is now for businessmen, corporation presidents and community cultural leaders. The trend-setting corporate clients of the 1950's established a selective standard that has had a hard time surviving the building boom and the cultural bandwagon. There is a bank like a split orange in Casper, Wyoming. There is a Kaiser Aluminum plant in Portsmouth, R.I., wearing a flashy gift wrap that promises to open if you lift up the box top and tear off the decorative vertical strip.

The trend ranges from irrationality, or novelty for its own sake, to dishonesty, or the complete vulgarization of art. It is followed by architects of large and small reputation, with more or less overtly awful results.

The sad fact is that public and patrons will accept anything quicker than rational simplicity, or the logical and sensitive solution to a problem. They are sick to death of plain, cheap, badly constructed speculative building, and their non-professional eyes are not always adept at distinguishing between simple statements of quality and simple junk.

The popular reaction is still largely *horror vacui*. Fill it up, busy it up, distort it, disguise it, make it look arty or different, but don't make it a logical, artistic expression of conscientiously considered structure, function and form. It wouldn't get published if you did.

There is no justification for this brand of self-seeking architectural exhibitionism. And yet the architect is asking for a larger share of the responsibility for designing the environment, at the same time that he faults and flouts it by demonstrating a lack of responsibility in his own work.

In Europe architecture is still primarily a social art, its highest and best expression frequently sublimated with sensitivity to larger human and environmental needs. In the United States there is no environment, in spite of all the talk about it. There are buildings that strut and fight and turn their backs on each other and the city—advertisements for architects and for an art in serious trouble.

Kicked a Building Lately?

To the public, the style called Supermannerism is best known in its more psychedelic entertainment or showcase aspects—the multimedia, sound-reinforced, flashing patterns of color and light in designs by the young, for the young, in discotheques and boutiques. It is largely an art of interiors and graphics.

But it is also turning some of the more "with it" architectural schools upside down. Yale architecture students agitated until their notably Supermannerist dean, Charles Moore, aided in the temporary destruction of one of the major areas of Paul Rudolph's Art and Architecture Building. They installed a pulsing white light display of fluorescent tubing and silver mylar for a space and mind-bending esthetic experiment and design *double entendre* that practically told Mr. Rudolph to get up on the shelf and stay there.

When young architects do something like The Drugstore in fashionably mod King's Row, Chelsea, it reverberates around the design world until it becomes a cliché. More impressively virtuoso interiors in the same idiom, such as Sergio Asti's incredibly suave tricks with mirrored walls and lights, transparency and reflection in a tiny shoe shop in Milan, are less well publicized.

At its worst, the style is superficial, tricky, repetitive and shallowly ornamental, overusing bright metallic surfaces, plastics, curved corners and liverish colors ad headache and ennui. But at its best, it is considerably more than that. In the words of C. Ray Smith in the October, 1968, issue of *Progressive Architecture*—devoted entirely to the style (with irate cancellations from architect-readers who consider it rubbish)—the movement is "a rebellious attempt to expand experience by breaking down the traditions of the Establishment." It has been called LSDesign. And in the violently drawn battle lines within the architecture profession there is one more demonstration of the generation gap.

The traditions of established modern architecture are order, meticulously proportioned lines and spaces, sensitively utilized color and puritanically austere style. All this is being broken down deliberately. Basic shapes and spaces are denied and insulted by Dayglo-bright designs of hard-edge geometry that cross right over windows and doors with consummately calculated arbitrariness in stripes, circles and abstractions. Existing elements are further fragmented by applications of mirror and mylar and dematerialized by light and kinetic effects. They are distorted by diagonal and bias installations and the deliberate camouflage of other materials. Lettering is larger than life size, suggesting an architecture of its own. "Environments" are created independently of their surroundings.

The results range from godawful to the genuinely revelatory expansion of visual and sensuous experience. Like all other styles that are primarily decorative and responsive to a particular moment in time and taste, this one will quickly be run into the ground. It happened with Art Nouveau, which ranged from the sublime to the atrocious and died of overexposure and overreaching after a very short life span. That one took half a century to be properly evaluated as more than slightly reprehensible, dismissable surface decoration. This one is being similarly pigeonholed by those who should know better.

In an exercise assigned to Yale architecture students by Super-graphicist Barbara Stauffacher, the students were to "explode" the dull box of the school elevator with color and pattern. Their painted designs were executed, two a week, until the end of the semester.

Certainly no one in the building was bored. Designs ranged from a "peace elevator," with stars and stripes inside and the elevator doors sliding together to present the image of a bomber outside, to pure space-expanding experiments in a fluorescent paint and flashing

Breaking down the tra-
ditions of the establish-
ment: "Op" elevators at
Yale Architectural School
(JAMES RIGHTER FOR PRO-
GRESSIVE ARCHITECTURE)

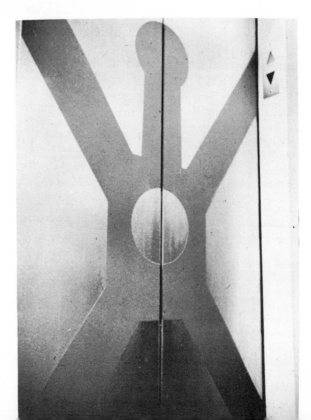

light. These are as legitimate exploratory exercises as any of the abstract study courses apotheosized by the Bauhaus as the heavenly road to architectural creativity.

Supermannerism is witty as well as wildly sense-awakening. This is not without significance at a time when black humor is the response to the grotesqueries of the bitterly self-defeating complexities of twentieth-century civilization. Maybe it is a form of black art. It is as volatile and fragile as revolution. Call it part of the state of revolution that seems to be the condition of our age.

What is upsetting the older professionals is that the style is an architecture destroyer—and what is destroyed, or mocked, is their architecture. What is even more upsetting, if anyone cares to face it, is that there is good reason for this. Look at any of the slick renderings of big building complexes by the big architectural offices. That one of Madison Square Garden and its companion office tower, for example, that was kicking around in ads for quite a while before it was built, looking like something dispensed from a machine, or like a giant can of tuna and box of crackers (tear off the box top and get Irving Felt). Or take any of those boardroom table-model models of new Sixth Avenue skyscrapers or big new commercial or cultural structures reproduced in newspapers and magazines. A wretched excess of computerized look alikes. Predictable banality on a supercolossal scale. Overwhelming square footage of nothing.

There is an impulse to kick them (ever tried kicking a building?) or to picket them (that has actually been done). Even much of the better work today has turned into a kind of Ikebana ritual of approved proportions and sterile relationships. What is really happening is that the present generation, full of beans, talent, revolt and defensible disrespect for the tasteful totems and the huge, hack symbols of the Establishment, is giving them a highly creative raspberry. You could call it productive protest.

For this is not nihilism, in spite of its blithe self-advertisements to that effect. It is a style going somewhere even if it is to a straight dead end. That won't matter, because in the process it will have opened important new doors of vision and experience. It is a way of breaking out of the depressingly minimal spaces and formulas that are laughingly called architecture in the name of today's economic pressures and expediency. It is the return of ornament, if you will, or an equivalent decorative enrichment, banished by Adolf

Loos and the early modern movement as "crime." It is the contemporary integration of the arts so falsely sought in more traditional terms, with the architect closer to the visual arts than he has been in a very long time.

Most important, it is the addition of still another useful tool to the architect's equipment, for, with the rest of us, he will never see the world in quite the same way again. Nor should he, because it will never be the same world again, and that is the truth behind the generation gap everywhere.

Don't Call It Kookie

The theory of Megastructure, or the gathering of many components into a single unit, implying largeness or greatness, as expressed in the Greek root of the word, is producing, in various modifications, some of today's most interesting architecture. It has been thoroughly explored by critics and intellectuals and its flashier aspects have been reduced to a kind of kicky high-fashion novelty by the stylish magazines.

What Megastructure amounts to, with considerable flexibility in interpretation, is a way of meeting the frighteningly enlarged scale and needs of today's building. It is proposed that this be done by means of huge structures that are actually made up of multiple small units that can be used over and over, serially or as accretions, in varieties of modules, through repetition and ultimately mass production. These units can be hung from or slid into or connected with some form of containing framework, but the implication always is of an ever-expanding number of smaller parts hooked into a general system of services and circulation.

Megastructure has a technological and functional rationale beyond cavil and a staggering creative and esthetic potential. At its highest reaches it is violently anti-Establishment, anti-formal, open-ended and non-centric (in the sense that classically conceived architecture is composed with a back, a front, a beginning and an end), deliberately rejecting symmetry, balance and focus and all of the time-honored conventions of architectural design. Bigger than any monument, it disclaims monumentality for a social and industrial image. It is "endless architecture," "action architecture," "anonymous architecture." It has "clip-on" parts for "plug-in" cities. It is also one of the most stimulating, promising and problematic architectural developments of the twentieth century. Results, in practice and on paper, range from the all-purpose university structure, having a big vogue right now, to Megastructure as the city of the future, a kind of erector-set environment with disposable parts. It goes all the way from a specific system of design being boldly explored here and abroad to the purest Utopian vision.

Perhaps the best of the flexible, expandable, university-in-one-building experiments is Scarborough College, a branch of the University of Toronto that is now an object of architectural pilgrimage. Designed by John Andrews, it combines two of architecture's most progressive trends: Megastructure and the New Brutalism. This single, stunning structure of rough concrete is a continuous circulatory system embracing classroom units and student spaces. An even more ambitious Megastructure by Candilis, Josic and Woods is going ahead for Berlin's Free University. A highly personal version of the principle has been constructed for the new arts center at the University of Illinois by Walter Netsch of Skidmore, Owings and Merrill. Others are under way.

The most notable exponents of Megastructure in its most extreme form have been a coalition of English architects in their twenties and thirties called the Archigram Group, whose theories were brought to international attention with a London exhibition in 1963, "The Living City." Interest has been whetted by occasional publication of the group's *Archigram* magazine.

Archigram's theories of a total Megastructure environment of expendable, industrialized components attached to a framework of circulation and services are richly buttressed by a spectacular abstract visualization of the kind of science fiction city that would be shaped by systems approaches, computerization and technology. Service-and-traffic grids fed by ducts contain rearrangeable, stacked housing and office units swung into place by cranes; the whole thing creeps across the land on giant metal legs. Awe-inspiring inhuman complexity has language to match. Peter Cook's magnificent mechanistic drawings are filled with "maximum pressure areas," "information silos" and "capsule-unit housing towers." This is Plug-In City.

Scarborough College's all-in-one building for
the all-purpose university (KEN BELL PHOTOS LTD.)

Critic Reyner Banham, writing in the *Walker Arts Center Design Quarterly*, called Archigram's "kit of interchangeable living cells and support structures the first effective image of the architecture of technology since Buckminster Fuller's Geodesic domes captivated the world." This is not, he warned, "a kookie teen-age Pop frivolity," no matter how many technological improbabilities it may contain. Utopia, after all, is Utopia. It deals in cosmic lessons, not instructions for do-it-yourself.

On a less cosmic level, Megastructure's more realistic versions offer provocative answers to large-scale building. In theory, these solutions to mass-produced housing or educational, commercial and cultural complexes are superbly, scientifically logical. In practice, their logic runs smack into the obscene obstacle course of tight money, artificially inflated land cost, archaic and restrictive union practices, obsolete and diverse building codes, astronomic costs of tooling for industrial production, politics, pigheadedness and the vicissitudes of public and personal taste. They collapse like a house of cards.

The process is being repeated, for example, for Habitat, Moshe Safdie's brainchild and beautiful obsession that was the showpiece of Montreal's Expo '67. What started there as serious Megastructure was completed, in a vastly reduced and compromised form, as something less than the inexpensive General Motors-type housing product intended. It was a hand-crafted Cadillac, an enormously costly, non-standardized, custom-made model. While it offered a tentative prototype demonstration of a handsome and rational design principle, it was also a sad case history of production realities.

New York City and the Federal Department of Housing and Urban Development have attempted Habitat studies. Attracted to the economic and technological promise of Megastructure housing, New York has come to the same economic and technological dead ends. How curious that those dead ends should be produced by the most progressive of all scientific civilizations. We can build small, sophisticated, exotic, demonstration mini-Megas only. The implicit mass-scale economics and efficiencies are unobtainable. The status quo wins hands down.

There are other objections to Megastructure. In the December issue of *Architectural Design*, guest-edited by Jonathan Miller, on the metaphors and myths of the city, Chris Abel severely criticizes every aspect of the theory from Scarborough to Plug-In City.

Megastructure does not, he says, take into account the adaptive processes of the living community, the organic adjustments to change that must inevitably be made. It is an orderly rigid concept. The Megastructure building or city is a "closely integrated or cohesive ordering of a system of multifarious activities" that insists on a "coherent image." Life, he says, using such currently "in" words as conurbation, homeostasis and cyclic processes, is just not like that. Megastructure ignores the "adaptive behaviour the planner cannot himself specify."

Touché. But the truth, as usual, is somewhere between the Gospel of Archigram and the Fallacy of the Esthetic Straightjacket. Megastructure is one more tool pertinent to our times and problems.

The Case for Chaos

To a public learning to look at its surroundings critically and seeing the physical effects of the confusions and vulgarities of modern life, the drive for order and elegance seems an irreproachable cause. Moreover, it has been the cause of concerned architects, planners and intellectuals representing the avant-garde of social and esthetic thought for the past fifty years.

On the other hand, there is the case for chaos. One can react in two ways. The first is to express indignation and horror at the perverseness of such an idea. Call it backsliding nihilism, part of a currently fashionable denial of existing standards and values. Or it is possible to look at it carefully and find some eye-opening observations on the urban scene. The eyes of the observers (youthful, of course) are being used with a surprising historical objectivity. At the same time, they are examining the phenomena of the present, not with the sweeping a priori attitudes of condemnation that have become pious clichés, but with a cool, analytical acuity.

Today's theory is tomorrow's practice. With the speedup characteristic of our age, it has a way of becoming today's practice. Any thinking, feeling citizen involved with his environment in this latter part of the twentieth century (that's right—latter—with all the "projections" to the once awesomely remote year 2000 no more than comfortable middle age for the present generation) must know the wave of the future or succumb to the undertow of the past. Another generation gap.

The theorists point out that there are sound sociological, technical and practical explanations for the look of today's world, like it or not. We are asked to examine the mess again. They claim that we can deal with the chaotic environment in constructive and even creative ways by admitting its conflicts, analyzing its components and recognizing the purposes they serve and the contributions they make to our way of life.

Is chaos really so chaotic, they ask? Does it not contain valuable elements of vitality and variety, complexity and contrast? Can we not learn from the organically evolving environment? What about planning by adaptive processes? Is there an esthetic of the Pop landscape? From this point on, you may have your choice of embracing chaos on any step of the scale from an instructive demonstration of contemporary realities to great art form, depending on the length of your hair.

Chaos may even contain an order of its own, we are told. It is an order of "inclusion" and "the difficult whole" rather than an order of "exclusion," or "rejection," which has been the teaching and operation of modern architecture to date. It offers a pluralistic esthetic of "both and" rather than the selective "either-or" decisions enforced by orthodox architectural theory. This is a far more complex approach to the environment than we have been taught to take.

Rejection or exclusion has been a basic tenet of the modern movement. Its pioneers preached against the chaos of the contemporary environment with the same breath in which they called for a new architecture. If they could not eliminate the setting, they turned their backs on it. They were fighting for release from an accretion of smothering, pseudo-arty Victorian clutter and to them slob city and the landscape of the superhighway were just updated versions of the old enemy. It has now become terribly clear that they rejected too much. There are lessons of sterility wherever their reductive principles have been scrupulously carried out. That prescription for order didn't work. The present search for order calls for acceptance of the irreconcilables of our complex existences, new values and a new vision.

This is fascinating, heady speculation and the best of it is to be found in a slim book called *Complexity and Contradiction in Architecture*, by Robert Venturi, published by the Museum of Modern Art in association with the Graham Foundation for Advanced Studies in the Fine Arts.

Mr. Venturi is the guru of chaos. The book is, as he calls it, a gentle manifesto. Its illustrations of great buildings of the past are rich demonstrations of ambiguity and complexity. Where the modern architect of the last generation turned to the simplicities of the anonymous and the primitive, this generation turns to the most sophisticated examples of history. In the present, Mr. Venturi finds Roadtown, U.S.A., and the Supermarket-Supermotel-Superhighway landscape, commonly inveighed against in the primers of a more beautiful America, exhilarating esthetic experiences. He takes his Yale students to Las Vegas much as an earlier generation made pilgrimages to Palladian villas.

He teaches a new scale created by the automobile and a new, bold architecture of communication grasped by the car in motion. The new architecture is the little building and the big sign on Route 66.

Learning from Pop Art, the conventional is accepted and given character by change of emphasis and context; the "valid and vivid" banalities that are so much the reality of the American scene are the new icons. Mr. Venturi is witty, brilliant and challenging; for a short course, read "Learning from Las Vegas," written with Denise Scott Brown, in the March, 1968, *Architectural Forum.*

All right. You don't buy it. Brought up on America the Beautiful, you find Pop landscape an affront. Reyner Banham, in lively critical essays, may embrace the fluorescent plastic environment but you still suffer vertigo in motels. Everyone to his own life-style. No significant proportion of Yale architecture graduates has moved to Las Vegas. And even if it is doctrine that every son reject the values of his father, there are circumstances in which the elements of the Pop landscape become outrage. There is always a dangerous tendency for reason and judgment to abdicate to fashionable ideas.

Still, one cannot sell this strong-stomached generation short. Quite aside from the controversial Pop Art aspects of the theory and the patent dangers of dogma, it is clear that a whole generation is rediscovering the umbrella. It is not just apotheosizing the Strip. It is bringing back into building and vision a challenging richness and

The Strip at Las Vegas, today's substitute
for the pilgrimage to Palladian villas
(THE NEW YORK TIMES BY CARL GOSSETT, JR.)

complexity that have been lost through the ritual purification of the modernists.

At present, as in all beginnings, the new doctrine is being pushed too hard to prove the point. In practice, it shows every sign of becoming a codified set of mannerisms. Its more arcane applications must be explained to the non-initiate, and that introduces the problem of the architect, like the artist, being reduced to talking to himself. Orthodox modernism could turn into orthodox ambiguity.

The very real promise, however, is of an architecture of adaptation and accommodation, two words that have been taboo in the modern movement. It would embrace existing contradictory realities, systems and programs, the complexities and conflicts of modern life, the growth and changes in physical form, taste and needs. It would, in a sense, roll with the punches.

Another, even gentler cultural guru of our time than Mr. Venturi, August Heckscher, has made the telling point that the doctrine of rationalism proves inadequate in times of upheaval. "Such inner peace as men gain must represent a tension among contradictions and uncertainties." This is true, say the rebels against orthodox modernism, of outer order, as well. The revolution is dead. Long live the revolution.

Monumental Questions

In the spring of 1967, at New York's cozy Museum of Contemporary Crafts, a tiny, tidy selection of models, photographs and sculpture called "Monuments, Tombstones and Trophies," set neatly among primly potted chrysanthemums, dealt with a huge, unsettling theme: the validity of memorial construction for our time.

It did not, ostensibly, start out to do this. The overt purpose of the exhibition was to explore the broad potential of twentieth-century commemorative art, from conventional memorialization to social protest. It was meant to demonstrate new forms, materials and meanings for an old, almost timeless use of art and architecture. But the question of why it seems to be so difficult today to produce a convincing or moving monument pertinent to our times seethed quietly beneath the surface of the show.

The examples, by artists, architects and engineers, ranged widely. There were photographs of Eero Saarinen's famous parabolic arch in St. Louis with the improbably Pop name of the Jefferson National Expansion Memorial. There were the even more improbable Pop baked potatoes and giant ice cream sticks proposed for public streets and squares by Claes Oldenburg, who also contributed the idea of a huge, monolithic cube as a memorial plug for the intersection of Broadway and Chambers Street. The monumental traffic backup would be as impressive as the monument itself, and one assumes that it was an implied part of the design. The subject was literally run into the ground in Michael Steiner's buried drainpipe, into which the viewer would peer for his symbolic kicks.

The show had moon monuments, portable monuments, temporary monuments and disposable monuments—a deliberate contradiction in terms. It included memorials and tombstones that did their level Pop best to put down society and its more tiresome conventions, an effort yielding diminishing returns as the once-shocking vocabulary of esthetic protest takes on an almost old-shoe acceptability. Shock is like dope; you have to keep increasing the jolt. The "trophies" ran the full familiar gamut of esthetic black humor from the satiric visual non sequitur to generously applied genitalia. Most were one-line, one-time sight gags.

But all served to focus on an inescapable, nagging, unasked and unanswered question—the legitimacy or visibility of monuments in today's culture and society. It is a sticky question, as almost a decade of unsuccessful effort on the part of the Franklin Delano Roosevelt Memorial Commission, for example, clearly demonstrates.

In that case, the basic issue was never faced. Matters of size and style, traditional representation versus abstract forms, were all superficial considerations. They were esthetic red herrings obscuring the pertinent problem of whether a traditional memorial stressing traditional values can be produced convincingly and responded to sincerely by our age. Even the best intentions of the best artists and architects seem consistently to fall flat, or at most to achieve a bland or lukewarm artistic or associative success. With few exceptions, the memorial vacuum is filled only with the most redundant and weary clichés.

The fact is that the emotional, intellectual and spiritual climate of the twentieth century has changed so much in response to a radically changing world that the familiar memorial is an anachronism. Mere structural mass does not impress when a miraculous technology has made superhuman scale the everyday norm. Simple nobility verging on pomposity or sentimentality reflects nothing of the strange and shifting values of these peculiarly transient revolutionary, violent and questioning times. This is an age of moral uncertainty, of strange twists of behavior and judgment, of hope, cynicism and despair, of horrible destructive potential and new cosmic frontiers. The old yardsticks for men or monuments simply do not apply.

When art does not reflect or contain the thought and standards of its own age, when it is not infused with the meaning or values of its time, it has no meaning or value at all. That is the dilemma of the conventional memorial built today. It offers false reassurance to the unsophisticated that the old values still exist, but the more aware are unmoved and unconvinced and even a little ashamed of its sham heroics. It seems spurious and oversimplified; at best, hollow; at worst, a mockery.

It is not surprising that the only modern monuments of any measurable impact are those dedicated to a particularly grim form of modern death. They are the memorials to twentieth-century group massacre that eschew most traditional figurative symbolism, such as the hovering slab of the Fosse Ardeatine in Rome.

This does not mean that there are no longer men or ideas worth honoring. There are heroes, even when the anti-hero is acknowledged and in vogue. There is beauty, even when the tastemakers look on it suspiciously as a deceptive instrument of sensuous depravity used to gull the unwary or the undiscriminating. But there are no longer the cultural absolutes, the emotional innocence, the intellectual faith and naiveté that legitimizes the kind of monument that correctly expressed that faith and naiveté in an earlier time. Thoughtful men are no less concerned with society; it is just that their faith and feelings are infinitely more vulnerable and complex.

The great memorial era really ended with the Victorian Age. Sentiment and the search for sublimity, intensification of feeling, were all nineteenth-century goals. It was the style to take one's Sunday stroll in a well-landscaped cemetery, with suitably dramatized intimations of mortality. And of immortality, as well. Emotions were large, elementary and exaggerated. Standards were literary and moralistic, and so was the full spectrum of the arts. Nobility rode high and noble heroes charged unremittingly across public spaces.

Today the nineteenth-century hero charges through a traffic jam or guards a slum, which says far more about the unheroic standards of our age. Esthetic puffery has little place in a time of tough questions and answers and terrible uncertainties. Man was never more mortal or his world more insecure. His values were never more in flux. The exhibition offers no better comment on today's human condition that Carl Andre's pile of sand, meant to sink invisibly into the surface of the grave.

All of the Arts but Architecture

The dedication of the Atlanta Memorial Arts Center raises issues that will have to be faced, not only in Atlanta, but in every city that has succumbed to the cultural center epidemic. Atlanta was one of the first communities to complete its version of the new breed of omnibus arts center of the sixties—the ambitious cultural catchall meant to serve a complete range of performing and visual arts with facilities of elaborate professionalism and sometimes stultifying nobility.

In some communities the new theaters and museums are obviously needed. But assuming that creativity and the audience for it are bottomless, an assumption totally without validity, there is still the perpetual care and feeding of these expensive, money-eating plants and the nagging matter of what will keep them filled when they are done.

The justification for putting all of one's cultural eggs into one monumental basket seems to be a childlike confusion of the monument with the product, of the container with the contained. The building itself is seen as a proclamation of the cultural virtues of the community. As some justification for this, it is a legitimate mark of culture for a community to want the enrichment of monumental architecture in an era when architecture has become a catalogue selection of manufacturers' substitutes for it and public sculpture has been supplanted by the Holiday Inn sign. This makes it all the sadder to see the best intentions go awry.

The Atlanta Memorial Arts Center—culture in a big box

It is significant that most of the centers seem to be going awry in the same way. To anyone getting the model photos and releases, they look as if a cultural center computer had designed them all. The computer has been programed with everything anyone else has done and with the classical nostalgia of an older generation that provides the money and sponsorship for the centers and is looking for a "palatable" modern style—something that is not "too modern" and reminds them of conventionally admired effects of grandeur, measured by traditional, unchanging standards of material and appearance.

This is, of course, a guaranteed way of missing the grandeur of our times—bold, rough, sometimes brutal, technologically marvelous, genuinely expressive of an age that is not smooth or classical at all. It has its own beauty, its own magnificence, as does the vital and troubled era in which we live. This moment in time is a unique point in every kind of history, including art history. In building for it, a miss is as good as a mile.

192

The State of the Art

The reason for singling out the Atlanta Arts Center as a case history is that it is complete and it is typical. This is not to hold it up as undeserving of respect. One respects the conscientious, intelligent, well-meaning people who work hard to make a dream come true. One simply questions the dream.

In the case of Atlanta, the result is representative of the current school of cultural center thought and design. It is the product of a community marked by gentility and courage. Atlanta lost 122 of its top cultural patrons in a tragic plane crash some years ago as a chartered air tour flight left Paris for home; the center is a memorial to them. The city not only picked up the pieces and developed new leadership, but it is clear to any visitor that there is a quality of mind and heart that few other communities can match.

The design process, however, offers a certain unhappy enlightenment that is applicable to almost any other case history one might care to choose. Atlanta decided on a monumental box to contain its High Museum of Art, the Symphony Guild, the Municipal Theater for drama, opera and ballet and the Atlanta School of Art. (They have it; the structure is 232 feet wide by 294 feet long and 50 feet high and covers six acres of Peachtree Street.)

Because the High Museum was already on the site and was to be incorporated into the new structure, the architects Toombs, Amisano and Wells, associated with Stevens and Wilkinson, decided to bridge the existing building with giant trusses from which other parts of the structure would be hung. This was a strong engineering concept that set the building's esthetics, as well. But the estimates came in too high.

There was a model and rendering of the scheme, and the sponsors liked some of the surface effects—what appeared, for example, as white exterior walls. They were interested in retaining the effects that pleased them even when the structural rationale was gone and change was indicated.

For financial reasons and pressured by sponsorial taste, a daring engineering solution became solid concrete walls—white walls. The transition was not accompanied by any understanding on the part of the patrons of the esthetic of modern concrete construction and it was gradually disguised, paneled and painted for a more acceptable "classical look."

One donor saw a newspaper photograph of the Atlanta Stadium

with its handsome, exposed concrete supports and mistook it for the Arts Center, reading the supports as an enclosing colonnade. He refused to give up that image, and since he contributed a substantial part of the $13 million cost, after a while the building got the colonnade. It holds up nothing except exterior lights but it does provide a pleasant promenade.

Ludicrous? The same thing is going on everywhere. These curious, backward-looking standards are being set and the debilitating compromises are being made by architects wherever cultural centers are going up. The design decisions are controlled by a respected and powerful generation that is completely innocent of the architecture of today. The last art that is being encouraged is the art of architecture.

The result is Caricature Classicism or Running Scared Modern. Then, having gotten a building signifying little except tasteful pomposity, the question still waits of what will be done with it in operation. It can be successful as a showcase of popular performances of a largely non-innovative character for a wide audience, with an occasional arts festival thrown in. In that respect, it does bring a lot of some kind of art to a lot of people. But art is based on creativity, and that is usually going on somewhere else.

The Atlanta Center hopes specifically for a lively interaction of the arts that have been housed together. The greatest chance of that happening may be through the students in the art school, who could, if the responses in other schools are any indication, tear the carefully programed place apart.

The only certainty is that there will be a large operating deficit every year that must be met by the unending commitment of the business community and annual fund-raising campaigns. Every one of the new centers will have to face the realities of continuing deficit financing on a very large scale.

It seems quite obvious that when all of the resources for culture are being channeled into one monumental effort that can absorb more than is ever available, the chance diminishes for support of other, non-affiliated, more experimental, non-Establishment arts. These enterprises never break even. All they do is provide the talent, style and new forms and meanings that are what culture is all about.

In Atlanta, for example, there is Theater Atlanta, known for its high caliber, free-ranging productions. Concurrent with the Arts Center opening, it put on a wonderfully sharp, witty, irreverent biting and pertinent satire called *Red, White and Maddox*, later brought to Broadway. (If you didn't expect it in Atlanta, you don't know Atlanta.) This show nearly didn't open. There were no funds. They were raised, at the last minute and only as a stopgap, by radio appeal. Right after the Arts Center's opening festivities. Theater Atlanta was evicted for arrears in its rent. Its season was over before it started.

The question that is not being asked or answered anywhere is whether the encouragement of culture has not been sadly confused with its memorialization. Will the expensive new Establishment showcases subsidize the arts that are most creative or pull the rug out from under them? There are signs of the latter already.*

Of Symbolism and Flying Saucers

How do you finish an anachronism? How do you complete a cathedral begun too late, beset by conflicts in symbolism, construction, art and costs, overshadowed by skyscrapers, clinging to obsolete crafts, mismeasured for glory and miscalculated for meaning in the modern world?

The Cathedral of St. John the Divine, on Morningside Heights, was conceived in 1891 as the world's largest and latest of the great medieval line that ran from Arles to Amiens. There was only one thing wrong. It was not the product of a cathedral-building age. The medieval cathedral was a superb structure, the creative flowering of a special confluence of forces at a particular moment in time. Its synthesis of technology, necessity, timeliness and expression is the basic formula of all great architectural art.

Out of context, the formula is not reproduceable. The same moment and the same results never come twice. Archeological

---

* The most pessimistic fears about the Atlanta Arts Center were confirmed a few months after opening. It was unable to meet its operating costs and rising expenses and the alliance of performing arts companies was broken up.

copying will not make it so. This is an ineluctable reality of art and life. Until it is understood, we will continue to have the pious reproductions, the dead reconstructions, the vacuum-packed imitations and the false, nostalgic standards that, at best, evoke only the second-hand suggestion of the artistic glories of some other age, or at worst, throttle creativity and subvert values in our own.

When the design for St. John the Divine was projected, the church spire was already losing out to the commercial tower—a kind of symbolism, if one wished to look for it, that the cathedral was no longer the physical capstone of the city or of society and could no longer offer the comforting assurances of an older, more familiar symbolism merely by increasing the size of its traditional forms. The medieval cathedral already belonged to history.

And so the cathedral sits unfinished, not through the inexorable process of the evolutionary architectural change of the Middle Ages, but through conflicts over aims, objectives, symbolism and commitment of church funds in the twentieth century.

The misconceptions of its builders are reflected accurately in the vicissitudes of its construction. When a church evolved from Romanesque to Gothic from the eleventh to the thirteenth centuries, art and history, not a board of trustees, made the decision. When St. John the Divine was redesigned from Romanesque to Gothic, Ralph Adams Cram, the Gothic revivalist who replaced the original firm of Heins and La Farge in 1911, opted for the change, and it really didn't matter.

It was not important because neither style grew out of the conditions of the time. Neither was a creative act. The game was archeological and the choice was arbitrary. The basis was personal taste. Art is never taste. It is the synthesis and catalyst of the complex factors of any cultural era, modified, if you will, by taste, but taste alone is cold, thin stuff, tenuously related to a genuine esthetic product.

What all this leads up to is the simple fact that it doesn't really matter how the cathedral is finished now—a subject that has been the cause of some little rarefied furore. It is merely, again, a matter of taste. The forms and meanings of the building are so totally removed from the social, spiritual and esthetic mainstream of the twentieth century that the result, whatever the decision, will inevitably be cold, thin stuff.

A careful and conscientious effort has been made by the firm of Adams and Woodbridge to solve the problems that exist. The cost of the central tower planned for the crossing and of the completion of the west towers would be prohibitive today, even if stonemasons were available for the work, which they are not. The "temporary" Guastavino dome, guaranteed for ten years and going for half a century—a testament to that fascinating and now equally historic form of tile construction—is to be replaced.

The architects have been forced, ironically enough, by that same evolutionary process of art and history that the cathedral ignored, to go to modern concrete construction in the name of cost and practicality. They are providing elevators in the piers that will support the beams for a "modern Gothic" glass and concrete lantern to substitute for the unbuildable crossing tower, because labor to change an electric light bulb, for example, is too costly today to permit the bulbchanger the inefficiency of toiling up stone steps. Count the anachronisms, architectural and otherwise, in that sentence. You can only finish a superanachronism like St. John the Divine with more of the same, and there is not much to be said in praise or blame.*

Which brings us to the final ecclesiastical architectural question of why religious building today is in such a curiously depressing and distressing state. Few religious institutions now fall into the trap of mock-medieval. They seem to be going for mock-modern instead. Almost all have adopted modern design as a kind of trademark of the contemporaneity of their outlook and needs.

And that is precisely the trouble. They distort today's architecture into a trademark, or gimmick, and not much else. Never has so much progressive technology ended up as so many visual tricks. Never has so much experimental structure been so decoratively misused. Never has the doctrine of free esthetic expression been so abused or engineering advances so superficially vulgarized for effect. There are exceptions, of course, but they are aggressively outnumbered by churches poised like moon rockets, synagogues of country-club luxe in jazzy concrete shells, and far-out flying saucer chapels.

* Not too long after this article was written the decision was made to leave the cathedral unfinished as a symbol of the extraordinary social pressures and problems of our time that the church must use all of its resources to meet.

Architecture

Perhaps it is still just a matter of taste. Or of a lot of bad architects. But more likely it has to do with the unresolved relationships of spiritual needs and physical symbolism in the twentieth century, for which no number of flashy cantilevers or catenary curves provides convincing answers. If St. John the Divine sought safe, standardized symbolism, the modern church pins its faith too often on specious novelty. The matter comes back once more to the validity of solutions that are a legitimate and natural expression of an age, as opposed to those that are wilfully or arbitrarily conceived. It is an area of pitfalls and complex philosophical possibilities. But it comes full circle to art and history again.

Art, Architecture and Museology

After eight long years of planning and fund raising for a total of slightly less than $3.5 million, the city of Syracuse, N.Y., a community of 300,000, has built an object lesson in art and museology.

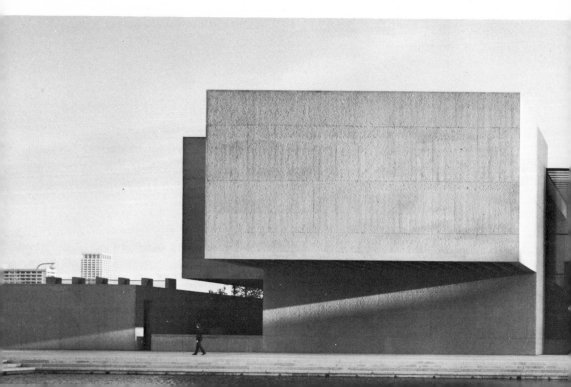

The State of the Art

The Everson Museum of Art sets a standard that other cities, embarked on a wave of museum and cultural center building of epic proportions and some historical significance, will now be called on to match.

Everson's building has been designed by I. M. Pei and Partners, with the sensitive collaboration of the museum's director Max Sullivan and the sensible backing of an obviously non-meddling board of trustees whose faith in professionalism has been justified by the results. They must be doing something right, because Mr. Pei has received the commission for the extension of the National Gallery in Washington on the strength of the Syracuse job.

This is the architecture of today as art history will eventually record it. It does not try to be pretty, or classical, or decorative, or evocative, or palatable to the cautious. In that overworked but accurate phrase of the now generation, it does its own thing.

Most important of all, it is a clear demonstration of the dramatic oneness of contemporary art and architecture.

This is a fact of art that has escaped those constantly calling for "integration of the arts." It has eluded the critics who deal in

The Everson Museum of Art in Syracuse, N.Y.
(EZRA STOLLER)

increasingly complicated treatises on increasingly minimal aspects of modern painting and sculpture without recognition oɪ ʰeir relationship to the contemporary environment.

It has been ignored by most museum directors who treat art of any kind as something to be maintained and displayed in a vacuum. No greater disservice or distortion could be inflicted on the art of this century.

Not since the age of fresco, to which the current phenomenon bears tenuous resemblance, have art and architecture provided such an esthetic and environmental whole. If the specialists would stop looking at their specialties long enough, they could see the shape and meaning of art in our time. Everson is a good place to see it.

The visitor will not find a notable permanent collection. There are other cities to go for that. But he will have what the contemporary art museum can, and should, uniquely provide: a fully dimensional esthetic experience in which the building and its contents interact on the highest plane.

Whether Everson has succeeded by design or accident or both, this esthetic totality is undoubtedly a more important and valuable objective for the small museum in the small city than the costly and competitive building of a large collection.

It gives that old chestnut, "art appreciation," new meaning. It should be the primary aim of any arts building program. If the point is missed, as it is being missed or muffed in so many of the new centers, the result is second-rate and compromise culture. It is the difference between being alive and half-dead.

The form of the Syracuse building is a squared pinwheel consisting of four gallery blocks around a sculpture court. Placed in the desolate limbo of center-city urban renewal, opposite an older sports and convention hall, next to a steam plant and with future neighbors amorphous, the museum gives style where none exists. It also connects with an underground parking garage, a planning plus.

The material is the same inside and out—reinforced concrete faced with a diagonally striated, bush-hammered aggregate that warms the gray with crushed rose granite. Exposed, natural concrete borders the panels and is used for stairs, balconies and bridges inside.

The identical exterior and interior finishes can be seen simultaneously through glass panels set in channels in the walls between the gallery blocks. The only additional material is oak, beautifully used for gallery floors, stair rails and display cabinets.

Outside, the small but massive blocks hover over a large, paved plaza. Aboveground, the whole structure is only 130 feet by 140 feet. Underground, it broadens to a 260-foot length to accommodate administrative and members' quarters and an elegant 320-seat auditorium.

Inside, the gallery blocks have controlled, artificial light. They are bridged continuously around the two-story, fifty-foot-square interior court, where natural light pours down from rimming skylights of clear glass, always visible from the galleries. Passing clouds and outdoor planting become part of the building through these and the glazing that joins them, running from ground to roof, at two corners.

The carefully arranged and detailed sequences and play of space and light, the changing views of art form and color, the way the pedestrian moves and experiences and enjoys all this, is architecture. The way in which abstract painting—such as the huge Morris Louis and Helen Frankenthaler canvases hung on the court wall—is enriched and completed by the setting, is integration of the arts. The interaction of the two is art at the highest level.

At its small scale, the building is comfortably monumental. It is timeless and classical without caricaturing classicism or compromising its contemporaneity. As art and culture Everson is today —and it is going to last a good long time.

The Seductive Virtues of Alvar Aalto

The twelfth-floor conference room of the Institute of International Education (a 1963 building by Harrison and Abramovitz) is probably one of the least-known landmarks in New York. Designed by the internationally honored architect Alvar Aalto and paid for by the Edgar J. Kaufmann Foundation, this top floor has been transformed for an undisclosed and probably formidable sum into the most beautiful and distinguished interior New York has seen in many years.

Aalto Conference Room—subtle and sumptuous

Here are the famous Aalto trademarks that have been admired by two generations of architects. Pale, laminated woods are used with the plasticity of sculpture; stepped, curved walls and ceilings turn ordinary rectangular spaces into a series of softened enclosures of seductive virtuosity; and deceptive simplicity belies a most sophisticated style.

But even if these contributions have already taken their place in architectural histories, there is nothing dated about them. The Kaufmann conference room is so far superior to corporate and institutional interior design here that they make the standardized, expensive ploys of teak-by-the-yard, carpet-by-the-vertical-inch and conference-table-by-the-ton seem flashy and cheap by comparison.

This superiority rests on a large talent and small details. First, and most important, there is Aalto's treatment of architectural space.

It might be called a sensitive and loving kind of manipulation that molds, instead of denying, the existing architectural shell. It is creative camouflage rather than destructive decoration. And it is frankly sensuous rather than severe.

Approximately 4,350 square feet of conventionally boxlike, low-ceilinged space has been divided into a lobby, reception room, conference room and a corridor. Much of the area can be opened or closed in a variety of ways by sliding doors.

The large conference-room ceiling sweeps upward in undulating stages to a window wall, an effect made possible by moving the heavy service machinery above. Side walls curve gently and unexpectedly, giving a diagonal focus. Even the cobalt-blue Finnish tile of the elevator entrance is rounded and smooth to the hand. Inside, the colors are white and ivory, accented by black, with the cool, elegant clarity of natural tones and materials.

Scarcely second to the resolution of space is the superb use of wood. It is quite possible, in this country, to forget that wood is so beautiful and that its appeal is due to its qualities as a natural material. American processes of manufacture frequently result in a mechanized and overfinished product that looks as if it had never known a tree.

The rooms glow with the pale warmth of white birch. White plaster walls are partly sheathed with white-birch panels, and slender, vertical battens of clustered, laminated birch rods tie both surfaces together.

This wall treatment breaks into a brief abstract fantasy at one point on the longest side of the main conference room, where a composition of straight and bent wood forms is meant to suggest a stylized forest. It was reduced to a small stand of "trees" by New York's fire laws.

All of these more sensitive elements, including the Aalto-designed furniture upholstered in soft black leather, an integral part of the interiors, were prefabricated or produced in Finland. The "forest" was studied at full size in the architect's Helsinki atelier and re-erected here. Large, plain sections, like the ash panels and sliding doors of the same white tone as the Finnish birch, were made in the United States.

There is no sign of the aggressive angularity or dynamic sharpness that is commonly labeled modern. Aalto might be called, to use the language of painting, a soft-edge architect. He continues to work, in increasingly subtle ways, with the free form, a concept he virtually invented in the 1920's. And he has seen it turned into the most abused of all clichés.

He himself is incapable of a cliché or a stereotype of any kind. A small, spry, sophisticated, impeccably tailored Finnish troll approaching a patriarchal age, with a gleam in his eye and a soft barb to his wit, Alvar Aalto still leads the field of design.

Mies: Lessons from the Master

Genius is seldom acknowledged by its own generation; we wait for the authentication of Charlton Heston playing Michelangelo as superman in supercolor.

But we have had our supermen: Frank Lloyd Wright playing himself, and Le Corbusier playing Scrooge while producing timeless spatial and sculptural delights, and Mies van der Rohe. This is the triumvirate that so decisively affected the course of architecture in the revolutionary years of the twentieth century, evolving the look, structure and function of a new kind of man-made world in natural and inevitable synthesis with society's other radical changes.

Mies was a massive, craggy man, given to few public pronouncements, whose person and work shared a tacit monumentality.

The Miesian esthetic—strict, strong and subtle—is a correct, ordered and logical architectural solution for our day. That it is not the only solution goes without saying; but each artist must have his personal vision which he carries as close as possible to its ultimate perfection. Mies's vision rested on the acceptance of modern technology as it stunningly appeared in his youth.

Trained as a stonemason, bricklayer and delineator of plaster ornament, he saw steel and glass as the fabric of a new world of shimmering skyscrapers and floating pavilions of stringently rational and elegant simplicity. He produced work of a purity and power as great as anything the art of building has ever known.

But technology is not art, and form only follows function as a starting point, or life and art would be much simpler than they are. The key to the art of architecture is the conviction and sensitivity with which technology and function are interpreted esthetically, in solutions of practical social purpose.

Mies's structure, often the hard, straight-lined strength of the steel frame, is reflected in exterior metal detailing of painstaking refinement that speaks directly and logically of his way of building. These details are often as expressive as Sullivan's foliate ornament was of its underlying structure, and it is the quality and effectiveness of this expressive balance that marks the good, or great, building.

The proportions of a Mies design are so sensitively adjusted, his understanding of the richness of marble, the brilliance of glass and the substantiality of bronze so sensuously sure, his feelings for the materials of our time so overwhelmingly rich and yet so far from vulgar, that no one has matched the precise and timeless beauty of his buildings. The Seagram Building, for example, is dignified, sumptuous, severe, sophisticated, cool, consummately elegant architecture—architecture for the twentieth century and for the ages.

The Miesian example is a lesson of principle. But in too many cases the Miesian principle has been ignored and the Miesian example simply "knocked off" in the cheapest Seventh Avenue terms.

Without fine materials and meticulous details, Mies's diamond-sharp doctrine of "less is more" becomes a most ordinary formula. Raised above the shoddy and speculative, however, it is a competent and appropriate formula and it is here that Mies's signal importance, as the source of a genuine popular style, has been so much misunderstood.

The "glass box" is the most maligned building idea of our time. It is also one of the best. Whatever its deficiencies, and there are many, due to the complex factors of architects who are less than perfectionists and businessmen who are less than philanthropists or sociologists, it is the genuine vernacular of the mid-twentieth century. It derives legitimately from Mies's masterful and meaningful innovations, and it serves legitimately the needs of a commercial society that builds on an industrial scale. It does this with sheer and brilliant modern magic and with as much validity and suitability as the last great vernacular style, the Georgian.

Mies stood for discipline, and this is becoming a lost architectural virtue. He stood for logic, which is now a contortionist's trick. He stood for style, in its highest and most valid meaning of the expression of standards and techniques of a particular historical time.

He came to work in Chicago in 1938. Except for a brief stop-over at Harvard after leaving Germany, Chicago is the city that he made his own. He built there a significant handful of handsome apartment houses, the start of a campus for the Illinois Institute of Technology, an impressive Federal court and office building that is one of the city's show pieces.

Two more buildings are in construction in the Federal Center, the first structure for the huge Illinois Central air rights tract is in work, as well as what may be the most important skyscraper in the country—an immense fifty-story I.B.M. building on the river, adjacent to those other show-stopping structures, Bertrand Goldberg's circular Marina City towers.

There are at least half a dozen very large, new, excellent buildings in Chicago influenced and executed by a second generation trained by Mies until the late fifties, during the period when he headed the I.I.T. School of Architecture. The outstanding example is the monumentally successful Civic Center with its Picasso-adorned plaza, its dramatic eighty-seven-foot spans faced with rusting steel designed by a combination of talents from three local offices: C. F. Murphy, Skidmore, Owings and Merrill, and Loebl, Schlossman and Bennett. The most radical designs of the Chicago branch of the top big business firm of Skidmore, Owings and Merrill, long firmly rooted in the Miesian esthetic, are here. The 100-story, tapered, diagonally trussed John Hancock Building is a distinctive, looming obelisk against Chicago's windy skies. Architecturally, Mies's Chicago is not the Second City anymore.

Thirty years after Mies's arrival in Chicago the world has caught up with him, but it still does not understand his work. His art is subtle, structural, professional. His remarkable refinements escape the casual observer. His buildings do not provide the cheap, easy effects of fake elegance with which the public gulls itself as a substitute for the real thing.

The world knows now, as the profession knew even forty years ago, that this quiet man of serenity and strength, whose art distills the deceptively simple essence of complete sensuous sophistication, was one of the great men and great artists of our age.

The Federal Court and Office Building
in Chicago by Mies van der Rohe
(BILL ENGDAHL, HEDRICH-BLESSING)

207

Architecture

Even without real understanding, it brought to him in his eighties the major commissions that were denied to his talents when he was younger: the Berlin Museum, the I.B.M. Building, a Lloyd's Bank building in London, the multi-structure Dominion Center in Toronto. It is now possible to live in Mies apartment houses in Chicago, Detroit, Newark, Montreal and Baltimore. It is not possible to do so in New York. (It remains a mystery how New York's status-symbol-conscious rich can continue to accept, at the nation's highest prices, residential architectural trash.)

What may well rank Mies as the most important of the form-giving triumvirate in the final analysis, is the fact that he did so much more than bring the highest art to architecture. He took the basic tools of the structural revolution that changed the world irrevocably and magnificently in the twentieth century—steel and glass—and turned them into a system of structural esthetics with subtle variations that belie any literal interpretation of his methods. He handled this system with such logic and beauty that he transformed both the building and the vision of our time.

His work is the refinement, over a lifetime, of a revolution. His buildings are not the sketches made on the backs of envelopes on high-flying jet planes between international construction sites that have become part of popular twentieth-century hard-sell architectural mythology. The pivotal skyscrapers, houses, museums, schools and office buildings cover over a half century in one of the most important periods of the building art. They are the end product of painstaking study and restudy of a theme that was explosively radical after the First World War and has been fully realized today. If city streets are lined with ordinary offspring, this is common to every creative age. They are preferable to the petty, picturesque vanities that pass for innovation.

Can anyone stand unmoved at the top of a steel-framed sky-scraper today, looking out across a city's glittering twentieth-century towers, glass walls reflecting clouds, sky and structures in a massed, changing pattern of light and color? This architecture is not static, any more than life is static. Can anyone fail to recognize and react to this miracle of our time? Mies is basic to the miracle.

In the natural pendulum swing of revolution and reaction, of stimulus and rejection—and twenty years is just par time for the course—an entire generation of architects has turned its back on

Mies. Twenty years have inevitably revealed the deficiencies of the First International Style; the limitations of a rigid functional esthetic applied to the complexity of later twentieth-century architectural needs, from planning to urban sociology, are clear. As always, the pendulum swings too far.

Only in Chicago has the Miesian lesson been properly learned. For Chicago proves that while Mies's personal brand of consummate elegance cannot be copied—the massive, subtle rhythms of the Federal Building are breathtaking—his basic philosophy can and does lead to significant further developments of structure and style.

Two of the most important buildings in modern architectural history are found in most of the basic textbooks on the subject: Mies's prismatic and curved glass skyscraper projects (unbuilt) of 1919 and 1920–21. On the Chicago horizon now there is a curved glass building, Lake Point Tower, by second-generation architects Schipporeit and Heinrich. It is, almost, the dream realized. It is still considerably less than the dream. Mies's dream of perfection is elusive and vulnerable and, except for fellow professionals, too rarely recognized by his contemporaries. History will see him as one of that small body of men after whom the world is never the same again.

Preservation

Lively Original Versus Dead Copy

SAN Francisco has finally demolished what may have been the world's most romantic modern ruin—Bernard Maybeck's crumbling chicken wire, lath and plaster Palace of Fine Arts, a beloved, elegant bit of Corinthian-classic pastry erected for the Panama Pacific Exposition of 1915. A replica in steel and concrete will replace it.

"Let the thing fall down in peace," said Maybeck before he died in 1957. But its admirers had other ideas. Why not raze the disintegrating old landmark and build a new one just like it?

Alas, we can think of many reasons why not. They have to do with the value of a lively original versus a dead copy, the integrity of a work of art as expressive of its time, the folly of second-hand substitutes for first-rate inventions, the esthetics and ethics of duplication measured against the creative act.

We can think of only one reason to justify rebuilding the lovely, evanescent structure. It can stand as a $7.7 million monument and symbol of a current attitude toward the architecture of the past so fallacious, so insidious and so dangerous that those of us who have helped nurture the preservation movement in this country can do little more than weep.

Theoretically, this is the moment of triumph. The preservation

210

ball is begining to roll after a long, uphill fight. New York City
has a landmarks law. The Federal Government has named Brooklyn
Heights a registered National Historic Landmark equal to Boston's
Beacon Hill. Concern for the national architectural heritage is flowering in the public consciousness and action has started in many
communities.

The tragedy is that it seems to be starting off briskly in the
wrong direction. The only triumph right now is the archaeological
fake, or reconstruction. This is a newly built scholarly copy of an
old building that does nothing to save anything from the bulldozer.

For every Brooklyn Heights, which preserves a historic continuity of real buildings of the real past, there are numerous projects that will put up brand-new "aged" imitations mixed with a
few dislocated victims of throughways or urban renewal for spuri-
ously quaint little groups of instant history in sterile isolation.
Across the country the genuine heritage of the nineteenth century
is still being razed to be replaced by elaborately rebuilt synthetic
eighteenth-century stage sets more pleasing to twentieth-century
taste.

This disease, which we have previously called galloping res-
torationitis, evades the sticky problem of saving the real thing by
letting it be bulldozed and putting up a copy at a more convenient
time or place. This way, the real estate man can have his cake,
and the preservationists can eat it. What they are eating, of course,
is crow. The result is a lot of sham history and sham art. And it
is receiving massive infusions of some of the country's best philanthropic money.

The unwitting source of the infection has been the suave,
scholarly and phenomenally successful restoration of Colonial Williamsburg. To point this out, as we have learned painfully, is equated
with a kind of treason.

Nevertheless, Williamsburg is an extraordinary, conscientious
and expensive exercise in historical playacting in which real and
imitation museum treasures and modern copies are carelessly confused in everyone's mind. Partly because it is so well done, the
end effect has been to devalue authenticity and denigrate the genuine heritage of less picturesque periods to which an era and a
people gave real life. This alone is history. The rest is wishful
thinking, or in plainer words, corruption of preservation's legitimate aims.

Architecture

Today a majority of the country's projected preservation proposals are heavily dependent on copies and costumed atmosphere. Ambitious plans start with restoration of existing buildings and then tip the balance to the deliberate manufacture of "authentically reconstructed" landmarks and synthetic style. In New York the outstanding quasi-historical monument is Fraunces Tavern. It is every schoolchild's eighteenth-century touchstone. Fraunces Tavern is not an eighteenth-century building at all. This "landmark" was built in 1907 virtually from scratch, starting with a few old timbers. It gives schoolchildren a fair idea of what a Georgian building looked like and it gives local businessmen a fair lunch. But it is not old, it is not authentic, and under no circumstances is this kind of thing preservation.

Preservation, according to the National Trust for Historical Preservation, which has listed official definitions and priorities, is the retention and repair of genuine old buildings that still stand.

Restoration, given second priority by the Trust, is the more extensive work of putting a deteriorated landmark back in condition.

Reconstruction, at the bottom of the Trust list, is the erection of a modern copy of a no longer existing structure on the basis of educational value. It is justified only when all else fails.

Preservation is the job of finding ways to keep those original buildings that provide the city's character and continuity and of incorporating them into its living mainstream. This is not easy. It is much simpler to move a few historical castoffs into quarantine, putting the curious little "enclave," or cultural red herring, off limits to the speculative developer while he gets destructive carte blanche in the rest of the city.

There is no cause for optimism in New York. In addition to the economic problem of making the past work in this peculiar city, there is also the chilling certainty that philosophically and nationally we are heading the wrong way.

A Vision of Rome Dies

Pennsylvania Station succumbed to progress at the age of fifty-six, after a lingering decline. The building's facade was shorn of its

Demolition of New York's Penn Station
(THE NEW YORK TIMES BY JACK MANNING)

eagles and ornament. The last wall went not with a bang, or a whimper, but to the rustle of real estate stock shares. The passing of Penn Station was more than the end of a landmark. It made the priority of real estate values over preservation conclusively clear. It confirmed the demise of an age of opulent elegance, of conspicuous, magnificent spaces, rich and enduring materials, the monumental civic gesture and extravagant expenditure for esthetic ends. Obsolescence is not limited to land use and building function in New York.

It was still the Gilded Age in 1910 when the building was completed by McKim, Mead and White, one of the turn-of-the-century's most gilt-edged architectural firms. There was plush in the Pullmans, crisp damask in the diners, silver bud vases on tables, and the New York-bound traveler debouched into a Roman tepidarium.

Modeled after the warm room of the Baths of Caracalla, the station's concourse was longer than the nave of St. Peter's in Rome. Its vaulted ceilings were 138 feet high, and its grand staircase was forty feet wide.

The soot-stained travertine of the interiors, reputed to be the first used in this country, was from quarries in Tivoli employed in building the Eternal City. Its mellow, golden-cream was used in the Colosseum in the first century A.D. and St. Peter's fifteen centuries later. New York could be called the Mortal Metropolis.

Six murals by Jules Guérin, huge topographical maps of Pennsy territory in sky blues, pale browns and yellow, high in the reaches of the massive walls, gradually disappeared under layers of the same soot. Generous deposits turned the exterior Massachusetts granite from warm pink to dingy gray. Now marble pomp has been reduced to rubble; stone to dust.

Today there are new symbols for a new age. The modern traveler, fed on frozen flight dinners, enters the city, not in Roman splendor, but through the bowels of a streamlined concrete bird, as at Trans World Airlines' Kennedy International airport terminal. Classical columns are replaced by catenary curves.

Architects' conceits may change, but businessmen remain the same. Alexander Cassatt, an extremely astute businessman and head of the Pennsylvania Railroad when the station was designed, wanted to build a hotel on the valuable air rights over the terminal.

214

His architect dissuaded him, arguing that the railroad owed the city a "thoroughly and distinctly monumental gateway."

As Lewis Mumford has observed. "Professional and civic pride won out over cupidity."

It was a shaky victory that lasted only fifty years. A soiled, symbolic gateway has been carted to the scrap heap and its replacement is the Madison Square Garden sports and entertainment center connected to a twenty-nine-story office building. Land values and air rights have pushed the main concourse completely underground. The style is not Roman Imperial, but Investment Modern.

The station's decline began long before demolition. As time passed and grime gathered, life and architecture became noticeably less grand.

The Great Depression made the once-elegant terminal a home for the homeless, its increasing shabbiness and sense of inert time and the stale chill of hopeless winter nights immortalized by William Faulkner when he wrote:

> In the rotunda, where the people appeared as small and intent as ants, the smell and sense of snow still lingered, though high now among the steel girders, spent and vitiated and filled with a weary and ceaseless murmuring, like the voices of pilgrims upon the infinite plain, like the voices of all the travelers who have ever passed through . . .

With the return of prosperity, and the traveler, demolition by commercialization began. Colored ads appeared like blasphemous utterances in the marbled halls; automobiles revolved on turntables; shops and stands were added in jazzy cacophony.

In 1958 a huge, lighted plastic clamshell was hung on wires from the Corinthian columns, hovering over a saw-tooth arrangement of new ticket booths. The result, according to Mr. Mumford, was sabotage, a "masterpiece of architectural and visual incongruity."

By 1963, when a group of prominent architects and citizens picketed the building to protest the announcement of the decision to demolish, it was hard to realize, with Philip Johnson, "that man can build nobly," in the light of the esthetic debris.

Functionally, the station was considerably less than noble. The complexity and ambiguity of its train levels and entrances and exits were a constant frustration. Except for its great glass and iron waiting room, it was a better expression of ancient Rome than of twentieth-century America.

But its great spaces and superb materials were genuinely noble, in a sense that architecture can no longer afford, in cubage costs alone. The new terminal has nine-to-twenty-two-foot ceilings, against the original 138, all below grade. And the concept was noble, in a sense that society now tragically undervalues.

In 1906, when the $25 million hole was dug in the old Tenderloin district for the $112 million terminal and landmark, the city's and the railroad's sights were high. Now dreams of urban glory and broken Doric columns lie shattered in the Secaucus Meadows.

Where Ghosts Can Be at Home

There are no flags flying to mark it, but a battle has been won in New York. After years of callous wholesale destruction of the city's architectural heritage there is now a near-total reversal of official policy toward the past.

The Housing and Development Agency, the city's superbuilding department, has asked for and is currently getting from the Landmarks Preservation Commission reports on what should be saved, historically and architecturally, in the city's twenty-five urban renewal areas. The City Planning Commission has selected a waterfront site for urban renewal designation in Lower Manhattan, with preservation as a prime objective.

In its lucid, readable report on the Washington Street renewal area, the Landmarks Commission makes this statement: "The report itself is a landmark. This is the first time in New York City that a government agency charged with the task of historic preservation has been required to report to the agency in charge of urban development."

Asking for professional guidance sounds about as simple and logical as coming in out of the rain. But although expertise has always been generously available in New York, it has been conspicuously unwanted in city circles.

The city's action comes only after twenty years of ruthless and indiscriminate bulldozing of Manhattan's most historic areas carried out with a singleminded insensitivity compounded about equally of bureaucracy and ignorance. It took fifteen years of that time to get a landmarks law and commission, an achievement that surprised a lot of professional New York cynics.

Remember Brooklyn Bridge South? The city crushed the life and color out of it and handed the wreckage to the developers for urban renewal superblocks. We won't bore you with the losses again; they are recorded in New York histories and architectural textbooks. They are also preserved on hundreds of feet of underground movies and uncounted photographs by artists, historians and observers of the New York scene who roamed the rosy brick rubble —there is no brick quite as handsome as that of the eighteenth and early nineteenth centuries—with recording film and grim despair. (You meet some of the most interesting people on demolition sites.)

Early-nineteenth-century houses
in Washington Market
(THE NEW YORK TIMES BY SAM FALK)

Architecture

In the old, established order of things the Washington Street site, which included the Washington Market, would have gone exactly the same way—and most of it did.

It may be an indulgence to point out, for that useless thing called history, that the old Washington Market, now semi-demolished as part of a thirty-eight-acre renewal area, was a very special place, like Covent Garden in London or Les Halles in Paris, the latter also on the way out. (There is already a frozen-food teeny-bopper generation that never knew it.)

Not only were its shabby "genteel" brick houses and commercial buildings, which ranged from the eighteenth through the mid-nineteenth centuries, similar in material, scale and style, but they had accumulated an extraordinarily handsome set of spontaneous graphics in the signs painted on the old houses.

The area was "redolent," in the Landmarks Commission's word, of old New York, and equally redolent of garlic and pearly onions, and gleaming with the fresh color of avocados, tomatoes and egg-plants. It was filled with the bustle of early dawn activity for a city still stonily asleep. Hopelessly non-functional for the twentieth century and, we assume, now happily transferred to safe, sanitary and totally steril in every sense of the word new accomodations in the Bronx, the old market had Hogarthian energy and Georgian style.

The Landmarks Preservation Commission has recommended strongly that a group of six virtually intact early-nineteenth-century houses in the market—some of the oldest in New York—be preserved and ultilized in any redevelopment scheme.

They are at 29, 31 and 33 Harrison Street and 327, 329 and 331 Washington Street, between Harrison and Jay. They form a corner and an almost complete block. It has also suggested that three more houses, 314, 315 and 317 Washington Street, on the block below, be moved, if possible, to fill out the block. It has further been urged that the city's earliest remaining cast-iron front, erected in 1848 by New York's innovating builder James Bogardus, be dismantled and re-used in some fashion.

The Housing and Development Agency has accepted these recommendations. It has announced officially that any "sponsor" will be required to find a use for the Harrison-Jay Street row and must restore the houses as part of its bargain with the city.

Certainly the houses are shabby and derelict to the average eye. But even to the average eye it is clear that this group of buildings, again in the words of the Landmarks Commission, suggest "an earlier time and a different way of life." Behind the grime and commercial remodeling are the dormered roofline, the domestic two and a half stories, the Flemish bond brick, the dentil cornices, splayed, double keystones and incised block lintels that are the delight of those who collect rare examples of the stylistic past.

Just across Lower Manhattan the City Planning Commission is including an eleven-block, thirty-eight-acre site for renewal that will focus on the early-nineteenth-century Schermerhorn row at Fulton and South streets on the East River. This group of buildings is one of the few that still evoke sailing-age New York. In this case, preservation is not incidental to the project; it is its purpose.

The restoration area, to include a South Street Maritime Museum and sailing ships anchored at the foot of Fulton Street, is being sponsored by the South Street Seaport, Inc., a private preservation group. The city's renewal role will be to make land assembly possible. The kind of faith, hope and civilized vision that New Yorkers are not supposed to have got the ball rolling, and now the city has picked it up.

We need both the South Street and Washington Street projects. They are only a drop in the bucket of what has already been destroyed. Both have the singular virtue of being *in situ* preservation—original buildings still on their original sites. Nothing beats keeping the old city where it belongs and where its ghosts are at home.

But unless enough instances of the old city are integrated with new construction, there will be no real urban continuity or economic reality. We will simply have acquired an occasional embalmed architectural freak. The objective of preservation is the retention of the full range of styles, sensations and references that record the city's history and achievements visually and environmentally to keep them in the city's vital mainstream.

So please, gentlemen, no horse-drawn cars, no costumes, no wigs, no stage sets, no cute-old-stores, no "re-creations" that never were, no phony little-old-New York. There is a tendency in American restoration for corn to conquer all. In Europe old buildings are

Old Fulton Street houses for Seaport Museum
(JERRY DAVIS)

used naturally and normally, not reduced to cultural kitsch. That is perversion, not preservation.

The past becomes real by its legitimate and handsome contrasts with the present. Give us the best of contemporary style, life and uses in the old buildings. Now that we have won the battle, let's not lose the war.

Where Did We Go Wrong?

The following item was not invented by some gifted pixie mentality; it is from *Preservation News,* published by the National Trust for Historic Preservation. The National Trust would not put you on. We quote:

> Babe Ruth's birthplace and a few neighboring properties were recently purchased by the city of Baltimore for $1,850. The home of one of baseball's immortals is located on Emory Street, a narrow alley of humble row houses. The Mayor's Committee for the Preservation of Babe Ruth's Birthplace is now debating whether to leave the house at its present location or to move it and the neighboring houses to a site adjoining Memorial Stadium, to be part of the Babe Ruth Plaza. Vandalism in the present neighborhood has prompted the committee to resolve "to restore the house at its present location only if environmental amenities are found to be reasonable." The inaccesibility of Emory Street is also cited as a reason to move the house elsewhere. However, Emory Street is too narrow to move the house intact and dismantling would be the only solution.

It reads exactly as if Lewis Carroll wrote it.

"Leave the house where it is," said the Red Queen. "I can't," said Alice. "It's inaccessible and there's vandalism." "Then get some environmental amenities," said the Red Queen, "and be quick about it." "What are environmental amenities?" asked Alice. "Don't ask foolish questions; just move the house," said the Red Queen. "But the street is too narrow," said Alice. "Nonsense," said the Red Queen, "don't you know anything? Take the house apart and put it back together again. And move the rest of the houses with it." "Poor things," said Alice. "Where to?" "To the Memorial Stadium, naturally," said the Red Queen, "and call it Babe Ruth Plaza." "Couldn't we just leave it?" asked Alice. "If you do," said the Red Queen, "you will have to take out the other houses and put up a sign, 'No Ball Playing Allowed.'" "Mightn't 'Ballplayers Welcome' be better?" said Alice.

Alas, it is not straight out of *Through the Looking-Glass;* it is straight out of life. And if it sounds like parody, that is exactly what much of the preservation movement has become. It is game-playing. The game as it is played—by a strict set of rules—is to seal off historic buildings from the contemporary environment in a vacuum of assiduous make-believe.

The process ranges from babes in Babe-Ruth-land to the phenomenon of Williamsburg, where the art of scholarly self-delusion reaches the extravagantly ($79 million) sublime. It deals in "cutoff dates," which means ruthlessly destroying anything later than a certain arbitrarily selected year that interferes with the illusion desired, and "restoring back," a horrendous process of faking the chosen period by removing all subsequent accumulations of time and history. The final perversion is "reconstruction," or rebuilding things that no longer exist, and that, if you take the blinders off for a moment, merely means putting up brand-new "old" buildings, which, no matter how carefully researched and how admirable the educational motives, is a contradiction in terms and values that shows how sick the whole thing has become.

"I say the moon is made of green cheese and this is the eighteenth century," the sponsors of these historical "enclaves" (a favorite euphemism) of the studiously unreal tell us. No matter how you slice it, it is still green cheese, and you can slice it many ways, from Strawberry Banke to Old Sacramento. The point is that the whole idea and purpose of preservation—saving the past because it is part of the living heritage of the present, so that the process of history enriches the city and the environment—has been lost.

The result is a cross between playacting in the name of history (and the lesson being taught is curiously subversive if one still equates education with traditional values of truth and, by extension, morality, or knowing what is true or false) and a museum of period arts. The inevitable conflict set up between the forms of the past and the uses of the present—a conflict denied overtly but carefully and often comically disguised to accommodate the tourist trade—is an abrasive anachronism. It all dead-ends in a head-on clash of new, old, and new-made-to-seem-old for which there is no solution except playing the game harder, increasing the make-believe and the confusions of real and reproduction, not for a living lie, but for something that is a dead lie at best.

The tragedy is that this concept has become so popular that it has almost totally aborted the proper approach to the conservation of our urban heritage. The purpose of preservation is not to "re-create" the past, a laughable impossibility filled with booby traps like the lady in saddle shoes, harlequin glasses and hoop skirt who shattered this observer's first schoolgirl visit to Williamsburg. (No, changing the shoes and glasses wouldn't fix up anything at all; you really couldn't restore the lady back.)

More shattering, on a much later visit, was the lack of information from guides as to what was authentic and what was not, since obviously no distinction was made in their own minds between copies and genuine survivals. Even the survivals have been so smoothed up that the line gets fuzzy. To them, it was all real. Actually, nothing is real except those buildings that have lasted a couple of centuries, gathering a significant patina of changing American culture (stripped, naturally) and the collections of furnishings that are curatorial triumphs, deliciously arranged to simulate someone's personal possessions by a well-researched extension of wishful-think.

It is all art and artifice and the finest green cheese. It is a beautifully hollow stage-set shell, totally removed from the life-force of the society that gave it form and meaning. A little fudging for effect hardly matters. (Please don't write, oh superpatriots, to tell me that I am simultaneously sullying both Williamsburg and the American flag; it is not treason to look art and history in the eye. I value both beyond the call of tourism.)

What preservation is really all about is the retention and active relationship of the buildings of the past to the community's functioning present. You don't erase history to get history; a city's character and quality are a product of continuity. You don't get any of it with "enclaves" in quarantine. What a cut-off date cuts off is any contact with the present at all. In urban terms, preservation is the saving of the essence and style of other eras, through their architecture and urban forms, so that the meaning and flavor of those other times and tastes are incorporated into the mainstream of the city's life. The accumulation is called culture.

In New York the sentiment for preservation is a relatively new thing. The city has never preserved anything. Its nature is to destroy, build and change. New Yorkers are not antiquarians and that is part of their pride and strength. To be successful in New York, preservation must strike a singular balance with this spirit; even the past must face the future.

The challenge is to make the city's heritage a working part of the dynamic vitality and brutal beauty of this strange and wonderful town. And above all, to make it New York.

This Time Everyone Wins

This tale is called how to have your cake and eat it, too. It is a classic American urban drama of the bulldozer versus progress in which, for a change, everybody wins. It is the story of the new Albany headquarters for the New York State Bar Association.

The story ended with the unveiling of a project for a building complex that is a sophisticated triumph in that most delicate, complex and poorly understood art of the environment: urban design. It did not start that way. It began with everyone on collision course, or completely normally for any American city.

In April, 1968, the New York State Bar Association announced that it had negotiated the purchase of 2, 3 and 4 Elk Street, adjacent to the State Capitol and to court buildings, and would demolish the houses for its new headquarters, to be designed by New York architect James Stewart Polshek. The lawyers were quite certain that they wanted a fine, new, modern building.

Elk Street, or what remains of its iron-trimmed, four-story brick-row houses of the 1830's, is Henry James Albany—evocations

224

Design for State Bar Building, Albany

of another age when the city combined traditional society and gubernatorial politics in more gracious surroundings and at a more stately pace. The houses face Academy Park and hold a tenuous line for period amenity against institutional encroachment. The street and its houses were designated as landmarks by Albany's Historic Sites Commission created in 1966.

Instant outcry followed the lawyers' announcement. With every "good" intention of making the new structure "blend" with

225

what would be left of a then totally decimated row—other parts have already been violated—the lawyers never knew what really hit them. What hit them immediately was the Albany Historic Sites Commission. This protest was followed by the concern of the Hudson River Valley Commission and a continuous barrage from the local papers, the *Times-Union* and the *Knickerbocker News*.

The Hudson River Valley Commission is a state agency that has the right to hold public hearings and review projects within one to two miles of the river from its source to Lower Manhattan, to determine whether they would have an "adverse effect on the valley's resources." Although its powers and recommendations are only advisory, its functions were invoked.

A hearing was held on April 15, and sentiment for preservation ran strong. The Albany Historic Sites Commission was joined by the New York State Council on the Arts, the Albany County Historical Association, the Center Square Association, the Schenectady Historical Society, the Eastern New York Association of Architects and an assortment of public and private persons from Mayor Erastus Corning to those who felt, not always with as much clarity as conviction, that there was something important on Elk Street that ought not to go.

Without the ultimate cooperation of those whose action is being questioned, this show of sentiment means nothing. The Hudson River Valley Commission held a similar hearing last fall in Troy, N.Y., where feeling ran just as high for keeping a far handsomer street of unified brownstones called Doctors' Row, which the local renewal agency planned to demolish for a dismal new doctors' building. The commission recommended against demolition, and after a brief academic pause for a non-materializing sponsor, the city bulldozed, anyway. (The neolithic planning policies and practices of small-city urban renewal in the United States is a sad subject in itself.)

The Albany houses individually are not architectural gems or notable historical monuments. The cry, as is so often the case in American cities, was "They may not be great, but they're the best we've got." The real point was made in hearing testimony by Bernd Foerster, professor of architecture at Troy's Rensselaer Polytechnic Institute, who stated that the significance of Elk Street far exceeds the importance of the separate structures. This was sensed by others who saw the street as the increasingly rare, still-living fabric of another, past life-style of the city that it would be infinitely poorer without.

To the trained eye it was a classic case of urban design. The values involved were the qualities of streetscape, through special period scale and character, and the role of the whole row as a "wall" or strengthening space enclosure for the park and as an "anchoring point" for the State Capitol complex and Albany's past. What was significant was the cultural, esthetic, historical and human sum of the parts. These are the concerns of the professional urban designer that add up to felicities of scale, style and ambience, which are a large part of what environment is all about. It is very rarely about monuments or single masterpieces.

To make a long story short, the lawyers got the message. They did more than that; their architect set to work to make a valid use of the old buildings without sacrificing a proper solution of the Bar Association's modern needs.

The result is a demonstration project of how to use the past without turning it into a charade and how to extend its fabric functionally into the twentieth century for the best kind of living environmental continuity. The philosophical and design lesson here is of national importance. So is the lesson for preservation.

There is, too, the inevitable note of irony. After fruitless attempts to find someone who would save its old, outgrown headquarters, the Bar Association sold its landmark building on Washington Street—built in 1789 and later remodeled—to a real estate developer who has demolished it for a twenty-two-story office building.

The idea of merely retaining the Elk Street facades and destroying everything behind them was rejected immediately as "false-face preservation" by the architect. What Mr. Polshek has done is to keep the main part of the houses, to a depth of about thirty feet, and to use those nineteenth-century front parlors for reception space, a conference room and the president's office.

Behind these handsome rooms there will be a glass-enclosed corridor, facing a multi-level open plaza and the new building, joined to the old ones by another connecting corridor. The landscaped plaza between will provide entrance to both new and old structures.

227

Architecture

The new building will be uncompromisingly new. Its deference to the old ones will not be in the kind of copying or "adapting" of style or details that leads to smug architectural pratfalls but in a basic sympathy for scale and compatible contrast. The bulk, for one thing, will be broken into three stepped, skylit structures: one for reception, the second for a thirty-five-to-forty-foot-high grand hall for meetings and group functions, the third for offices. The design is a conscious accommodation of the best of both worlds.

There will be approximately 30,000 square feet of space and the cost will be something over $1 million. The cost is higher than for demolishing and building new, but the Bar Association could not buy the luster added to its institutional image. About 85 per cent of its functions will be in the carefully programed new space, the rest in the old houses. There is no sacrifice of utility to antiquarianism. And it all works.

It works in a creative, contemporary solution of sensibility and cultural maturity that promises richness, interest and a variety of pleasurable environmental experiences embracing past and present that should be a prime objective of twentieth-century urban design. We hope the lawyers live happily ever after.

Culture Is as Culture Does

After fifty years of life and twenty years of death the great Adler and Sullivan Auditorium in Chicago is back in business again. Orchestra Hall, also in Chicago, was beautifully spruced up for its sixty-eighth birthday. In St. Louis a 1925 movie palace has been successfully transformed into Powell Symphony Hall, complete with handsome bar from New York's demolished Metropolitan Opera House.

In New York a few years ago, Carnegie Hall was rescued from the developers and refurbished. A lot of musicians would still rather play there than in the new, acoustically and esthetically controversial Philharmonic Hall that almost sealed its doom. In Brooklyn the Academy of Music is being quietly restored to its original turn-of-the-century elegance.

Restored Auditorium Theater in Chicago
(RICHARD NICKEL)

Sentimentalism? Hardly. This is no more than a practical coming of cultural age, a belated recognition that fine old buildings frequently offer the most for the money in an assortment of values, including cost, and above all, that new cultural centers do not a culture make. It indicates the dawning of certain sensibilities, perspectives and standards without which arts programs are mockeries of everything the arts stand for.

229

Architecture

The last decade has seen city after city rush pell-mell into the promotion of great gobs of cultural real estate. It has seen a few good new theaters and a lot of bad ones, temples to bourgeois muses with all the panache of suburban shopping centers. The practice has been to treat the arts in chamber of commerce, rather than in creative, terms. That is just as tragic as it sounds.

The trend toward preservation is significant not only because it is saving and restoring some superior buildings that are testimonials to the creative achievements of other times, but also because it is bucking the conventional wisdom of the conventional power structure that provides the backing for conventional cultural centers to do it.

That wisdom, as it comes true-blue from the hearts and minds of real estate dealers and investment bankers, is that you don't keep old buildings; they are obsolete. Anything new is better than anything old and anything big is better than anything small and if a few cultural values are lost along the way it is not too large a price to pay. In addition, the new, big buildings must be all in one place so they will show. They'll not only serve the arts, they'll improve the surrounding property values. Build now, and fill them later.

At the same time, tear down the past, rip out cultural roots, erase tradition, rub out the architectural evidence that the arts flowered earlier in our cities and enriched them and that this enrichment is culture. Substitute a safe and sanitary status symbol for the loss. Put up the shiny mediocrities of the present and demolish the shabby masterpieces of the past. This is the ironic other side of the "cultural explosion" coin. In drama, and in life, irony and tragedy go hand in hand.

Chicago's Auditorium is such a masterpiece. With its glowing, golden ambiance, its soaring arches and superstage from which whispers can be heard in the peanut gallery, it became a legend in its own time. One of the great nineteenth-century works of Louis Sullivan and Dankmar Adler and an anchor point of modern architectural history, it has been an acknowledged model of acoustical and esthetic excellence. (Interestingly, it is a hard theater to "mike" today, and many modern performers, untrained in balance and projection and reliant on technical mixing of sound, find it hard to function in a near-perfect house.)

230

Until October, 1967, the last performance at the Auditorium was of *Hellzapoppin'* in 1941, and the last use of the great stage was for U.S.O. bowling alleys during the war. Closed after that, it settled into decay for the next twenty years. Falling plaster filled the hall and the golden ceiling was partly ruined by broken roof drains.

Last fall the Auditorium reopened, not quite in its old glory, but close to it. The splendors of the house were traced in the eight-candlepower glory of carbon filament light bulbs of the same kind used in 1889 when the theater, and electricity, were new. Their gentle brilliance picked out restored arches, balcony curves, frescoed lunettes, stenciled traceries and plaster friezes in warm gilt and umber.

The story of the Auditorium's death and resurrection is another of life's little cultural ironies.

In 1904 the Chicago Symphony moved to the new, smaller Orchestra Hall. In 1929 the Chicago Opera pulled out for Samuel Insull's opera house on Wacker Drive. A 4,237-seat house, minus symphony and opera, was hard to fill, then and now. But the Auditorium was never meant to be profitable; that was why Adler and Sullivan encased it in a hotel and office structure to carry it commercially, and this did work for a while. Then only the Auditorium's formidable granite walls kept it from being torn down.

In 1957 the building was acquired and the commercial parts used by Roosevelt University. In 1960 the university created the Auditorium Theater Council, a legal act that made it possible to turn the theater over to a private group for restoration and operation. The council was headed by Mrs. John V. Spachner, whose lifelong dream it had been to bring the Auditorium back to life.

It took seven years, against all kinds of odds, to do the job. It had to be done on a hard cash, pay-as-you-go basis, because the council, in order to protect the university, its trustees and council members from liabilities due to loans, contracts or theater operation, is prohibited legally from spending anything except money actually in hand. This is a continuing impediment.

Fund-raising ran into trouble immediately when it was announced that the new McCormack Place convention hall would include a 5,000-seat theater. When it was built, it turned out to be an acoustical dud, and the whole thing subsequently burned down. But the biggest blow came in 1962, with the feasibility study of the council's architectural consultants, Skidmore, Owings and Merrill. For a fee of $50,000 they told the group that it would cost $4¼ million to restore the building and that it was structurally unsound.

Another Chicago architect and Auditorium buff, Harry Weese, who has also refurbished Orchestra Hall, was certain that the building was solid. He wrote to the council, offering to help without charge, and his answer was his appointment as head of the building committee. The final answer, with theater and engineering consultants George Izenour and Fred N. Severud, using valuable information in the S.O.M. study and historical research by Crombie Taylor, is a sound, functioning house for just over $2 million. It raises a healthy skepticism about other it-can't-be-done preservation studies.

Pay as you go has left some gaps. Originally, almost every inch of flat wall was covered with Sullivan's characteristic laced, gold stencil ornament, and the luster of the house is considerably dimmer without it. Mechanical features are incomplete. But the work will go on.

In New York the same kind of thing is being achieved without fanfare at the Brooklyn Academy of Music. A quasi-public institution, it is being restored over a ten-year period by a team of young architects, MacFadyen and Knowles, with city money, under Parks Department aegis.

We have never had greater technical means or expertise to make our landmarks bloom. The question is no longer whether we can bring old theaters back to new brilliance but whether we can fill them when they're done. As with the new centers, that will be the acid cultural test.

Anatomy of a Failure

There is no art as impermanent as architecture. All that solid brick and stone mean nothing. Concrete is as evanescent as air. The monuments of our civilization stand, usually, on negotiable real estate; their value goes down as land value goes up.

A typical statement of a major corporation, made with the utmost candor and the conviction of the true faith, is that land value is the whole bit. It would be irrelevant if the site contained the Kingdom of God. The logic and the mathematics are immutable.

In addition to land economics, buildings, even great ones, become obsolete. Their functions and technology date. They reach a point of comparative inefficiency, and inefficiency today is both a financial and a mortal sin.

It would be so simple if art also became obsolete. But a building that may no longer work well or pay its way may still be a superb creative and cultural achievement. It may be the irreproducible record of the art and ideals of a master or an age. Its concept, craft, materials and details may be irreplaceable at any price (yes, some things are without price and that puts them at a distinct disadvantage) and therein lies the conflict and dilemma of preservation.

Frank Lloyd Wright's Imperial Hotel in Tokyo was an extraordinary record of the coordinated architectural and decorative arts of a single period, carried out in 1,009 days of on-site work by one of the great architects of all time. Fifty years later it was obsolete by current standards, as land use and as an operating hotel. It took less than four months to demolish what took four years and an astronomical, for that time, $4,750,000 to build.

What is the point in writing about it now? Does it have any more than the grisly fascination of post-mortem? Actually, it is a terrifyingly revealing chronicle of some of the preservation problems of our time. It could be called the anatomy of failure.

The wrecking ball swung from 8 A.M. to midnight from November 15 until almost the day that ground was broken, with appropriate Shinto rites, for a new, seventeen-story, $55 million, 1,000-room hotel, on February 28, 1968.

Furnishings, including some of the famous Wright-designed fittings, were rushed without notice to a Nagoya department store and sold as second-hand goods. It all went in forty-five minutes, cheap; Wright's peacock chairs sold for a dollar. Almost everything else, with classic Japanese neatness and efficiency, was baled, wrapped or tied in piles of copper (cornices, lighting fixtures), wood (grills, trim) or whatever, and sold as scrap. The heavier rubble made landfill. Some carved stone was saved; examples will go to

the State University at Buffalo, where Wright's Martin House of 1904 is being restored.

As a result of desperate preservation efforts which read like a bad script, part of a central section of the building may be re-erected in the Meiji Village fifteen miles north of Nagoya. This is a 128-acre outdoor museum of eighteen reconstructed buildings of the period from 1868 to 1912. (This equivocal triumph hung fire for a while because the Wright building was too late in date, but it was finally accepted.) Even that gesture is contingent on rais-ing funds.

For once, everyone had been well alerted by the press, begin-ning with Tokyo newspapers in March of last year. After some initial difficulty in getting interested persons together, the Commit-tee for the Preservation of the Imperial Hotel was organized and met in July. In October Mrs. Wright arrived on the scene, as head of the American branch of the committee. She was followed by a stream of visitors who came with everything but money.

Even as late as November, the committee's pitch was for re-taining the whole structure on its site. In November the Architec-tural Institute of Japan supported the cause with a report and reso-lutions also urging *in situ* preservation.

No one had spoken officially to the hotel management, which was understandably skittish. A meeting was finally arranged in November through the Ministry of Education's National Committee for Protection of Important Cultural Properties. Imperial President Tetsuzo Inumaru was adamant. The hotel was coming down. The committee proposed an alternative: move the whole structure to another site. Estimates were over $4 million. The committee was given until January 15 to arrange to move at least part of the build-ing; after that date demolition would be completed.

The timetable, of course, was impossible. So were the eco-nomics. Less than $10,000 had been raised internationally by the committee. Even the cost of saving ninety-seven carved stone samples came to $135,000, or about $1,350 for each piece, and the committee could not cover that.

The first failure, therefore, was one of objectives. At too late a date, totally unrealistic goals were being pursued. A hard look should have been taken at the facts of the situation and a feasible plan established. Some of the vast rambling building's interiors

Demolition of Frank Lloyd Wright's Imperial Hotel
in Tokyo (SETSUO SAITO)

with their remarkable architectural and sculptural details and furnishings—the peacock alleys, parts of public spaces—might have lent themselves to selective preservation. Under the pressures of time and money, this was the only sensible procedure.

There was a failure of communication, as well. Japanese bureaucracy is rigid; different government agencies that controlled land or museums or other possible aids simply did not negotiate. Moreover, as Professor Bunji Kobayashi, an architect closely involved in the preservation effort, points out, bureaucrats control the government tightly and "the voice of the intellectual community is seldom heeded. Some government figures feel that they lose face if they follow such outside voices."

There were also procedural failures. As the deadline approached, the committee found that it did not have the legal status to accept donations beyond small gifts. It was helpless either to take over the building or move it to another site, even if time or money had made either more than the wildest dream.

But the most tragic failure is of the whole American art and cultural establishment. It seems incredible that not a single foundation, not a single major museum, not a single large university, not a single cultural institution or agency, not a single philanthropist, saw the opportunity to select and preserve one part of one major spatial element, with its crafts and accessories, of one of the major works in American art history.

It was an unparalleled opportunity. While museums squabbled over acquiring the not-quite-prime glories of the Temple of Dendur and grants were given for still more theoretical studies, all were blind to the chance to add a meaningful part of a work of American creative genius, by one of the masters of the modern movement, to an American collection, at a moment in time when it could have been plucked for posterity. In the final analysis, the worst failure of all was the total absence of vision and value judgment where it should have existed, a serious and shameful indictment of our most illustrious institutions.

Anatomy of a Success

There is a ghost in the New York Shakespeare Festival Public Theatre at 425 Lafayette Street in New York, a most un-Shakespearean
ghost with the unlikely name of Austin L. Sands. Mr. Sands was
a nineteenth-century New York merchant and insurance man. As
reported by the diarist George Templeton Strong, "old Sands
spook" appeared to Joseph Cogswell, director of the Astor Library,
now Joseph Papp's New York Shakespeare Festival Public Theater,
three times in 1860.

By rights, Mr. Sands and Mr. Cogswell should have been
present at the opening of Mr. Papp's theater. This opening was a
very special occasion. It marked the transformation of the old Astor
Library into the new home of the Shakespeare Festival—the first
structure saved and remodeled for re-use under the New York Landmarks Law.

The merits of Mr. Papp's plays and the technical qualities of
the theater are the drama critic's responsibility. But as architectural
preservation—that combination of civilized sentiment and historic
sensibility that makes cities rich and real and has nothing to do with
real estate values that make cities rich and sterile—the new theater
is a heart-warming hit.

In the Astor Library's former main hall, a handsome, fifty-
foot-high, skylit chamber with a two-tiered row of classical cast-
iron colonnades built in 1851 and scheduled for demolition in 1965,
there is now one of the most delightful small theaters in New York.

(House seats, Mr. Papp, for John Jacob Astor, who left $400,000
in his will to construct the original building on then-fashionable
Lafayette Street, for William B. Astor, who added the south section
in 1859, and the later John Jacob Astor, who built the north wing
in 1881.)

The theater seats 299, not counting ghosts, and cost $445,000,
roughly the same price as the original building. "We were going
to have an 800-seat theater," Mr. Papp says, "but we got to love
that room. We were showing everyone that room and then we
were showing the plans that destroyed the room and we decided
against it."

Under the Landmarks Law, the exterior of a landmark building must be preserved, but there are no restrictions on interior remodeling.

Program credits should read architecture by Giorgio Cavaglieri; mechanical engineer, Nicola Ginzburg; structural engineer, James Hufnagle; contractor, Yorke Construction Company; theater designer, Ming Cho Lee; theater lighting, Martin Aronstein; acoustical consultant, Christopher Jaffe.

In what is now called the Florence Sutro Anspacher Theatre, steeply ranged red velvet seats lead down on three sides of the virtually intact main hall to a floor-level stage. Cream-white Victorian balustrades and columns with leafy cast-capitals have been restored and picked out in real gold leaf. "A quality decision," Mr. Papp explains. "The building kept forcing us into quality decision." (Sorry to add one more crack to the tiresome total about Lincoln Center, but most of the gold leaf there is fake.)

The old skylights in the gently curved ceiling have been cleaned and lit softly from behind. Red velvet curtains draw on motorized tracks backing the second-level colonnades.

On the fourth side of the room, behind the stage, two of the classical columns have been stripped down to their iron shafts and made part of a supporting structure for lights, sound baffles and a second-story catwalk.

All this "working equipment" is left bare and painted a deliberately contrasting black: modern structural "brutalism" played against genteel Victorian propriety. It is a theatrical exercise in the esthetics of contrast, and it works. The theater has beauty and charm. It says a lot, in succinct architectural terms, of change and continuity in slightly more than a century—one of the most fascinating centuries in the history of the adventure called civilization. Why does New York continue to throw it away?

During that century, visiting celebrities toured the Astor Library as one of the city's chief cultural attractions and found its skylit halls "bright as a house of glass." The building closed at sundown because it had no artificial light. Mr. Sands came later.

The book collections, according to a guide of the period, did not contain "all the treasures of the British Museum and the Bibliothèque Nationale," but, it added sanguinely, "that fact is not easily discovered." It scarcely matters now. The 200,000 books are scat-

Main hall of New York Shakespeare Festival Public Theater, formerly old Astor Library
(THE NEW YORK TIMES BY NEAL BOENZI)

tered to other library branches and the thousands of refugees are gone who passed through the building's halls from 1920 to 1965, when it served as headquarters for HIAS, the Hebrew Immigrant Aid Society.

What remains is the continuum called culture, the mixture of past and present, of art, history and humanity, of creative experiment and monumental elegance, that brings people to cities like lemmings to the sea. The strong survive and add to the urban heritage; the weak disappear forever into Uris buildings.

In January 1966, just after the Shakespeare Theater had arranged to purchase the Astor Library from an apartment house developer who had bought it from HIAS, with the eighteen-month-old Landmarks Commission as intermediary, this writer stood in the bone-cracking chill of the deserted and grimy north hall. There is nothing colder than death, and a dead landmark is no exception.

For $2,535 the north hall has been given fresh paint, gold curtains and new life. Some $61,490 will turn it into a fully rehabilitated rehearsal and recital hall. The almost identical south hall, still grimy, is a shop for sets. Both are acoustically excellent, spatially extravagant period gems, unreproduceable now, with the same skylit ceilings and double-tiered rows of classical colonnades as the new theater in the central hall.

In the partly refurbished lobby, brick arches at the rear are left pointedly bare. That will be $71,590 more. Below, carved out of solid masonry piers and arches, is the shell of a second 299-seat theater, shored up by wooden scaffolding while it waits for funds. With structural steel needed, it will cost $784,713. Approximately $1 million of an estimated total of $3 million has been spent; one year of a three-year restoration job is complete.

Outside, the solid brick and brownstone structure is untouched. It has been called "Italianate," "Byzantine," "Rundbogenstil" and "German Renaissance" by 113 years of scholars, admirers and detractors. Call it anything, but call it a success.

Coming of Architectural Age

Ten years ago, the two square blocks of solid sandstone, granite, brick and marble built and rebuilt as the Patent Office by Robert

240

Library of Smithsonian National Collection
of Fine Arts in the Old Patent Office
(THE NEW YORK TIMES BY GEORGE TAMES)

Mills, William Elliot, Edward Clark and others from 1836 through the 1880's, a monument in the noblest of Washington's classical styles, were scheduled to be pulverized and replaced by blacktop. To a lot of people, particularly parking lot operators, blacktop is the most beautiful thing in the world.

Ten years ago, the choice between landmark preservation and parking was made almost automatically in favor of the latter, and the ghosts of monuments past occupy parking lots in every American city. But the Old Patent Office cheated fate. Today it houses the Smithsonian Institution's National Collection of Fine Arts and the National Portrait Gallery.

In 1958 the Old Patent Office was given to the Smithsonian Institution. Six years and $6 million after conversion to a museum began, give or take a few unhappy Government Issue design details, the orphan Smithsonian art collection has acquired a stunning home, its first since the collection's founding in 1846.

To architectural historians, the building is a fine example of nineteenth-century style from Greek Revival to Victorian Renaissance. To management experts, whose pragmatism is usually matched only by their spiritual poverty, the name of the style is Waste Space.

Corridors, used as galleries, average seventeen feet wide and seventeen feet high. Where cool abstractions now hang, beds for the wounded and dying were improvised on the marble floors after Antietam and Bull Run.

The Lincoln Gallery, named for its use as the promenade for Lincoln's second inaugural ball, is approximately 60 by 300 feet and has sixty-four white marble columns and pilasters rising in cathedral-like groined vaults.

The present library, three stories high, elaborately balconied, colonnaded and skylit, is sumptuously Victorian; the kind of waste space (*vide* also the high-rising, marble-clad, mural-decorated rotundas of old courthouses and city halls) that makes men at least seem noble.

The building had been unbelievably abused. The great spaces were cut up into small Federal offices. One-eighth of an inch of government green paint had to come off those marble columns. The Granite Gallery, now used for sculpture, has heavy, square, gray granite columns and architraves that support solid brick barrel vaults, rediscovered in the paint-removing process.

The graceful stairs had elevators rammed into the stairwells. Marble floors were all but destroyed by partitions and electrical and heating conduits.

In the restoration and conversion, the government almost ruined the building again. As the Federal agency in charge of construction, the General Services Administration had the job of turning the Old Patent Office into a museum for the Smithsonian. Most of their work has had to be undone by the museum administration and its architectural consultant, Bayard Underwood.

The GSA knows how to build the world's most banal office buildings. It has cornered the market on all of the ugliest standard fixtures made anywhere, and no matter what architect designs the buildings it constructs in any city of the country, the G.I. equipment appears and covers them like a slow ooze. The thought of its warehouses is numbing.

As work proceeded on the new museum, office clocks were suddenly and mysteriously smacked into the center of sixty-foot exhibition walls. Fire hoses, alarms and air grilles were dotted about like Pop Art in prime exhibition spaces. Standard anemostats for the air-conditioning appeared like tin platters as the focal point where the handsome groined ceiling vaults meet.

But what should really be preserved in some branch of the Smithsonian (they were removed as rapidly as possible) is the all-purpose monster of a museum ceiling fixture devised by the GSA which runs on by the mile embroidered with endless outlets for plugging in the worst of everything ever designed for museum use. Its greatest feature was instant and total interior sabotage.

The new museum, therefore, is virtually a rescue operation. The clocks were pulled out and safety equipment moved when possible. Fluorescent fixtures by the yard have been replaced by curved lighting tracks that follow the line of the vaulted ceilings to hold a variety of incandescent spots. Considering the building's conversion history, the majority of the struggles between archeology and adaptation to modern use have been resolved successfully.

Until recently, mere magnificence was no reason for keeping an old landmark around. The Smithsonian has not only brought this

243

prime Robert Mills building back to life (he was also the architect of the Treasury Building and the Washington Monument) but has also undertaken the restoration of James Renwick's original Corcoran Gallery, the old Court of Claims, on Pennsylvania Avenue.

This may not be a preservation avalanche, but in government circles, where change comes like treacle and culture is often equally sticky, it is an indication that the United States is coming of architectural age.

The Past

The Curiously Contemporary Case of Sir John Soane

So you've seen swinging London. You've been to The Drugstore with its miniature mod rotunda wrapped in shiny brass walls, its pop clutter and vertical space bathed in rock sound—the multi-dimensional environment, the "now" esthetic, the new, new world. And because you're a card-carrying member of the over-thirty generation, you have the feeling that although it's fresh, and fun, it is scarcely revolutionary and that somewhere you've seen it all before.

Well, you have. In that early nineteenth-century swinger's pad, Sir John Soane's Museum—the curious house the famous English architect built and occupied from 1812 to 1837 for his home and personal collection of art and antiquities, preserved by an endowment in his will and by an act of Parliament.

Here are the miniature rotunda with its multi-dimensional effects of light and surface, the dramatic tricks with scale and space, the collector's clutter that outpops camp, the "now" esthetic of circa 1825. No rock—just a cacophony of clock chimes on the hour. There you have it, plus a few tricks the now generation still hasn't learned. The point here is not to offer redundant proof of that old chestnut that there is nothing new under the sun but that when Chelsea palls, non-swinging London still has a lot to offer and Sir John can make the present generation look pale.

The remarkable thing about the Soane Museum is not that this beautiful oddity is so little known but that it has become a pilgrim-

age point for today's architects, who find much to admire and to learn from this intensely personal memorial.

Soane is the English exemplar of the phase of late-eighteenth- and early-nineteenth-century transitional architecture known as romantic classicism. In France this movement produced Boullée's dreams of supercolossal funerary grandeur and Ledoux's colonnaded spheres; in England it is embodied in Soane's domed, skylit spaces that were the fruit of his search for "the poetry of architecture." The unorthodox work of this group is considered by architectural historians to be one of the significant moments in esthetic theory and practice. Its geometric severity and austerely smooth planes, the play of light on simplified, aggrandized classical forms used with bold and striking originality, made the break with tradition that opened the door to the modern revolution.

Soane's reputation has been higher outside of England than at home, and his influence is greater now than it ever was in the past. Few of his buildings still stand; of his masterpiece, the Bank of England, only the outside walls remain unchanged. His work has been characterized by Dorothy Stroud, author of *The Architecture of Sir John Soane,* as "highly idiosyncratic, sometimes hard to comprehend and always of interest."

The idiosyncrasies and interest are all present in the museum at 13 Lincoln's Inn Fields. The museum's curator, a position occupied by custom by a scholar of particular architectural eminence, is Sir John Summerson, historian, philosopher and critic of notable literary grace.

The building is a curiosity of such endearing strangeness, with passages of such imaginative fancy, that one feels oddly as if one might have dreamed the whole thing. But who could dream a monk's parlor and crypt and sepulchral chamber on the basement level, a passage of classical columns on the ground floor holding aloft a wall-less mezzanine drafting room, light shafting down from lateral skylights, a miniaturized dome over an open circular well surrounded by arched passages at two levels, every surface covered with fragments of antiquities and sculptural and architectural memorabilia overflowing into a monument court and monk's yard and tomb?

Soane had the magpie acquisitiveness of the cultivated nineteenth-century gentleman and professional with the means and taste to collect what the current sensibility admired. Coins, casts, columns and corbels, everything, from pieces of Greek friezes to an Egyptian

Sir John Soane's house and museum—
legacy of a nineteenth-century cultural magpie
(TRUSTEES OF SIR JOHN SOANE'S MUSEUM)

247

sarcophagus, is piled up with ordered surrealist splendor. Today's "environments" can't beat it.

The beauties as well as the curiosities are there, too. One notes the breakfast parlor in particular, with its delicately embellished flat-domed ceiling "like a rich canopy," in Soane's words, the room gently light-washed from a central lantern and high skylights at two sides, mirrors studding the arches and dome. This is an interior of magically controlled spatial and sensuous effect.

No one can fault the superb library in Pompeian colors, where segmental and circular arches with mirrors set behind them suggest rooms beyond rooms and worlds beyond a nineteenth-century London town house.

The house is a primer, in surprisingly small scale, of many of those creative devices that can lead to the elusive environmental "poetry" Soane sought and that define the architect's basic techniques and objectives in the manipulation of space, light and form. This is the essence of the art of architecture of any period or style.

Not a few of today's architects have learned Soane's lessons well. Philip Johnson puts his gratitude on public record. His sheer delight in tricks to be played with shallow domes, *trompe l'oeil* scale and colonnades, sources of light and progressions of space, make the Soanian debt quite clear.

He offers, in fact, a fascinating twentieth-century parallel to Soane, the architect-collector of means and taste, with his own domestic museum. Soane's famous picture room has cleverly hinged panels that swing open to reveal layers of paintings; Johnson's underground gallery has panels that pivot to reveal his collection.

Non-swinging London has much to teach the interested observer, architect or not. There is the lesson of urban excellence, with every street offering buildings of irreplaceable magnificence or streetscapes of notable quality. Expendable cities add nothing to the dignity of man.

Much has already been destroyed here, including Soane's buildings, and Londoners are vocally concerned. This is the kind of city that puts planning news on page one, and where a press conference on the release of a new city scheme turns into a knowledgeable planning debate.

"What insurance is there of continuing architectural elegance?"

248

asked one member of the press at a recent briefing, objecting to demolition of older buildings of character for new construction. "Will the area be swamped by architectural monstrosities?"

"We can't save every nineteenth-century building," replied a city official, "even if John Betjeman wants it," with no further identification of the poet and preservationist apparently necessary. "I would like to correct that, sir," another press member objected. "Betjeman and the Victorian Society are quite selective." It couldn't happen in New York.

Mackintosh: Revolution and the Scent of Heliotrope

A hundred years, or even fifty years, becomes a landmark and a time for looking back, and what we look back at now are the roots of the modern movement in architecture and design. We are examining history with the beginnings of some kind of a perspective about it, which means that we are embarking on voyages of re-discovery.

There is nothing like a retrospective exhibition to create that sense of rediscovery and re-evaluation. First, the fiftieth anniversary documentation of the Bauhaus came as a surprise to those either old enough to be shocked by the flight of a half-century or young enough to think of the beginnings of the Bauhaus as shrouded in the mists of time. Next, an exhibition organized by the Scottish Arts Council to celebrate the centenary of the Scottish architect Charles Rennie Mackintosh (1868–1928) was shown first at the Edinburgh Festival and later at the Victoria and Albert Museum.

To those who have simply taken Nikolaus Pevsner's word and the pictures beginning to fade in the classroom art histories that Mackintosh was a genius to be reckoned with, this exhibition was indeed a revelation. Whatever its shortcomings, it was the first retrospective of his work outside Scotland. The show consisted largely of re-creations of those famous interiors of 1900 to 1917 that startled turn-of-the-century professionals. These "rooms" used original furnishings and accessories, so that the effect was fresh and immediate and the impact tremendous. We are undoubtedly in for a Mackintosh revival, if in nothing more than shades of mauve floating in a sea of sculptured white.

Re-evaluation is hardly necessary. This is merely stunning affirmation that Mackintosh was one of the major innovative talents of modern times, with a deep and definitive influence on the forms of architecture and design that set the scene of the contemporary world.

Charles Rennie Mackintosh was the leader of the "Glasgow School," a small group of sensitive men and women who renounced the decorative excesses of long-entrenched Victorian taste. This movement was one of several short but significant revolts that recurred from the time of William Morris well into the twentieth century, to leave their mark on history and the world.

The contrasts could not be more splendidly revealed than they are in the permanent upstairs collection at the V and A where the exhibition was held. The Victorian room, with a huge ceramic centerpiece of unclear, elaborate function covered with roses, held by straining cupids and topped by writhing gold snakes, leads directly to the William Morris room and the ascetic works of Voysey and Mackintosh.

The moment of Art Nouveau paralleled the Glasgow School. There are connections—beautiful ones—between Mackintosh and those seductive forms, but he used them rarely and with exquisite sensitivity in a far stricter geometry. It is a geometry of intensely personal style and skill, brilliantly prefiguring movements as decorative as the modernistic and as basic as the Bauhaus.

Andrew McLaren Young, director of the exhibition and author of the catalogue, notes that Mackintosh "did not reject the need for decoration. But for him decoration was new clothing for new ideas: new ideas on the role of function and the geometry of architectural space."

Mies van der Rohe has described Mackintosh as a "purifier." He was that, and to be in his presence in this show makes one realize that purity need not be sterility. It can be a flowering rather than a repression of the senses. He makes one feel color more because he uses it with such supremely refined intensity: white becomes a mass of nuances, violet glows through a teardrop in a silver lamp or melts against mirror or glass in traceries of lead, red is a declamation in a

250

black, white and yellow wall. This is something that. cannot be experienced in the scholarly journals.

His influence went directly from Glasgow to Vienna, where the architects of the Secession admired him extravagantly and invited him to participate in the Exhibition of 1900. Josef Hofmann became his friend; Olbrich and Behrens were indebted to him; the line extends to Wagner and Loos, to the Bauhaus and Gropius and Mies, to everything that we call modern today.

A lot has been lost along the way. One has gotten awfully tired of Bauhaus blue, of the tubular clichés, of the safe design formulas. Only now is a less puritanical and intellectualized sensuousness coming back into architecture and design with a younger generation involved with the full spectrum of color and dimensional experience. These are often hard and chic optical exercises, even esthetic throwaways; Mackintosh was involved in a reformation that was also a gentle exploration of beauty and a probing analysis of architectonic surfaces and space.

He is sometimes paired, or paralleled, with Frank Lloyd Wright, but beyond the climate of the time which led men of genius to strip beauty bare, their talents are individual and unlike. In 1896, when his Glasgow Art School was designed, it was, in many ways, ahead of Wright.

One begins to call the art school a great proto-modern building, but it was proto-nothing; with its expressive functional modernity enriched by the spatial definition of the remarkable decoration, and a touch of sound Scottish traditionalism, this is a great building in quite absolute terms, by any measurement of time or style. The drawings for it were further enlivened by sample furnishings in the show, including a well-worn reading stand with a sign warning users not to take the periodicals out of the room.

The exhibition also included watercolors, flower drawings, textile designs, posters and an assortment of objects, such as the unsurpassed silver flatware that museums vie for, and other work of the Glasgow School, including that of Margaret Macdonald, Mackintosh's wife. But it would all be a ripple on the surface of art history if it were not for the strict, lyrical power of this one man. His almost equally celebrated fellow reformer, Voysey, is a craftsman next to him. Mackintosh worked for an elite few, but something of the changes he inaugurated pervades every life today.

Glasgow School of Art by Charles Rennie Mackintosh

Whether it is the art school, the domestic interiors or the series of tearooms for Miss Cranston, the designs are as curiously affecting now as they must have been when they first appeared. This has been expressed with particular effect by Ahlers-Hestermann quoted by Pevsner:

> These rooms were like dreams . . . white and serious looking, as if they were young girls ready to go to their first Holy Communion. Here was mysticism and asceticism, but with much of a scent of heliotrope, with well-manicured hands and a delicate sensuousness . . . two straight chairs with backs as tall as a man on a white carpet looking silently and spectrally at each other across a little table.

Romantic Classicism: Buildings That Stretch the Mind

The 148 drawings and prints of the late-eighteenth- and early-nineteenth-century work of Etienne-Louis Boullée, Claude-Nicolas

252

Ledoux and Jean-Jacques Lequeu, which belong to the Bibliothèque Nationale in Paris and have been touring this country as the show "Visionary Architects," have never been seen here before, except in reproduction. They are being circulated by the Art Department of the University of St. Thomas in Houston, which has also produced a very complete catalogue. Three drawings were added by L'Ecole Supérieure des Beaux Arts.

Any idea of human scale in this work—a current architectural preoccupation—is crushed by the sheer size, severity and strangeness of the forbidding, Euclidean concepts. Environment for people? This is a morbid landscape of death, of funerary fascination, of cenotaphs, cemeteries and monuments on a scale to dwarf the planets and belittle the gods. It is an imaginary world of fantasies that push creative reason to the vertiginous edge of beauty and understanding. Styles in thought and feeling change as radically as styles in art.

"The architect's mission," said Boullée, "is to orchestrate nature." That particular trick was not attempted again with comparable grandeur until Bruno Taut redesigned the Alps (on paper) in 1917. "Architecture puts on the spectator the spell of the marvelous," wrote Ledoux, and he did not mean fun places like Disneyland. What he and his colleagues had in mind were temples and tombs, a superhuman scenery of the sinister and the symbolic.

Drawing for a fort by Etienne-Louis Boullée

Some of the most extraordinary of these late-eighteenth- and early-nineteenth-century projects, Ledoux's scheme for a saltworks city at Chaux, for example, are familiar from standard architectural histories. Each succeeding generation has looked at these works with awe and differing interpretations, depending on its particular hangup. But few have looked at them except in reproduction.

The experience of the exhibition proves that this remarkable *oeuvre*, in its technical, esthetic and conceptual aspects, is unreproducible. Its actuality is overwhelming. In an age that favors instant shock, its impact comes slowly. The drawings are precise architectural renderings in somber black and gray washes; the style is neoclassical and formal. Many examples are much larger than reproduction ever hinted, containing details that have never been visible. All stretch the mind.

There are pyramids that make Cheops miniscule. Cemeteries are cities of the dead. A stadium for 300,000 is approached only by Leningrad's 100,000-spectator stadium today. Leningrad's stadium is built relatively cozily into an earth embankment; Boullée's would have been raised as a masonry monument to a kind of insane stylography of non-stop colonnades. (Only totalitarian vision has embraced this numbing excess. Massed spectator humanity hovers at about 50,000 in the United States.)

In the world of Boullée and Ledoux, lightning flashes from lowering clouds and illuminating shafts break through *grisaille* gloom to strike across gigantic walls and endless steps and columns repeated to infinity. The "architecture of shadows," Boullée named it; of shadows on flat surface planes that banished currently popular Baroque rhythms and decoration as "sterile riches," for the "immutability" of independent masses and a new "poetry of architecture."

Newton's cenotaph as conceived by Boullée in 1784 is the earth's sphere itself, the sarcophagus inside miniaturized by a soaring, celestial replica of sky and stars at night, an artificial sun by day. Ledoux also used a sphere for a suggested caretaker's house at Chaux. To both men, its continuous contour was "the expression of the sublime."

This eerie landscape of giant geometry, with clouds floating across the tops of pyramids and cones, was not propelled, as today's visions are, by a revolutionary technology. It stretched the limits of classical elements and traditional masonry construction. In the words of George Collins, who has written a fine, perceptive article about the show for the Museum Bulletin, it "defied both man's comprehensions and his building techniques." Its scale also defied economics, even in prerevolutionary France.

But if these visions remained unbuilt, their architects were not non-builders. They produced lesser, but still quite splendid works, of which few stand today. Boullée was architect to the Comte d'Artois, brother of Louis XVI. Madame du Barry became Ledoux's patron, and with royal help he even got started on his saltworks at Chaux. After the revolution he was reduced to editing and engraving his lifework.

Architecture parlante, these strange and symbolic buildings were called in the eighteenth century. They ranged from Boullée's tomb for a soldier in the form of a supercolossal sarcophagus and Ledoux's bold house for the director of a waterworks, designed as a cylinder or tube through which a river flows, to Lequeu's stable in the shape of a royally caparisoned cow.

Lequeu's more intimate never-never-land is tinted with pastel pinks, blues and greens. His *délices* hover between dream and nightmare: the columns of a gardener's cottage are in the process of transmutation from stone to decaying tree trunks; a gate to a hunting park is a strange abstraction of obelisks topped by realistic animal heads with disturbingly human expressions.

His is a world much closer to Disneyland, but infinitely more elegant and erotic, of Gothic dairies and chicken houses with onion domes, topped by delicate spires and roosters, underwater salons to delight de Sade, Indian pagodas as temples of thought.

There are several ways to look at this. One is for just what it was: a revolutionary moment in architectural history when top talents rejected the prevailing Baroque and Rococo styles for a fantastically enlarged vision served by a radical reshaping of the classical vocabulary. The new style, Romantic Classicism, was enormously influential.

The second way to look at it is as the forerunner of modernism, and this has been extremely popular in our time. Emil Kaufmann's *From Ledoux to Le Corbusier* is a basic text. "This was a turning point in the history of modern architecture," says J. C. Lemagny of the Bibliothèque Nationale. "A handful of men began to sense that there was poetry in a smooth surface, in two lines meeting at a right angle."

It can also be looked at as a kind of psychedelic experience, or just as art. These are wonderful pictures, masterpieces of draftsmanship and rendering, expressionistic marvels of stone, light and landscape. It will be a long time before they are seen again. And it will be a long time before the twentieth century develops its own kind of poetry to match that of the eighteenth.

Old Town Blues

St. Paul de Vence, France, is ripe for urban renewal. The buildings are at least 300 years old and the toilet count is low. To say nothing of the density. All those old stone buildings huddled together on top of a hill, packed so tight they nearly touch over narrow, crooked streets.

Any planner knows that anything over a hundred years old with that kind of density and toilet count is substandard. That's the key word, substandard. It's in all the urban renewal studies and it means that things need to be improved.

The trouble is, some ministry in Paris declared this place a historical monument. There's even a law that protects it. The ramparts that Francis I built around the town can't be taken down and the old houses have to stay. No tall buildings can be constructed on the hillsides to spoil the view. All changes must be "in character." No smart little stainless steel awnings or neon signs. No Carrara glass fronts or aluminum siding. They can't even widen the streets or bulldoze a few buildings for parking lots. No one can do anything progressive.

Of course, it's picturesque. It's really quite dramatic, silhouetted against the sky. You might even say it's quaint. Walking through those curving, stone-walled, stone-paved streets, there are some nice surprises, like coming into tiny squares with splashing fountains or suddenly glimpsing far-off sunlit hills through twisted, shadowed alleys. The light in the town is stopped down, filtered and subdued, captured in narrow spaces and reflected from masonry walls. Beyond those walls it washes hills of olive, oak and pine with brilliant luminosity and fields of roses and carnations spread out like an illuminated cyclorama.

Ni vitesse, ni bruit, the sign says on the approach road. No speed or noise. They pull the ramparts in at ten o'clock at night. It's picturesque, all right, but any planner would know in a minute that it hasn't got the amenities. Dance hall, cinema, bowling—ask the English New Town builders. You're dead without amenities. They've proved in England that you get the New Town Blues without amenities. Obviously someone has overlooked the need for a survey to see if they've got the Old Town Blues in St. Paul.

Nothing to do at night except walk around those ramparts in the moonlight. You can almost touch the moon. Or climb to the top of the southern ramparts to see the distant silver glimmer of the Mediterranean. Count the figs, pomegranates and oranges on the trees. Even Michelin only gives St. Paul an hour; a stroll around the town and out.

Any open-space expert could tell you that those views and protected fields and hills are useless. According to the latest theories, they should be utilized for active recreation. There could be people tramping, camping, swimming, playing touch football and pursuing organized physical activities out there. It's almost as big a waste as not letting the developers build villas.

Of course, if the French are serious about this national monument thing, there's a way to do that right, too. They could "Williamsburg" St. Paul. It would be easy to have some archeologists dig out some shards and stones from under the ramparts to prove that some buildings were once there that aren't there any more. They could make new copies just like the old ones. That's called reconstruction. Another key word.

Or you could "restore it back" to its prime period. But that would be hard to decide. If you really took it back to its beginnings, it would be necessary to get rid of a lot of the stuff that's there now, including the ramparts. Maybe it would be best to make it all Francis I period. With hostesses in appropriate costumes.

But then that would bring a lot more tourist trade and something would have to be done about the roads. They would have to be widened and straightened out. No American car can get in and turn around on these streets, and all they've got now is a man with a cap

(OVERLEAF)
Saint Paul de Vence: not for planners but for people

and a whistle and a large assortment of Gallic shrugs and signs to heaven. He could be kept for local color. The rest could be fixed by any up-to-date traffic engineer.

Even now, the tourists pour in locally on Sundays and from all of France in July and the International crowd takes over in August. The hills around are full of big-name artists like Chagall and Picasso. But anyone knows an artist is some kind of nut and obviously nobody gives a fig or a pomegranate for city planning.

Funny people, the French. They must be doing something right. Or could we be doing something wrong? Funny place, the world of the absurd.

DATES OF ORIGINAL PUBLICATION

262

Index

Index

264

Index

Index